Edited by John Lane and
Gerald Thurmond

The Woods
Stretched
for Miles

NEW
NATURE WRITING
FROM THE
SOUTH

The University of Georgia Press
Athens and London

Acknowledgments for the use of previously published materials
appear on pages xvi–xvii, which constitute an extension of the
copyright page.

© 1999 by the University of Georgia Press
Athens, Georgia 30602
All rights reserved
Designed by Sandra Strother Hudson
Set in 10.5 on 13 Cycles by G & S Typesetters, Inc.
Printed and bound by McNaughton & Gunn
The paper in this book meets the guidelines for permanence
and durability of the Committee on Production Guidelines for
Book Longevity of the Council on Library Resources.
Printed in the United States of America
03 02 01 00 99 C 5 4 3 2 1
03 02 01 00 99 P 5 4 3 2 1

Library of Congress Cataloging in Publication Data
The woods stretched for miles : new nature writing from the
South / edited by John Lane and Gerald Thurmond.
p.   cm.
ISBN 0-8203-2087-0 (alk. paper). — ISBN 0-8203-2088-9 (pbk. :
alk. paper)
1. Nature.   2. Natural history—Southern States.   3. Lane,
John, 1954–   I. Thurmond, Gerald.
QH81.W765   1999
508.75—DC21   98-20339

British Library Cataloging in Publication Data available

For Ab Abercrombie *and* David Scott,

who taught me how to walk the edges

of wild southern country.

For TK *in remembrance of Belize, Mexico,*

and for the long haul. And for my children,

Ben, Nathan, *and* Meg, *in hopes that*

for them the woods will still stretch for miles.

Contents

Preface

In his 1960 memoir, *The Road Home,* James McBride Dabbs remembers the wilderness of his South Carolina home: "Behind the house the woods stretched for miles, long leaf and short leaf pines interspersed with hardwoods ... virgin timber, never turpentined." Today, if you drive from Sumter toward Columbia, South Carolina, you pass through the land James McBride Dabbs could see out behind his house. The light still blends the trees together in the distance. If you stop your car by the side of the road and stare into the woods you can feel for a moment a haunting presence in the distance, what William Faulkner described in "The Bear" as a sense of your own "fragility and impotence against the timeless woods."

The region we call the South stayed rural a long time, but one tends to forget there were vast stretches of southern wilderness well into this century. Scholars have defined the South geographically, historically, and as a place in the imagination, but usually the notion of the South as "wild land" doesn't figure in this description. In this anthology, the region we are considering the South—the states of Virginia, North Carolina, South Carolina, Georgia, Florida, Alabama,

Tennessee, Mississippi, Louisiana, Texas, Arkansas, and Kentucky—is one of the first places settled by Europeans on this continent, and it can be argued that some southern landscapes (such as Oklahoma) remained "territorial" in our imagination until recently. Even in the most developed southern states, such as Florida and Virginia, the ghost of wilderness still survives. Bears still stop traffic on the Shenandoah Mountain Skyline Drive. Florida panthers still hunt and mate in the Big Cypress Swamp.

This anthology is the first of its kind to pull together the various voices writing about the southern landscape. It is a step toward returning to the South a reputation not only of writing praised for its "sense of place," but also for strong literary voices (such as William Bartram and John James Audubon) speaking for wildness and natural history.

In his book *The Environmental Imagination* Lawrence Buell writes that one of the primary reasons for nature writing is what he calls restorationism. For a biologist restoration means reestablishing the ecological integrity of an area. For Buell restoration means recreating the meaning and value of places the significance of which may have been lost to us or never recognized. Or, as Buell puts it, nature writers "practice restorationism by calling places into being . . . not just by naming objects, but by dramatizing in the process how they matter."

Both of the editors have benefited from such imaginative acts of restoration. For John Lane it was James McBride Dabbs, the author quoted above, who taught him that the southern landscape mattered and was a fit subject for writing. For Gerald Thurmond it was the old Texas naturalist and writer Roy Bedichek who legitimated his passion for hiking and natural history. Each of the contemporary authors collected here has that power of reviving a sense of place Faulkner describes and Buell writes about, although each of them practices that power in a somewhat different way.

Some of the writings collected here are directly connected with the biological as well as the more figurative notion of restoration. Susan Cerulean's essay describes biologists' work with swallow-tailed kites in Florida; Wendell Berry writes about his attempts to return the land of his small Kentucky farm, and, by extension, himself and his community, to health. Biologist Archie Carr is faced with one of the more awkward consequences of biological restoration in the form of a very large alligator in his front yard pond.

Other writers draw on older, non-European traditions to find meaning. Christopher Camuto and Marilou Awiakta explore Cherokee thought. In the selection from Christopher Camuto the usual western emphasis of observer-privileged-over-object-perceived breaks down in the presence of that rarest of habitats in the east, the old-growth forest. In Marilou Awiakta's piece the European separation of individual and community and of land and spirit are blurred in her beautiful and hypnotic description of an imagined Cherokee ceremony.

The selection from E. O. Wilson reverses the usual direction of people's influence on nature and shows how his boyhood experiences of nature (and an unfortunate accident) helped set him on his path to becoming one of our most significant evolutionary biologists.

At times the writer is not so much required to dramatize the meaning of nature as to sort out and probe our various and extreme responses to it. Stephen Harrigan's essay does this in his description of his own and others' reactions to the poisoning and dying of the massive and centuries-old Treaty Oak.

This is a collection of writings about the South, and as such some themes are perhaps more likely to occur in this literature than in work about regions with a shorter history of European settlement and a less exceptional parcel of American history. An example of a theme often encountered in these essays is religion. The South is called the "Bible Belt" for good reason, and so it should not be surprising that religion or at least the rumor of God is found lurking in literature about the southern landscape. In the selection from Eddy L. Harris the writer encounters a floating Jeremiah driven by God to the Mississippi River. In other selections Harry Middleton converses with his Smoky Mountain prophet and spins his prayer wheel and Franklin Burroughs passes by a river baptism. Religion may be central to family traditions in the South, as it is in the funeral service described by Janisse Ray, or it may be part of the principles by which you respond to nature, as in James Kilgo's reaction to wading waist deep into the muck of a rookery. In these essays, religion seems as much a part of the South as red clay.

The southern literary landscape is peopled, has a history, and discloses complicated personal and family loyalties. Franklin Burroughs's essay reveals his river trip to be as much a journey through family and regional history as a trip on the Waccamaw. The "theft" in Barry Lopez's essay takes place in the context of his uncle's sense of history and morality, and Janet Lembke's essay is as much about her little community on the river Neuse as it is about its seasons. Janisse Ray finds herself in the nature writers' paradise of Montana only to be drawn back to the scrub pine of her south Georgia home, and Bland Simpson concludes his piece with an image of his wife and himself as lovers in the Great Dismal Swamp and his twin children as infants being introduced to the swamp.

It is a complicated thing for nature writers to consider such a landscape, for after all, what is natural and wild in a land so transformed by human activity? Our writers answer this in a variety of ways. Jan DeBlieu finds wildness and risk in the approaching hurricane. Should she leave or ride out the storm? Mary Q. Steele's selection reveals her to be quite content with the ordinary offerings of suburban nature, such as a close encounter with a young June thrush in her garden. As the bird flies off to its parents' call of alarm she expresses satisfaction: "Who would want a longer or closer inspection than I had had of it? What is wildness for if not to make some difference and erect some barriers between us?"

Some of our writers struggle more with the concepts of wild and wilderness. In his essay Rick Bass offers the idea of a "buffered wilderness" to characterize the Black Creek Wilderness area in Mississippi, an area which is wilderness not in the sense of a place isolated and unchanged, but in the sense that it maintains its same biological integrity after centuries of Native American and European habitation. In contrast Christopher Camuto wants us to understand our loss from the almost complete destruction of old-growth forest in the Smoky Mountains, while Harry Middleton finds solace in the fact that these mountains endure in the face of so much human shortsightedness and heedless greed.

It is obvious from our selection of essays that we believe the wild South still exists, though we admit it has been transformed by cellular phone towers, satellite TV, air-conditioning, interstate highways, corporate farms, and mini-marts. Recently a black bear showed up on the outskirts of Spartanburg, South Carolina, sixty miles from the nearest national forest land. The bear, a young boar, eluded the authorities for three days, crossing and recrossing suburb after suburb, staying close to a ragged creek drainage. Some of us listened nightly to reports of sightings on the evening news. Hope was loose in the treeless backyards.

There are still bears, alligators, rattlesnakes, and deer (plenty of them) in the South. There are mountain gorges with walls of granite impossible to descend and waterfalls isolated and hard to describe. Even the rural landscape—that ragged land compromised by commerce and agriculture—is still mostly trees and fields, and for many southerners, behind the house the woods still stretch for miles.

JOHN LANE AND GERALD THURMOND
Spartanburg, South Carolina

Acknowledgments

Putting together an anthology may seem a simple enough task for those who have not tried it, but as we discovered, any anthology is a work of persistence and mutual aid. Many people have helped along the way. Dean Dan Maultsby and the Academic Planning and Research Committee of Wofford College provided us with summer grants to begin the work. The library staff at the college, especially Kay Barry, Ellen Tillet, and Roger Niles, helped us locate many of the essays and books that we collected in our search. Scott Slovic, Michael Branch, Dan Philippon, and Thomas Rain Crowe gave us valuable advice. David Taylor and Betsy Teter endured long discussions about the anthology, helped us formulate our thoughts, and proofread our copy. Joyce Blackwell performed the miracle of transforming scanned essays into readable text. Barbara Ras, Jennifer Comeau, Jennifer Rogers, Courtney Denney, and everyone at the University of Georgia Press worked with great patience to guide us through this project and put up with our delays. Finally, we would like to thank our students, who read many of these essays and, through their reactions, helped us choose. We put this anthology together with them in mind. Our thanks to them all.

The editors and publisher gratefully acknowledge the following publications and publishers in which these essays first appeared:

Rick Bass, "Good Day at Black Creek," *Wild to the Heart*, Stackpole Books: Harrisburg, Pa.: 1987.

Jan DeBlieu, "Hurricane," *Hatterus Journal*, Fulcrum Books: Golden, Colo.: 1987.

Wendell Berry, "The Making of a Marginal Farm," *Recollected Essays, 1965–1980*, copyright © 1981 by Wendell Berry. Reprinted by permission of North Point Press, a division of Farrar, Straus & Giroux, Inc., San Francisco, Calif., 1987.

Eddy L. Harris, "Vicksburg," *Mississippi Solo*, HarperCollins, New York, N.Y.: 1988.

James Kilgo, "Actual Field Conditions," *Deep Enough for Ivorybills*, Algonquin Books, Chapel Hill, N.C.: 1988.

Janet Lembke, "River Time," *River Time*, Lyons & Burford, Publishers, New York, N.Y.: 1989.

Archie Carr, "Living with an Alligator," *A Naturalist in Florida*, Yale University Press, New Haven, Conn.: 1994.

Harry Middleton, "Bagpipes on Hazel Creek," *On the Spine of Time*, Simon & Schuster, New York, N.Y.: 1991.

Franklin Burroughs, "Lake Waccamaw to Freedlands," *The River Home*, W. W. Norton, New York, N.Y.: 1992.

E. O. Wilson, "Paradise Beach," *Naturalist*, Island Press, Washington, D.C.: 1994.

Marilou Awiakta, "Daydreaming Primal Space," *Selu*, Fulcrum Press, Golden, Colo.: 1993. Originally published in *The Poetics of Appalachian Space*, ed. Parks Lanier Jr., Knoxville: University of Tennessee Press, 1991.

Bland Simpson, "The Great Dismal," *The Great Dismal: A Carolinian's Swamp Memoir*, copyright © 1990, 1998 by the University of North Carolina Press. Used by permission of the publisher and the author.

Excerpt from "The Oven Bird" from *The Poetry of Robert Frost*, edited by Edward Connery Lathem, copyright 1944 by Robert Frost, copyright 1916, 1969 by Henry Holt and Company. Reprinted by permission of Henry Holt and Company, Inc.

Barry Lopez, "Theft: A Memoir," *About This Life: Journeys on the Threshold of Memory,* Alfred A. Knopf, New York, N.Y.: 1998.

Mary Q. Steele, from *The Living Year,* Quill, New York, N.Y.: 1982.

Christopher Camuto, "Old Growth," *Another Country: Journeying Toward the Cherokee Mountains,* Henry Holt, New York, N.Y.: 1997.

Rick Bass

Good Day at
Black Creek

(MISSISSIPPI)

You would really like Jim Trunzler, I know
you would. In fact, it is hard to imagine anyone
not liking him; the thought of someone frowning
when his name is mentioned, or—get this!—of
someone calling him a name in anger is so unimaginable that it is ludicrous. He is just one of
those types. Ask someone who knows him to describe him to you and inevitably the description
will begin with a chuckle-chuckle or a heh, heh.
In his younger days, Jim used to be a bit of a card.
A rather large bit of one. He will be thirty-eight
years old this January first.

He looks like a big gnome. He has curly red
hair and a wild red beard and eyes that are ever
twinkling, as if he had just ducked around the
corner after playing a massive practical joke on
somebody; many times this is precisely the case.
He smokes a pipe and has large beefy shoulders
and thick strong biceps. He is a foreign car me-
chanic and an avid whitewater kayaker-canoer.
He is chairman of the Central Mississippi Sierra
Club and he invited me to go backpacking with
him one day while I was in his shop having my
car worked on. I had never met him before.

"I'd love to," I said. "When are you going?"

"Tomorrow morning."

"I'll be there."

1

There are ten of us going, I discover; Jim mills around, talking with everyone before we leave, offering them coffee, disgruntled when they defer, ecstatic when they accept. Not knowing about his coffee, I make the mistake of falling into the acceptor category. I taste it, make a face, and when he is not looking, pour it out in the street. It tastes like india ink. Packs are transferred to the cars that will be making the trip. Tires are thumped, hoods checked, and windshields cleaned. Jim's slender black cat, Ender, watches from under a hedge; all we can see of him is wide wondering eyes as round as saucers and as green as limes, looking at us as if he cannot, for some reason, believe what he is seeing. We try to coax him out to come with us, but it is no go; he is too smart. We get in the cars and wave good-bye to him. I have, luck of all lucks, managed to be in Jim's car. He has an ancient golden Volvo that he has rebuilt himself. It has a fantastic radio-cassette system, worth easily as much as the car itself. The morning sky is blue and crisp and cloudless: it is mid-February and a good morning for driving. We crack the windows a bit to let the cold fresh air whirl around, and the sweet melodic strains of James Taylor fill the air. He is singing a song about going to Carolina in his mind. It is mountain music; it is good music. For the first time I think to ask Jim where we are going to backpack. Black Creek, he tells me.

Located about 120 miles south of Jackson, about 50 miles north of the Gulf of Mexico, the Black Creek Wilderness Area is not yet officially a real wilderness area, not a designated one anyway, but it is trying to be. If approved and accepted into the National Wilderness Preservation system as was originally suggested by the Roadless Area Review & Evaluation program (RARE II), it will become Mississippi's first and only national wilderness area. The Black Creek wilderness is comprised of thousands of acres of swamps, hills, valleys, meadows, ridges, hardwood bottoms, and pine plantations through which the wide and deep and dark and cool Black Creek wanders, heading south, south to the Big Water. Broad-leaved cottonwoods and great thick sycamores line the banks of the river; the water is rich and golden black, tangy with the taste of fallen acorn tannin, and out in the still pools, behind the riffles and log jams, sulk great bull-headed catfish. Bullfrogs as big as waste baskets sit like green boulders on the banks and drum in the summertime; at dusk, cautious deer and bold raccoons can be seen coming right down to the crystal white sandbars that bound the meandering river. Bobcats pad silently through the leaves, stalking terrified, prolific cottontails, and red-tailed hawks wheel overhead in lazy figure eights. Some of the scattered handfuls of farmers who live near the borders of the proposed wilderness area swear they have heard mountain lions screaming back in the swamps; one man says he saw a bear. The Black Creek region, Jim tells us, is the wildest, most unspoiled land in the entire state; if indeed there are black bears remaining in Mississippi, Black Creek is almost certainly where they will be holed up.

We pass through Hattiesburg an hour and a half later; we begin to stir. A peppy, springy pop tune by Emmylou Harris is playing, and Jim drums his hands on the steering wheel—I noticed later that he seems to be happiest when he is moving, whether he is in a car, in a kayak, or even just walking—and he asks Curt, his copilot, to please pour him another cup of that delicious coffee from the thermos stashed on the floorboard. Curt obliges; there is plenty left. Curt pours while Jim steers with one hand and holds the cup with the other, watching the road nervously. Looking for excitement, cramped and restless after ninety minutes of riding, I lean forward, waiting for the car to hit a bump and make Curt pour it in Jim's lap, but it doesn't, and I sit back, disappointed. Thank you, says Jim. Curt says that it is nothing. It is Mardi Gras weekend in New Orleans, and the interstate is deserted: we are the only car on the road.

We exit the interstate and drive down a bumpy two-lane back-country road until we reach a sleepy little crossroads town with the unlikely name of Brooklyn, where we pull into a gravel parking lot and wait for Ron Fralik, who is supposed to be coming up from the coast to meet us there.

With a population of almost a thousand, Brooklyn is the last civilization before entering the Black Creek Wilderness Area, and at 10 : 00 A.M. on this sunny February morning it is awhirl with activity. A pale, long-legged, houndish dog walks down a side street, casting glances from side to side at all the stores. Farther down the road, a boy on a three-wheeler races figure eights around two oak trees in someone's front yard. Roosters are crowing somewhere; the flag over the post office hangs motionless. I go in the little store whose parking lot we are parked in—there is a screen door; a bell jingles when I enter—and buy a pint of chocolate milk and a moon pie. The girl at the counter gives me six cents too much change, and I can tell that it is going to be a beautiful day.

We gather around the cars, sitting on bumpers and hoods, and drink our chocolate milks and Mountain Dews and Bubbly-Fizz root beers and watch the boy down the street on the three-wheeler for a while, glancing occasionally at the sun or at our watches. Late ourselves, we were supposed to have met Ron at the store between nine-thirty and ten o'clock; it is now ten minutes after. Susan Haskins begins a series of stretching exercises that culminates in her placing one foot up on top of Louis McCool's pickup, the roof of which is taller than she is, and touching her head to her knee: we are all properly amazed. We glance at our watches again. The sun is warm, the day pretty; we wait four minutes and then leave.

"He knows where to find us," says Jim.

But do we know where to find him? We are supposed to catch the trail at a remote backwoods crossing called Janice Landing. We miss the turn: we find ourselves on a red gravel road that noses up and down steep pine-studded ridges, carrying us past greying farm shacks and collapsing chicken coops. Ancient tractors sit quietly abandoned in the small stumpy fields, overcome at last by time and rust; we are lost, but at least it is pretty. The road winds and loops and bends back and forth through the forest, so that each corner brings something new. The sun is warm, it is like summertime in February. We leave a cloud of swirling red dust behind us wherever we go and must roll up the windows. The Volvo climbs hills easily; the woods slide by.

We reach the top of a ridge and look down on the road we are supposed to be on. We turn around and head back down the road we just came up, looking for a turn-off. Jim begins to draw harder and faster on his cigarette. Gears clash sometimes now when he shifts, and surprised chickens squawk and cluck angrily and scatter to either side of the road as we blow past them again, anxious to be back on the trail. We find it twenty minutes later. Jim smiles, appeased now, and we unload the cars and lock up.

Black Creek is a different sort of wilderness from what most people are used to. It is not as remote as the sprawling thousand-square-mile chains of mountain spurs and subranges up in the Rockies, nor is it as isolated as the deserts of the Southwest. It is a buffered sort of wilderness. It is not Precambrian virginal, not like a peak up above treeline a hundred miles from even the nearest mining camp out West, but rather, it is an 1800s sort of wilderness: it is probably as close as is possible to being identical to what the country's first settlers encountered when they ventured into the southeastern hardwood bottoms two hundred years ago, when there were only brief, short-lived, and thinly populated little fishing camps, little trading posts, and little settlements scattered throughout the South: Rabun Gap, Georgia; Smoke Holler, Alabama; Janice Landing, Mississippi. . . .

It is not wilderness in the sense that it is five hundred miles from a telephone or a hard-topped road or a farm with running water and electricity, but it is wilderness in the sense that it has never been wilder, that this is how it was and always has been, even in prehistoric food-gathering-tribal times. Small, even tiny patches of the great forest are frequently cut over and harvested for management purposes, but again, this is how it has been since the country's beginnings: settlers felling logs for cabins, and clearing tiny openings deep in the thick forest depths for subsistence farming. At night, camped on a sandbar, you can still hear hounds running coons far away, running through the swamp bottoms all night long, and it is possible to imagine their men sitting up on a knoll around a small fire, telling stories and listening to their dogs, waiting for the right kind of bay, the right kind of frenzied *awoooooh!* that will tell them they've found one, so they can snatch up their guns and kerosene lanterns and go hurrying off through the bottoms in the direction of the dogs, stumbling over logs, clawing briars and vines out of the way . . .

It is not wilderness in the sense that other people, such as the coon hunters, never venture into it, but it is wilderness in the sense that it is still wild, and in the sense that it is unchanged: that it is, essentially, as it always has been.

On the trail I follow Jim so I can smell his pipe smoke. It is cherry scented; it is delicious. It fills the entire woods with a gruff yet mild benign aura; it makes the woods seem even friendlier, and it relaxes me. It is mellow. I myself do not smoke because it cuts down on my wind.

Hiking behind Jim, I shift and jiggle my pack; it feels good to be carrying a pack through the woods on a warm winter day; it feels good to have all I need on my back. Ahead of us both trudges sturdy Ron Fralik with calves like diamonds; he climbs hills as does the Volvo—effortlessly. After a while I notice that Jim's pack is getting smaller and smaller; I hurry to catch up.

I watch for armadillos as I go. Not found in Mississippi ten years ago, they are now fairly common in the Black Creek wilderness, having migrated up from Mexico and into Texas around the turn of the nineteenth century, spilling slowly northward ever since then, and Jim has offered a five-dollar reward to anyone who can catch one before dinner. Originally from Texas himself, Jim claims they are not only edible, but tasty. We do not know if he is joking or not, but we keep a watch anyway.

We stop and have lunch on a tall vertical bluff looking straight down into Black Creek. White wine, Swiss cheese, California golden raisins, dried apricots and sardines and apples and stone-ground wheat crackers—I am impressed. I chew thoughtfully on my squashed peanut butter and jelly sandwich and think to myself that next time I will have to do better: this crowd travels in style. I take a sip of warm water from my canteen and lean back against a thick-trunked white oak and close my eyes and doze. Peanut butter and jelly sandwiches almost always make me sleepy, and especially so on warm afternoons in the woods in February. I notice that everyone else is doing the same, even though they have not had the p b and j. Perhaps it is something in the air: it settles over us like a net, like a malaise, only it is pleasant. No one says anything; everyone dozes and listens to the woods. It is a group that believes firmly in proper digestion; it is a group after my own heart.

Dozing, it strikes me that if another group of hikers were to come trudging up the trail and find us leaning against trees like this, they would think we had all been poisoned, and I smile lazily without opening my eyes. Down in a creek branch somewhere below us, a blue jay scolds; out on the river, two wood ducks squeal as they rocket down its length. I have always believed in proper digestion.

An hour later we are hiking again, roaring up and down the trails as if the woods are on fire. These bearded Southerners with their long loping strides are leaving me fast behind. I am not originally from Mississippi. I am from northern Utah, where it begins snowing up above treeline in late August and where the backpacking trails often hug skylines so high that the air turns purple, almost black, and the wind blows hard and strong twelve months out of the year, and where a three-mile hike is often a day's work, and all uphill. Different muscles are used, and a different pace: different physiologies are developed. Rocky Mountain backpackers are often short and squatty, like tanks.

But tanks do not fare well in the delta woodlands; I practice unlearning my short, shuffling, power-climbing steps and try to smooth them out into steady and rhythmic ground-eating ones, and by the end of the day, I am beginning to get the hang of it.

We camp, of course, on the river, on a white sandbar. Firewood is gathered, and tents are pitched; dusk descends like a grey curtain. Owls boom, and bats chitter and swoop overhead, darting across the river, always altering their flights at the last microsecond to swerve and snap at some invisible insect. A fish breaks water out on the river, but there are no mosquitoes; it is still too cool, too crisp.

Half disappointed and half relieved that no armadillos were sighted, we all cook on the one big community fire, comparing recipes and dinners. Tim has four servings of spaghetti, three more than he needs, and we all sample it; Larry has brought too many hot dogs and distributes them freely. Coleman is on a diet, and plays his harmonica. Louis and Susan, to be married in June, walk off down the river holding hands: we tell Susan to watch out for bears.

"And panthers," calls out Jim.

"And alligators," says Curt.

Susan hesitates and moves in a little closer to Louis and looks back and then relaxes. Surely we are kidding. An owl booms again, and then they disappear around a bend in the river.

Because none of us really knew each other, there had not been a lot of talking on the trail this first day. Jim had led a blistering (literally) pace; whether he did this on purpose or not, I do not know, but that night we are all much closer, much more sociable and relaxed as we sit around the fire in varying states of shared exhaustion, massaging our feet and making up names for different stars. Jim sits back away from us and puffs benignly on his pipe and tells funny jokes from time to time. The sweet sure scent of cherry pipe smoke fills the night woods. We watch the fire and talk about everything. Louis and Susan return, and they too come over and sit down with us and watch the fire, and then, sure enough, we hear dogs. So for an hour or so we listen to them. They sound wild; they sound happy.

After a while, Jim says, "I believe one of them is coming this way."

It is true: one of the barks is growing louder.

"It sounds like he's on the other side of the creek," says Larry.

After a while the baying stops.

"That'll be him crossing the creek," Larry says casually. Susan edges closer to Louis and asks if perhaps we shouldn't douse the fire.

"What if he chases whatever it is he's chasing right through camp?" she asks, somewhat fearfully.

"Maybe it'll be an armadillo," Jim says hopefully. The baying starts up again.

"That'll be him on our side of the creek, coming towards us now," Larry tells her.

Soon we can hear the rustling of leaves and crash of vines as he scrambles up the ravine toward us; he is no longer barking. Sitting around the fire, our eyes straining into the darkness, we all—except for Susan—know it is just an old stray hound mistaking our fire for his owner's, but still, forgotten pre-Neanderthal genes stir uneasily within us, and we squint out into the blackness. The rustling stops, and we can hear him standing there, panting. Coleman flicks on a flashlight and shines it into the woods, and two fiery red orbs gaze back at us.

"What a beast," Jeff marvels.

"Look at his legs," Larry whispers.

"C'm here, boy," Jim whistles. The dog slinks forward, wagging his tail ecstatically, delighted to be taking this brief respite from the hunt, unbeknownst to his master. Off in the woods, maybe three or four miles away, we can barely hear the rest of the pack, headed in what sounds to be the opposite direction.

The dog heads straight for Larry. He must know that Larry still has a leftover hot dog. Larry feeds it to him; the dog snaps it up. We shine a flashlight on his collar and discover that his name is Vernon Mitchell and that he lives in Wiggins, Mississippi. The fire dies and the coals flicker: we watch them until they too are gone, and then we go to bed, with Vernon Mitchell lying outside Larry's tent, standing guard, dreaming simple dog dreams of unexpected but delicious frankfurters doled out by total strangers in the middle of the night deep in the Mississippi wilderness.

Lazy Sunday mornings, both sunny and smoky-steamy with burning-off fog, are when Black Creek is at its best. Summer afternoons in the deep cool swimming holes are almost as fun, and evenings are beautiful too, but the difference between morning and evening is the difference between a beautiful smiling woman and a beautiful angry one. The mornings are the smilers; gentler than the evenings, they are sun dappled and refreshing, and offer up great hope for the day no matter what yesterday was like.

This lazy Sunday morning is no different; amidst Jim's exhortations to "get vertical," we are off, plodding along our southeasterly course a good two hours before the crack of noon. Vernon follows.

We get lost right from the start. It is our own fault; we flush a wild turkey scratching in the sand in the middle of the trail and take the wrong fork, the unmarked one, watching where he has flown instead of where we should be going, and after fifteen minutes we realize we have stopped seeing the small white blazes marked on trees every one hundred yards that characterized the other trail. We are lost.

The rest is welcome; we sit down in the warm sun and close our eyes. Jim consults his map and tries to look worried. Ron and Coleman take off in opposite directions, looking for the white blazes; Tim and Curt go back down the trail to see if we missed a turn-off. Jim studies his map a little more, and lights up his pipe; smoke rises. Jeff and Larry begin humming the theme from "The Twilight Zone."

"We need to backtrack," Jim says finally, and rolls up his map and stuffs it in his pack and waits for the others to return. Ron and Coleman come trotting back in, luckless, but Tim and Curt come back up the trail and inform us that we need to backtrack.

Back on the trail again, we jump a big buck deer, and Vernon starts off in glorious pursuit, but with sharp, indignant cries we call him back: does he not know it is Sunday? Incredulous, he gives up the chase and returns, sulking, glowering even, and contents himself with casting back and forth across the trail for rabbit scents.

Sunday's pace is more leisurely. We drink from fast-running streams, and watch for armadillos again, and try to identify bird calls; lunch, held in a grassy meadow, once again makes allowances for proper digestion. We reach the cars around midafternoon, our feet sore but our spirits stronger than when we came; we are ready once more to face the rigors of Jackson. We wave good-bye to Vernon and then load our packs in the trunks and get in the cars and drive off. He stands back in the woods and watches us leave and then turns and pads on back down the trail, back toward Wiggins. There is no telling what he was thinking.

Jan DeBlieu

Hurricane

(NORTH CAROLINA)

In late September a tropical depression in the Caribbean attracted the alarmed attention of meteorologists at the Cape Hatteras weather station in Buxton. The system had formed off the coast of northern Africa, and it gathered strength at an unusual rate as it moved east toward the Lesser Antilles. Its spinning, counterclockwise winds accelerated, then slowed, then doubled in force, skimming salty moisture from the ocean and tossing it into the clouds. At the center of the storm warm air plunged downward, causing drastic shifts in pressure. Like the iris in an eye, the core widened and narrowed. By September 23 the storm had become Gloria, the largest hurricane ever to develop in the Atlantic Ocean.

On Hatteras news of Gloria's northward movement was greeted at first with little interest. The summer rentals had begun to empty for the season, and the pace of life had slackened. The ponds at the Pea Island refuge had filled with widgeons, teals, and a smattering of migrant shorebirds. The slant of sunlight had changed in a matter of days from the direct glare of summer to the more diffused sheen of autumn, staining the sand orange and streaking the sky with vermilion and mauve. The waxy tassels of sea oats had dried a crisp brown. As the wind shifted from southwest to northeast and back, the ocean color changed from celadon to a cold, broody blue and then to jade. During the third week of the month, the surf spread up the beach with unusual force as the moon slid directly between the earth and the sun to create the year's greatest tidal pull. At night, black waves crept almost to the dunes, wetting my feet with a velvety hiss.

Early evenings I relaxed on my back porch and counted the lime-colored tree frogs that hopped among the pieces of wood and piles of shells I had collected during the summer. Brittle, cone-shaped cocoons constructed by bagworm moths hung like ornaments from the cedar outside the kitchen window. The air, fresh and slightly damp, was full of the melancholy that signals that the hottest days of summer have passed. It was far too pleasant to dwell on the possibility of a major storm. Besides, Gloria was the third hurricane of the season that forecasters had said might swing our way. The others had not come close.

By Tuesday, September 24, Gloria had become enough of a threat to the Atlantic seaboard to merit comment among my neighbors. The next morning I wandered over to the Island Convenience, a small store owned by Mac and Marilyn Midgett. A sprawling complex by Rodanthe standards, it includes a quick-stop grocery, gas station, garage, crane hoisting service, storage yard for broken-down cars, and a real estate office. It is also the place neighborhood residents cash checks and catch up on gossip. The newspaper I picked up had a small story about Gloria on page one. I glanced at it as I pushed my quarter across the counter toward Mac's sister, Mildred Midgett, a solid island woman who is perpetually calm and pleasant.

"How are you, Mildred?" I asked absently, leafing to the paper's back sections.

"I'm fine, but I'm already tired of people talking about this storm. Seems like that's all anyone can think about this morning."

"Really?" I turned to the front page for a closer look. At press time Gloria had been eight hundred miles south of Cape Hatteras.

"One man already came in and said he was evacuating. He said it wasn't worth waiting until the last minute. I guess we'll have some sort of big storm tomorrow, whether it's a hurricane or not."

"Huh. I didn't realize it was that much of a threat. You think you'd leave if it started coming this way?"

"I haven't left for a storm yet."

"I don't know. If the forecasters said it was going to hit us dead on, I think I'd leave. I don't trust my house to stand up in a-hundred-and-thirty-mile-an-hour winds."

Mildred, one of the kindest souls I had met on Hatteras, looked at me askance. "That house has stood through more storms than you have," she said.

Outside, Randy Hall and Debbie Bell, my next-door neighbors, were talking to a car full of surfers, all of whom wore sunglasses with white frames. Hall had been leaning into the car, absorbed in conversation, but he extracted his hand and waved when he saw me. "It's coming. There's no doubt about it," he hollered. "There's a high-pressure system that's going to suck it right up the coast."

The day was cloudy and warm, but the air felt dry. I dropped the paper on the kitchen table and made a pot of coffee. I had no television, no reliable radio, no way to monitor Gloria's progress. Neither could I force myself to concentrate on the work I had scheduled for the day. If Gloria did drift toward Hatteras, I would have only a few hours to decide which of my possessions I most cherished and pack them up. But I was letting myself get rattled; I needed to get down to work. I would feel better if I got down to work.

After an hour of staring out the kitchen window at five gulls that circled and swooped above the myrtle, I walked across the street to see Mike Halminski, a wildlife photographer. He emerged from his darkroom with a marine radio and set it on the back porch.

The announcer reported that Gloria was 680 miles south of Cape Hatteras and moving north at fifteen miles an hour. If the storm followed the predicted course, it would make landfall on the cape sometime Thursday night. "Hurricane Gloria is a dangerous hurricane with winds gusting to a hundred and fifty miles an hour. Residents of the Outer Banks should be aware of its progress. . . . Windows should be boarded or taped, and objects outside that could serve as missiles in hurricane-force winds should be secured. . . . The biggest loss of life in hurricanes results not from high winds but from drowning. . . . Heavy surf already threatens to overwash portions of Highway Twelve at Pea Island, the S curves north of Rodanthe, portions of Hatteras Island north of Buxton . . ."

"Pretty scary," Halminski said.

The clouds had grown thicker, and the air was now heavy and damp. "Maybe I'm imagining it," I said, "but there's a really strange feeling in the air."

Halminski looked south toward the Chicamacomico station. "Maybe I should park my truck on that little hill and go on up into the station. It's stood through a lot of storms."

"If it starts to look bad I'm leaving. It's not worth taking the chance."

Robin Gerald, a local jack-of-all-trades, appeared in the doorway. "Anyone want to buy some pictures to remember this place?"

"Or some oceanfront property?" Halminski asked.

The two friends had moved to Hatteras more than a decade before, when they were in their early twenties and the island was only beginning to be developed. Both loved the violence of the Hatteras weather, but neither had ever experienced a major hurricane.

"She blows through here, my house is gone," Gerald said loudly. "That property over there's one of the lowest points on the island. Your house might be okay, might not." He was enjoying himself.

"It would be something to see a storm like that blow in if you knew for sure you were in a safe place," Halminski said.

"I don't have anywhere to go even if I did evacuate," Gerald said. "Nowhere's safe from them things, nowhere that I can go. Better to stay here and go down thrashing."

My stomach churned as I walked back to the house. There was nothing to be concerned about, not yet. Gerald had a knack for embellishment, and I was letting it overpower my common sense. The previous year Hurricane Diana had stalled south of Hatteras for two days, and park service rangers had cleared the beaches of tourists under fair skies, even as Diana lost much of her power and turned inland two hundred miles south of Ocracoke. Something similar could happen with Gloria. Above all I wanted to avoid being an alarmist. I got the keys to my pickup and pulled into the line that had started to form at the Island Convenience's gas pumps. Inside Mildred and Marilyn were ringing up purchases with studied efficiency, as if nothing unusual was going on. A balding man I had seen but couldn't place walked in behind me. "I'm getting ready to evacuate," he announced.

"You are?" Mildred asked. She seemed surprised.

"Yes. If it was just me I could take care of myself, but I have to think of mother, you know."

At home I called Wally DeMaurice, the meteorologist I had talked with about hurricanes and northeasters the previous spring. Gloria had been declared a Category Five storm, the worst on the scale, with winds of 150 miles an hour or greater. "Looks like your predictions of doom may come true," I said when DeMaurice reached the phone. "But really—is this storm any different from Diana?"

"Oh, very much so. It has the potential to be a real killer. There's no reason to expect it to lose strength, and it will be approaching our area at about twenty-five miles an hour. That's five times faster than Diana. And one of the complicating factors is that we're in a period of astronomically high tides. We're already running about three feet above normal, which with heavy northeast winds is enough to cause overwashes in several sections of the island. I'm going to send my wife and son off the island tomorrow if things keep looking like they look now. I've got to stay. Get back in touch with me after the storm, if I'm still around." He chuckled grimly.

I hung up with a shaky hand. For the first time I looked hard at the photographs of my family, the porcelain jewelry box on my dresser, the jeans and sweaters in my overflowing closet. Which of these could not be replaced? I had far too many things to take, but how would I whittle down my list of valuables to a manageable size? To calm myself I began gathering notebooks, sorting papers, making mental lists. The framed pictures would have to come off the walls in case the house started shaking—which seemed more than likely in hurricane-force winds. The stereo could be moved to a cabinet in the dining room. Did I have enough water in jugs for after the storm? I took down a kerosene lantern, filled it, and checked the wick. The electricity could go off at any moment, hurricane or no. Outside, I unlashed the bird feeders I had hung on the clothesline supports, and I piled cinder blocks on top of two doors I had stored on the back porch. Could a hurricane hurl a cinder block through a wall? Maybe, but if the wind reached that strength the house would probably break up.

Nearby I could hear the whirr of saws and the hammering of nails as a cottage owner boarded his windows. I had no plywood, but most of my windows contained small mullions that might withstand the wind. It was barely afternoon, anyway, and I would probably not leave until the next morning, if at all. For something to do I wandered down to the beach. The steel-gray water swelled fully but broke with little force. In recent weeks the beach had steepened. Now it dropped to the water in three steps: a six-inch ledge at the high-tide mark, a thirty-degree incline at the low-tide line, and a final scarp ten yards below that caused incoming waves to break a second time. Beyond that, the bottom had built and flattened as the weaker summer surf carried sand inland from nearby shoals. Nothing appeared the least unusual.

A wave glided toward me, and the sand began to bubble with mole crabs. In the past month they had doubled in length and weight. They would probably survive if a hurricane hit full force, but what would happen to the houses on the beach? It occurred to me that in a mere six months I had grown inordinately fond of the two miles of beach to the north, where I had climbed dunes, watched ghost crabs, and puzzled over the spread of shells across the sand. In a matter of hours a hurricane conceivably could render it unrecognizable. I went home and turned my dilapidated radio to an AM channel, which was blurred with static.

Gloria had moved fifty miles closer and was expected to pick up speed. The Dare County Commissioners advised Hatteras Island residents to prepare for evacuation before sunset. A mandatory evacuation had already been ordered for Ocracoke Island, since rough water was expected to suspend ferry operations by midnight, and it was not unlikely that Highway 12 would be flooded by dawn. If the storm continued on its predicted course, the Outer Banks might receive ocean surges of up to eighteen feet. The ground beneath my house was only four feet above sea level. An eighteen-foot tide would put the first floor under water.

I had no choice but to leave. Hurrying to the kitchen, I pulled from the cabinets a hand-painted platter that had been a gift from a friend and a pair of delft candlesticks my father had brought me from Holland. In my office I moved a clock, a vase, and an antique microscope away from the windows and stuffed my most important files into boxes to be put in the truck. I considered carrying a few things upstairs to protect them from flooding, but remembered that the roof could possibly come off.

I lowered the storm windows, moved furniture away from outside walls, stuffed a suitcase with clothes, packed a single box of mementos. The rest could be replaced. I had heard that a few windows should be left cracked to relieve sudden, drastic pressure changes as the eye of the hurricane passed over, so I raised two of the storms. The telephone rang with calls from anxious friends: I was leaving, wasn't I? I opened the door to the freezer and looked at my stockpile of food. All of it would be lost if the power went out for days. But if that were all I lost, I would feel exceedingly lucky.

I paused on the front porch long enough to wave to Halminski, who was loading boxes into his truck. "I'm going tonight," he called. "No sense hanging around and taking a chance on the roads." He was not alone. A steady flow of cars, campers, and trucks with trailered boats had begun moving north.

Near 8 o'clock, an hour after dark, I surveyed the rooms a

final time to check for items that needed to be secured. The sounds of sawing and hammering had grown louder; probably they would continue well into the night. I glanced briefly at two posters tacked to the kitchen wall and a ceramic pitcher on top of the hutch—they really could be replaced—before breezing through the living room and bedroom. On my dresser I spied a roll of film I had taken the previous week. Dropping it into my purse, I turned out the lights and locked the front door. As I drove away a feeling of nausea and fear settled firmly in my gut.

I drove only as far as Nags Head that night, bedding down on a friend's floor and making plans to turn inland the next day. By 11 P.M. the pace of the storm had slowed, and it was still five hundred miles south of the cape. I went to sleep feeling calmer and slightly foolish for fleeing so soon.

At daybreak the air was motionless, the sky cast with a textureless layer of cloud. The morning felt ominously empty, like the sudden, heavy silence that precedes an explosion of temper. Every television channel was filled with news about Gloria's move to within four hundred miles of the cape. I called the National Park Service and learned that Highway 12 had not flooded; as I had feared, I had been spooked into leaving too soon. I wondered about the condition of Pamlico Sound and the height of the surf. It seemed ridiculous to leave when the storm was not due for twelve hours or more. At the very least I had time for a trip back across the Oregon Inlet bridge.

I could see the tide washing high on the beach as I crossed the first leg of the bridge and began to climb to its crest. Below, the sound glistened, glassy and flat. The breakers at the inlet appeared small and less frenzied than usual. Great egrets crooked their necks to spear fish in the marsh beneath the bridge, and a tri-colored heron dashed across a mud flat on skinny legs, as if trying to chase down a crab. Above the north shore of Hatteras, a kingfisher perched on a wire with its bill pointed west. The scene was so calm and normal as to be spooky. I pulled into the parking lot at the bridge's southern edge and turned my truck back to the north.

At the time I began my drive inland, Halminski and Gerald sat on the porch of Mac and Marilyn's store and debated whether to leave. Despite his intention to evacuate the evening before, Halminski had worked until 1 o'clock moving his camera equipment to higher ground. Now he and Gerald—neither of whom had evacuated during the long threat of Hurricane Diana—quietly watched as Coast Guard vans and the last trickle of tourists and residents headed north. Neither wanted to go, but each was hesitant to stay alone. Debbie Bell, Randy Hall, and the rest of the immediate neighbors had already left. Finally Mac Midgett wandered out of the garage. A burly man with thick, curly sideburns that creep to his chin, Mac is known on Hatteras for his physical strength and fearlessness. "Looks like the whole island's gone," he said.

"Fleeing like a pack o' rats," Gerald said.

"I guess I'll load up and go."

"*You're* leaving?"

In the end only about four hundred people would stay on Hatteras, most of them in Buxton. More than two thousand residents, including the most weatherworn Hatterasmen, fled by dusk. As I drove west, past motels with "No Vacancy" signs in Columbia and Plymouth, past crowded emergency shelters in Williamston, Gloria neared shore and began to threaten Morehead City, fifty miles southwest of Ocracoke. As I arrived at a friend's house in Kinston and unloaded my gear, the hurricane turned north, directly toward Hatteras. The wind rose. The heavy rains expected all day began just after dark. I sagged into bed at 10:30 with Gloria ninety miles off the cape and moving north at twenty-five miles an hour.

If the storm traveled up Pamlico Sound, Hatteras Island would be to its east. The greatest winds and most dangerous storm surges occur in the northeast quadrant of a hurricane, where the forward motion of the storm boosts the power of the gusts. If the wind speed alone was 120 miles an hour and the storm moved north at 25 miles an hour, the combined winds would be 145—strong enough to destroy most buildings. Even if it passed east of the island, the damage could be significant.

Maybe, I thought, maybe it will still stall and go out to sea. The branches of two red maples scraped the roof as I fell asleep.

At 2:30 I woke up, startled by the quietness. The wind had quit, and my head felt stuffed with cotton. I crept downstairs to the living room and turned on the television. A weatherman was pointing to a map of the United States that had giant snowflakes pasted on top of Utah and Colorado. I kept the volume down until a map of eastern North Carolina flashed on the screen. "And as we reported an hour ago, Gloria did make landfall at Buxton on Hatteras Island about one-fifteen and is making her way up the coast," the weatherman said. "Reconnaissance flights show that she has already passed through the town of Avon, and the eye is about ten miles north of there at this time. It appears that the serious damage from the storm will be limited to the Outer Banks. So most of us in eastern North Carolina have a lot to be thankful for this evening."

Ten miles north of Avon! Five miles south of Rodanthe! Right now the winds would be blowing hard out of the east, three times as hard as during the northeaster that had kept me awake all night in April. The house would be shaking; dishes might be crashing out of cabinets. Gloria had been downgraded to a low Category Four hurricane, which meant gusts of only 130. A difference of twenty miles an hour did not strike me, just then, as significant. At least the storm had hit near low tide; the strong lunar pull meant that tides would be unusually low as well as unusually high. Low tide at Hatteras Inlet had occurred a few minutes after 1:00. Still, the ocean would be splashing over the dunes at the S curves and flowing down Highway 12, which would become a riverbed. Water would be lapping at my front door, my back door, maybe trickling into cracks. As the eye passed over, the air would grow still for perhaps twenty minutes. Then a hard west wind would slam the house, bringing a flood from the sound. I should have boarded the windows. I should have boxed up the ceramic pitcher.

I am standing in the kitchen. The wind has ripped my favorite posters off the wall. A spray of rain is blowing through a shattered window, and the water in the house is already six inches deep. Two

plastic cups bob next to the hutch, which is lying on its side. An
avalanche of broken glass spills from its open door. The flood is
rising fast, but it hasn't reached the paintings I piled on top of the
pub table in the dining room. Maybe it won't. The table's no great
loss; it needed to be refinished, anyway. . . . I am in my bedroom
shaking my head at the twisted frame of my iron bed. A minute ago
the dresser fell over and bent the footboard so badly it can never be
straightened. The house is still vibrating, and it looks like the two
northeast windows will be broken out by waves any time. Upstairs
the roof is leaking; water has begun to drip down the stairs.

The light the next day was a splendid yellow glaze that rico-
cheted from puddles and stabbed at my chafed, swollen eyes.
The sky was cloudless, the weather unseasonably warm. By the
time I reached Nags Head, the day had attained a peacefulness
that only heightened the numb sensation produced by my lack
of sleep. The waves that had swamped the causeway between
Manteo and Nags Head drained off before noon. By 1 o'clock
a line had formed at Whalebone Junction, the crossroads in
south Nags Head where Highway 12 forks to the south. Some
Hatteras residents had been able to return home by boat, but
the rest of us were told we would have to wait until the highway was reopened at 6 : 00.

The information available about conditions on the island
was sketchy, and certain details only heightened my worry.
Most of Hatteras had flooded; there was talk, in fact, that a
new inlet had been cut through. Rumors circulated that three
houses had burned in electrical fires. Other rumors reported
that damages were surprisingly light. Telephone calls to the
Buxton weather station and the Dare County sheriff's office in
Buxton brought news that the wind speed had reached only
eighty-seven miles an hour on the island and that no one had
been killed. Nevertheless, the force of the winds that preceded
the storm had pushed most of the water in Pamlico Sound
northward into the mainland's rivers and creeks. The harbors
at Hatteras and Avon had been sucked dry; then, after the eye
of the storm passed, the water had gushed back in a twelve-foot
wave. Many homes had been badly flooded; a few had col-

lapsed. A radio station in Kinston reported that two houses in Rodanthe had exploded. My heart lodged firmly in my throat.

By midafternoon tempers had begun to boil among the people who waited at Whalebone Junction. Many telephones were working on Hatteras, and calls to people who had ridden out the storm produced reports that Highway 12 was easily passable by four-wheel-drive truck. Still, the county commissioners had ordered that the highway remain closed until 6:00 to give workers time to scrape away sand and debris. Not even firemen would be allowed through. It was a dictum several Rodanthe men did not look upon kindly.

Shortly before 2 o'clock, a state highway trooper stationed at the turn-off to Hatteras Island looked up to see a line of pickups and jeeps speeding toward two patrol cars being used to barricade the highway. The shoulders of the road, although soggy, were clear on either side. The trucks whipped around the cars in a spray of water and continued south. The tactic signaled that Hatteras residents were determined to protect their property from fire and thieves—and that lawmen had best not stand in their way. Within the hour county officials had a change of heart; by 3 o'clock firemen and emergency service workers were granted permission to return to their homes.

The rest of us sat in our cars, grudgingly, as the sun began to set. Just before 6:00—forty-five minutes before dark—the barricades were moved aside and a mile-long string of traffic unleashed. Cars and trucks crowded behind recreational vehicles that slowed for four-inch-deep puddles. I drove three miles, then stopped dead behind an airstream trailer. Five minutes later, the line of traffic moved on.

Muddy water washed beneath my truck and sloshed to its bumper. On dry sections of highway, streaks of sand showed where dunes had eroded, and pockets of myrtle leaned to the east as if punched in by a fist. Otherwise, little damage was visible north of Oregon Inlet. But as I began the descent from the bridge I could see water lapping into the ridge of shrubs along the sound. The six-yard-wide beach in front of the shrubs was submerged. Farther south a line of telephone poles keeled badly to the east, and wire tangled on the ground. Thick swirls of eelgrass and rushes marked where the sound had crashed across the road and into the fields, almost to the primary dunes. Patches of mud, rippled in a pattern left by waves, covered the pavement. To my surprise, the tall, stately dunes on Pea Island appeared unscathed.

The sun had become a leaking red globe. Shadows stretched across the land as the sky turned to rose. I passed North Pond, only glancing at the squat profiles of two black-crowned night herons against the north dike. Normally they stuck to more secluded areas of the pond; normally I would have hit the brakes at the sight of them. Water from the pond brimmed close to the highway, as close as I had ever seen it. Birds appeared everywhere—hawks and herons, kingfishers and kestrels—but for once I did not care. Cars began to pass me at more than seventy miles an hour.

Bulldozers had scraped sand off the road at the S curves and piled it into six-foot mounds, next to chunks of wood and piles of rush stems. I braked briefly for the turns and accelerated in a burst. The roof of my house was still there and still shingled. I pulled carefully into the driveway—numb, anxious, afraid to go inside.

Flounder, pike, and croaker carcasses were strewn among the reeds, and the standing water smelled of marsh and mud. A wave had deposited a line of eelgrass on the top step, but the front porch was dry. Still aware of the traffic streaking by, I unlocked the door in the diminishing light, sucked in my breath, kicked off my sandals, and stepped into the living room. The rug was dry. I shined my flashlight on the windows, across the sofa to the stairs, and back into the kitchen. Except for a small puddle in the kitchen that had blown under the back door, the entire downstairs was dry. The second story was also undamaged. This cannot be, I thought, letting my gaze float around the rooms, to the paintings on the pub table, the posters in the kitchen, the ceramic pitcher. I lit the kerosene lamp and sat down, slowly, in the kitchen. The last light of evening I had come to love so well seeped through salt-sprayed windows.

On the beach that night, a waxing moon tickled the waves with bright ribbons of white. Where two days before the beach had been scarped and steep, it now sloped gradually to the surf.

The breeze was light and from the southwest, the water as tepid as tea. Pulses of lightning turned the few clouds that remained on the horizon a fleeting, burning orange.

"We should have stayed. Man, think of the waves we could have had yesterday morning."

"One of my cottage owners, a window of his blew in and he had glass literally embedded in his carpet."

"Nobody wants to go look in the graveyards. In this much water them bodies are likely to come floating up. They'll have to figure out who's who and rebury 'em."

"There was so much salt in the air you felt like you were standing on the deck of a ship in the middle of the blowing ocean."

"We were damn lucky, that's all I've got to say."

*

The next morning, when finally I pulled myself out of bed, the grass in my yard was an ashen gray from salt and mud. Traffic cruised slowly past the house as the first groups of sightseers trickled into town. Most declared Rodanthe a disappointment—nothing to see except residents drying out clothes and carpets—but in Avon the damage was more sensational. At least two houses lay in shreds. Eelgrass festooned the tops of beacons in the sound and the tips of six-foot shrubs on the east side of the road. In places, planks of fine-grade lumber had been carried by water from construction sites and strewn along the road.

The towns of the cape began to buzz with the camaraderie and good will that accompany disasters. Normally taciturn neighbors toured each other's houses, inspecting the damage and trading tales. People whose homes had not been flooded made up spare beds for the less fortunate, then pooled their foodstuffs and cleaning supplies. My house had been one of the few ground-level structures to escape flooding as Gloria pushed four feet of water through town. A fish house on the creek near my backyard marsh had exploded, its walls apparently pushed out by changes in pressure. Beyond it lay a swath of reed stems and trash thrown to the northeast—directly toward my house—by the surge from the sound. In the old village of Avon, two hundred houses had flooded, some by as much as seven feet, and the reported damages would exceed one million dollars. But the towns of Hatteras had stood, had even suffered remarkably little damage. Like several of my neighbors, I began to wish I had stayed through the storm.

I went to see Wally DeMaurice at the weather station, where he and two of his staff had worked through the night of the storm in a reinforced concrete-block building. During the twenty-six minutes that Gloria's eye passed over Buxton, DeMaurice had taken time away from his instruments only to dash outside and release a weather balloon. He pulled a paper from a file and slapped it on the table where I sat. It was a chart of barometric pressure during Gloria's approach. By 6 P.M. the pressure had begun a nearly vertical decline. At midnight it dropped completely off the chart.

"Never in twenty-six years of weather watching have I seen the barometer drop so fast," he said. "I know some people are wondering what all the commotion was. But keep in mind that we were extremely lucky. There were about six factors that worked in our favor. If any one of them had been different, the damage would have been much, much worse. That storm traveled from the west coast of Africa. If it had passed twenty miles to the west of us, up the sound, we would have been in the maximum energy field. It would have raped the Outer Banks. If it had hit at high tide, we would have had twelve feet more water than the predicted tide for that date. As it was, we only got about three to four feet more over most of the island, maybe five to eight feet in Avon.

"Remember, at one point this was the biggest storm ever to develop in the open Atlantic. Now, it lost a lot of its strength, but it still had the power to push all the water in Pamlico Sound to the north. When you think how much that amount of water weighs, you know the force behind it was staggering."

Whatever thrills I may have missed, I had been wise to leave. And for the next several days the residents of Hatteras would be granted a reprieve from work, since life would not return to normal as long as the electricity remained off. Why not relax and enjoy the commotion?

Meals became unusually festive as freezers defrosted and stocks of food thawed. Saturday night Halminski boiled ten pounds of shrimp, and Debbie Bell grilled eight pounds of steak raised at her father's farm on the mainland. In the absence of normal life, people organized their days around meals. Only minimal clean-up work could be done without electricity to pump water, and even when the power was restored, many wells would be salty from the tide and polluted from overflowing septic tanks.

Stories began circulating of people who had stayed through the storm, what they had witnessed, and how they had reacted. In Avon, where wind gauges had recorded gusts of more than a hundred miles an hour, residents retreated to the second stories of their houses as water poured into their living rooms and dens. Many of the oldest houses in town had been bolted to their foundations after the hurricanes of 1933 and 1944 had floated them to the beach. As Gloria pushed water from the sound through the village, a few residents cracked open their doors to allow it to flow through their houses rather than splinter the frames.

Rachel Austin pried loose two floorboards in her living room to prevent the flood from pushing up her entire first floor. As the sound tide swept through their front yard and toward the swaybacked house where the Austins had lived for forty years, the seventy-two-year-old woman and her husband, Willie, began piling up their furniture and appliances. Within ten minutes after water began gushing through the floor it had crested the window sills, turning Rachel's flowered wallpaper and yellow curtains a muddy gray. The refrigerator toppled over, and the stove twisted from its pipe. A mantel fell out from the wall. But the house was one of the oldest residences on the Outer Banks. Assuming it would stand through one more storm, they retired for the evening in their second-story bedroom after securing as many of their possessions as they could. All night they could hear water slopping against their furniture. They slept fitfully, but were content to be dry and warm. The next morning they went downstairs to find the kitchen blown off the house.

Again and again I heard people relate tales of stepping out into the eye of the storm and seeing stars, of walking to a neighbor's house in the worst of the wind, of drifting off to sleep and waking disappointed to find Gloria past. A few admitted twinges of anxiety after the sound flooded the island. Only once did I hear a resident express unbridled fright.

Brad Nash has yellow-white hair and a face so tan his blue eyes seem to shine through it like those in a jack-o'-lantern. A crabber and furniture builder who lives with his parents in Avon, he has resided on Hatteras full-time for seven years. As Gloria moved up the coast, he dismissed his parents' pleas to evacuate and settled into the third floor of his house, with his dog and two cats. The fourteen-year-old wood structure sits on three-foot pilings on a canal near the sound.

Nash had tracked Gloria as it moved up the coast and had noticed it was losing strength. As dusk approached and the winds rose, he tuned his maritime radio to the Cape Hatteras station and positioned himself in the living area at the southeast corner of the house. Nearby he had a wind gauge, a telephone, a life preserver, and an open notebook.

"At some point I decided I needed to keep a journal, if only to keep myself sane. I'm not sure when it became clear to me that the storm was actually going to hit. But by seven-thirty or eight I knew I was on Hatteras for good, that there was no getting off."

Nash's notes began at 8 P.M.

Winds NE, steady 50 to 65. Gusts to 85. I feel very much alone. House shaking, pets okay.

8:07—Winds 60 to 75.

"It occurred to me about this time that the buildings around me might pose a big threat. I wasn't worried about this house blowing apart on its own. It's too solid. But there's a house next door on stilts, and I began thinking that its windows might blow out and it might fall over, like a sprung umbrella."

9:00—Gloria 140 miles south of Hatteras. Gusts to 90.

As the hurricane approached, Nash began to receive phone calls from his anxious parents and from a friend who was driving east from Chicago to Maryland. The conversations eased his tension; as long as the phones continued to work, things couldn't be too bad. Periodically he ventured outside, where he used a large floodlight to watch the water level drop in the sound. By 11:00 the canal beside his house was empty. He remembered that his neighbor had moored a forty-five-foot fishing boat on the far side of the canal. The thought suddenly made his stomach flip. If the boat broke from its mooring after Gloria's eye passed, it would probably ram his house.

The winds increased until Nash could no longer open the east-facing door to a third-story deck.

11:30—Winds 80 to 90, gusts way past 100. House rumbling and shaking bad.

11:50—Something crashed and broke downstairs. Winds steady at 100+. Much wind noise—whistling and shrieking.

"At one point I jammed tissues in my ears because I couldn't stand the noise. It was very shrill. About this time too, an ash tray jumped across a desk and fell on the floor. That's how bad the house was vibrating. It would move considerably; it was like being on board a ship."

12:30—Barometer down to 29.

1:12—Ears starting to pop. Must yawn to help.

1:35—Eye here, with winds at 10 mph. Seems dead calm. Barometer at 27.8.

1:55—Eye gone. Winds west at 40. Very west. Still bone dry outside.

2:24—100+ west winds.

2:56—Strongest winds so far. House moving badly.

3:22—Phone dead. House being blasted.

Nash's journal did not make note of what time the sound tide rushed back in from the north. By then, however, he had opened the east-facing door to relieve changes in pressure and had gone outside to survey his immediate surroundings with the floodlight. He watched as a twelve- to fourteen-foot wave approached, lifting debris to its crest and slinging it forward.

"Everything started bobbing and dancing. There was debris all over the place, and the water was just sloshing violently. I had some piles of juniper six inches wide and sixteen feet long; they were flying around like Fritos. Waves started hitting the upstairs window.

"The thing that worried me the most was the big boat across

the canal. It was straining at its ropes; I thought it had gotten loose. It would pull toward me during a lull, and then a gust would get it and flip it back away from me, like a slingshot. It danced around like crazy, like the tail on a kite. Sometimes I could barely see it, it was moving so fast. And then it would whip toward me again.

"It was about this time that I put on the life preserver."

Around 3:40 Nash crawled out the eastern door, digging his fingers in between the planks on the deck. He could hear bangs and thumps coming from the sound side of the house, but without his floodlight he could not tell if the structure was being damaged. He wore a pair of goggles to protect his eyes. Slowly he slid his head and shoulders around the corner of the house to the west, bracing himself for the impact of Gloria's gusts. The wind caught him in the chest and threw him against the deck railing. He crawled back to safety, but not before he had seen that waves were tossing the fishing boat very close to the house.

3:44—Big boat hitting house. Wind won't die. Can hear lumber cracking and breaking. House might go down.

4:15—Helpless. Wind won't stop. House can't stand the damage. I'll have a Dr. Pepper and a cigarette.

4:39—Wind down some. It'll be daybreak and nice weather soon.

4:40—It will subside.

Before dawn he realized the fishing boat had rammed into a pile of lumber and lodged several yards from the house. By 5 o'clock the wind had dropped to between seventy and eighty, and the sound had begun to recede. Three feet of water still churned through his yard. Two lower-story windows had blown out, and water had washed into his shop on the first floor. But the building was intact.

"At that point," Nash said, "I kissed my pets, I went downstairs, I got on my very wet mattress, and I went to sleep."

Wendell Berry

The Making of a
Marginal Farm

(KENTUCKY)

One day in the summer of 1956, leaving home for school, I stopped on the side of the road directly above the house where I now live. From there you could see a mile or so across the Kentucky River Valley, and perhaps six miles along the length of it. The valley was a green trough full of sunlight, blue in its distances. I often stopped here in my comings and goings, just to look, for it was all familiar to me from before the time my memory began: woodlands and pastures on the hillsides; fields and croplands, wooded slew-edges and hollows in the bottoms; and through the midst of it the tree-lined river passing down from its headwaters near the Virginia line toward its mouth at Carrollton on the Ohio.

Standing there, I was looking at land where one of my great-great-great-grandfathers settled in 1803, and at the scene of some of the happiest times of my own life, where in my growing-up years I camped, hunted, fished, boated, swam, and wandered—where, in short, I did whatever escaping I felt called upon to do. It was a place where I had happily been, and where I always wanted to be. And I remember gesturing toward the valley that day and saying to the friend who was with me: "That's all I need."

I meant it. It was an honest enough response to my recognition of its beauty, the abundance of its lives and possibilities, and of my own love for it and interest in it. And in the sense that I continue to recognize all that, and feel that what I most need is here, I can still say the same thing.

And yet I am aware that I must necessarily mean differently—or at least a great deal more—when I say it now. Then I was speaking mostly from affection, and did not know, by half, what I was talking about. I was speaking of a place that in some ways I knew and in some ways cared for, but did not live in. The differences between knowing a place and living in it, between cherishing a place and living responsibly in it, had not begun to occur to me. But they are critical differences, and understanding them has been perhaps the chief necessity of my experience since then.

I married in the following summer, and in the next seven years lived in a number of distant places. But, largely because I continued to feel that what I needed was here, I could never bring myself to want to live in any other place. And so we returned to live in Kentucky in the summer of 1964, and that autumn bought the house whose roof my friend and I had looked down on eight years before, and with it "twelve acres more or less." Thus I began a profound change in my life. Before, I had lived according to expectation rooted in ambition. Now I began to live according to a kind of destiny rooted in my origins and in my life. One should not speak too confidently of one's "destiny"; I use the word to refer to causes that lie deeper in history and character than mere intention or desire. In buying the little place known as Lanes Landing, it seems to me, I began to obey the deeper causes.

We had returned so that I could take a job at the University of Kentucky in Lexington. And we expected to live pretty much the usual academic life: I would teach and write; my "subject matter" would be, as it had been, the few square miles in Henry County where I grew up. We bought the tiny farm at Lanes Landing, thinking that we would use it as a "summer place," and on that understanding I began, with the help of two carpenter friends, to make some necessary repairs on the house. I no longer remember exactly how it was decided, but that work had hardly begun when it became a full-scale overhaul. By so little our minds had been changed: this was not going to be a house to visit, but a house to live in. It was as though, having put our hand to the plow, we not only did not look back, but could not. We renewed the old house, equipped it with plumbing, bathroom, and oil furnace, and moved in on July 4, 1965.

Once the house was whole again, we came under the influence of the "twelve acres more or less." This acreage included a steep hillside pasture, two small pastures by the river, and a "garden spot" of less than half an acre. We had, besides the house, a small barn in bad shape, a good large building that once had been a general store, and a small garage also in usable condition. This was hardly a farm by modern standards, but it was land that could be used, and it was unthinkable that we would not use it. The land was not good enough to afford the possibility of a cash income, but it would allow us to grow our food—or most of it. And that is what we set out to do.

In the early spring of 1965 I had planted a small orchard; the next spring we planted our first garden. Within the following six or seven years we reclaimed the pastures, converted the garage into a henhouse, rebuilt the barn, greatly improved the garden soil, planted berry bushes, acquired a milk cow—and were producing, except for hay and grain for our animals, nearly everything that we ate: fruit, vegetables, eggs, meat, milk, cream, and butter. We built an outbuilding with a meat room and a food-storage cellar. Because we did not want to pollute our land and water with sewage, and in the process waste nutrients that should be returned to the soil, we built a composting privy. And so we began to attempt a life that, in addition to whatever else it was, would be responsibly agricultural. We used no chemical fertilizers. Except for a little rotenone, we used no insecticides. As our land and our food became healthier, so did we. And our food was of better quality than any that we could have bought.

We were not, of course, living an idyll. What we had done could not have been accomplished without difficulty and a great deal of work. And we had made some mistakes and false starts. But there was great satisfaction, too, in restoring the neglected land, and in feeding ourselves from it.

Meanwhile, the forty-acre place adjoining ours on the downriver side had been sold to a "developer," who planned to divide it into lots for "second homes." This project was probably doomed by the steepness of the ground and the difficulty of access, but a lot of bulldozing—and a lot of damage—was done before it was given up. In the fall of 1972, the place was offered for sale and we were able to buy it.

We now began to deal with larger agricultural problems. Some of this new land was usable; some would have to be left in trees. There were perhaps fifteen acres of hillside that could be reclaimed for pasture, and about two and a half acres of excellent bottomland on which we would grow alfalfa for hay. But it was a mess, all of it badly neglected, and a considerable portion of it badly abused by the developer's bulldozers. The hillsides were covered with thicket growth; the bottom was shoulder high in weeds; the diversion ditches had to be restored; a bulldozed gash meant for "building sites" had to be mended; the barn needed a new foundation, and the cistern a new top; there were no fences. What we had bought was less a farm than a reclamation project—which has now, with a later purchase, grown to seventy-five acres.

While we had only the small place, I had got along very well with a Gravely "walking tractor" that I owned, and an old Farmall A that I occasionally borrowed from my Uncle Jimmy. But now that we had increased our acreage, it was clear that I could not continue to depend on a borrowed tractor. For a while I assumed that I would buy a tractor of my own. But because our land was steep, and there was already talk of a fuel shortage—and because I liked the idea—I finally decided to buy a team of horses instead. By the spring of 1973, after a lot of inquiring and looking, I had found and bought a team of five-year-old sorrel mares. And—again by the generosity of my Uncle Jimmy, who has never thrown any good thing away—I had enough equipment to make a start.

Though I had worked horses and mules during the time I was growing up, I had never worked over ground so steep and problematical as this, and it had been twenty years since I had worked a team over ground of any kind. Getting started again, I anticipated every new task with uneasiness, and sometimes with dread. But to my relief and delight, the team and I did all that needed to be done that year, getting better as we went along. And over the years since then, with that team and others, my son and I have carried on our farming the way it was carried on in my boyhood, doing everything with our horses except baling the hay. And we have done work in places and in weather in which a tractor would have been useless. Experience has shown us—or re-shown us—that horses are not only a satisfactory and economical means of power, especially on such small places as ours, but are probably *necessary* to the most conservative use of steep land. Our farm, in fact, is surrounded by potentially excellent hillsides that were maintained in pasture until tractors replaced the teams.

Another change in our economy (and our lives) was accomplished in the fall of 1973 with the purchase of our first wood-burning stove. Again the petroleum shortage was on our minds, but we also knew that from the pasture-clearing we had ahead of us we would have an abundance of wood that otherwise would go to waste—and when that was gone we would still have our permanent wood lots. We thus expanded our subsistence income to include heating fuel, and since then have used our furnace only as a "backup system" in the coldest weather and in our absences from home. The horses also contribute significantly to the work of fuel-gathering; they will go easily into difficult places and over soft ground or snow where a truck or a tractor could not move.

As we have continued to live on and from our place, we have slowly begun its restoration and healing. Most of the scars have now been mended and grassed over, most of the washes stopped, most of the buildings made sound; many loads of rocks have been hauled out of the fields and used to pave entrances or fill hollows; we have done perhaps half of the necessary fencing. A great deal of work is still left to do, and some of it—the rebuilding of fertility in the depleted hillsides—will take longer than we will live. But in doing these things we have begun a restoration and a healing in ourselves.

I should say plainly that this has not been a "paying proposition." As a reclamation project, it has been costly both in money and in effort. It seems at least possible that, in any other place, I might have had little interest in doing any such thing. The reason I have been interested in doing it here, I think, is that I have felt implicated in the history, the uses, and the attitudes that have depleted such places as ours and made them "marginal."

I had not worked long on our "twelve acres more or less" before I saw that such places were explained almost as much by their human history as by their nature. I saw that they were not "marginal" because they ever were unfit for human use, but because in both culture and character *we* had been unfit to use them. Originally, even such steep slopes as these along the lower Kentucky River Valley were deep-soiled and abundantly fertile; "jumper" plows and generations of carelessness impoverished them. Where yellow clay is at the surface now, five feet of good soil may be gone. I once wrote that on some of the nearby uplands one walks as if "knee-deep" in the absence of the original soil. On these steeper slopes, I now know, that absence is shoulder-deep.

That is a loss that is horrifying as soon as it is imagined. It happened easily, by ignorance, indifference, "a little folding of the hands to sleep." It cannot be remedied in human time; to build five feet of soil takes perhaps fifty or sixty thousand years. This loss, once imagined, is potent with despair. If a people in adding a hundred and fifty years to itself subtracts fifty thousand from its land, what is there to hope?

And so our reclamation project has been, for me, less a matter of idealism or morality than a kind of self-preservation. A destructive history, once it is understood as such, is a nearly insupportable burden. Understanding it is a disease of understanding, depleting the sense of efficacy and paralyzing effort, unless it finds healing work. For me that work has been partly of the mind, in what I have written, but that seems to have depended inescapably on work of the body and of the ground. In order to affirm the values most native and necessary to me—indeed, to affirm my own life as a thing decent in possibility—I needed to know in my own experience that this place did not have to be abused in the past, and that it can be kindly and conservingly used now.

With certain reservations that must be strictly borne in mind, our work here has begun to offer some of the needed proofs.

Bountiful as the vanished original soil of the hillsides may have been, what remains is good. It responds well—sometimes astonishingly well—to good treatment. It never should have been plowed (some of it never should have been cleared), and it never should be plowed again. But it can be put in pasture without plowing, and it will support an excellent grass sod that will in turn protect it from erosion, if properly managed and not overgrazed.

Land so steep as this cannot be preserved in row crop cultivation. To subject it to such an expectation is simply to ruin it, as its history shows. Our rule, generally, has been to plow no steep ground, to maintain in pasture only such slopes as can be safely mowed with a horse-drawn mower, and to leave the rest in trees. We have increased the numbers of livestock on our pastures gradually, and have carefully rotated the animals from field to field, in order to avoid overgrazing. Under this use and care, our hillsides have mended and they produce more and better pasturage every year.

As a child I always intended to be a farmer. As a young man, I gave up that intention, assuming that I could not farm and do the other things I wanted to do. And then I became a farmer almost unintentionally and by a kind of necessity. That wayward and necessary becoming—along with my marriage, which has been intimately a part of it—is the major event of my life. It has changed me profoundly from the man and the writer I would otherwise have been.

There was a time, after I had left home and before I came back, when this place was my "subject matter." I meant that too, I think, on the day in 1956 when I told my friend, "That's all I need." I was regarding it, in a way too easy for a writer, as a mirror in which I saw myself. There was obviously a sort of narcissism in that—and an inevitable superficiality, for only the surface can reflect.

In coming home and settling on this place, I began to *live* in my subject, and to learn that living in one's subject is not at all the same as "having" a subject. To live in the place that is one's subject is to pass through the surface. The simplifications of distance and mere observation are thus destroyed. The obsessively regarded reflection is broken and dissolved. One sees that the mirror was a blinder; one can now begin to see where one is. One's relation to one's subject ceases to be merely emotional or esthetical, or even merely critical, and becomes problematical, practical, and responsible as well. Because it must. It is like marrying your sweetheart.

Though our farm has not been an economic success, as such success is usually reckoned, it is nevertheless beginning to make a kind of economic sense that is consoling and hopeful. Now that the largest expenses of purchase and repair are behind us, our income from the place is beginning to run ahead of expenses. As income I am counting the value of shelter, subsistence, heating fuel, and money earned by the sale of livestock. As expenses I am counting maintenance, newly purchased equipment, extra livestock feed, newly purchased animals, reclamation work, fencing materials, taxes, and insurance.

If our land had been in better shape when we bought it, our expenses would obviously be much smaller. As it is, once we have completed its restoration, our farm will provide us a home, produce our subsistence, keep us warm in winter, and earn a modest cash income. The significance of this becomes apparent when one considers that most of this land is "unfarmable" by the standards of conventional agriculture, and that most of it was producing nothing at the time we bought it.

And so, contrary to some people's opinion, it *is* possible for a family to live on such "marginal" land, to take a bountiful subsistence and some cash income from it, and, in doing so, to improve both the land and themselves. (I believe, however, that, at least in the present economy, this should not be attempted without a source of income other than the farm. It is now extremely difficult to pay for the best of farmland by farming it, and even "marginal" land has become unreasonably expensive. To attempt to make a living from such land is to impose a severe strain on land and people alike.)

I said earlier that the success of our work here is subject to reservations. There are only two of these, but both are serious.

The first is that land like ours—and there are many acres of such land in this country—can be conserved in use only by competent knowledge, by a great deal more work than is required by leveler land, by a devotion more particular and disciplined than patriotism, and by ceaseless watchfulness and care. All these are cultural values and resources, never sufficiently abundant in this country, and now almost obliterated by the contrary values of the so-called "affluent society."

One of my own mistakes will suggest the difficulty. In 1974 I dug a small pond on a wooded hillside that I wanted to pasture occasionally. The excavation for that pond—as I should have anticipated, for I had better reason than I used—caused the hillside to slump both above and below. After six years the slope has not stabilized, and more expense and trouble will be required to stabilize it. A small hillside farm will not survive many mistakes of that order. Nor will a modest income.

The true remedy for mistakes is to keep from making them. It is not in the piecemeal technological solutions that our society now offers, but in a change of cultural (and economic) values that will encourage in the whole population the necessary respect, restraint, and care. Even more important, it is in the possibility of settled families and local communities, in which the knowledge of proper means and methods, proper moderations and restraints, can be handed down, and so accumulate in place and stay alive; the experience of one generation is not adequate to inform and control its actions. Such possibilities are not now in sight in this country.

The second reservation is that we live at the lower end of the Kentucky River watershed, which has long been intensively used, and is increasingly abused. Strip mining, logging, extractive farming, and the digging, draining, roofing, and paving that go with industrial and urban "development," all have seriously depleted the capacity of the watershed to retain water. This means not only that floods are higher and more frequent than they would be if the watershed were healthy, but that the floods subside too quickly, the watershed being far less a sponge, now, than it is a roof. The floodwater drops suddenly out of the river, leaving the steep banks soggy, heavy, and soft. As a result, great strips and blocks of land crack loose and slump, or they give way entirely and disappear into the river in what people here call "slips."

The flood of December 1978, which was unusually high, also went down extremely fast, falling from bank top almost to pool stage within a couple of days. In the aftermath of this rapid "drawdown," we lost a block of bottomland an acre square. This slip, which is still crumbling, severely damaged our place, and may eventually undermine two buildings. The same flood started a slip in another place, which threatens a third building. We have yet another building situated on a huge (but, so far, very gradual) slide that starts at the river and, aggravated by two state highway cuts, goes almost to the hilltop. And we have serious river bank erosion the whole length of our place.

What this means is that, no matter how successfully we may control erosion on our hillsides, our land remains susceptible to a more serious cause of erosion that we cannot control. Our river bank stands literally at the cutting edge of our nation's consumptive economy. This, I think, is true of many "marginal" places—it is true, in fact, of many places that are not marginal. In its consciousness, ours is an upland society; the ruin of watersheds, and what that involves and means, is little considered. And so the land is heavily taxed to subsidize an "affluence" that consists, in reality, of health and goods stolen from the unborn.

Living at the lower end of the Kentucky River watershed is what is now known as "an educational experience"—and not an easy one. A lot of information comes with it that is severely damaging to the reputation of our people and our time. From where I live and work, I never have to look far to see that the earth does indeed pass away. But however that is taught, and however bitterly learned, it is something that should be known, and there is a certain good strength in knowing it. To spend one's life farming a piece of the earth so passing is, as many would say, a hard lot. But it is, in an ancient sense, the human lot. What saves it is to love the farming.

Eddy L. Harris

Vicksburg

(MISSISSIPPI)

Too many marvelous days in a row and you begin to get used to it, to think that's the way it's supposed to be. Too many good days, too many bad days—you need some break in the monotony of one to appreciate the other. If you only get sunshine, someone said, you end up in a desert.

I guess I'd had enough hard days to last me for a while, enough scary times to be able to appreciate the peaceful, easy, glorious days. On the way to Natchez, I had another one and I took full advantage of it to do absolutely nothing. No singing, no thinking, no talking to myself. Just feeling. Watching the river, noticing the changes in color, seeing the way it rises and falls depending on the wind and on what lay on the river bed. Each change had something to say, and I listened to the river. The river was talking to me, changing colors from puce to brown to thick murky green. Saying nothing. The idle chatter you get when you walk with your favorite niece or nephew going no place in particular with nothing special on your minds and the little kid just jabbers away because it's comfortable and he feels like it. The river was like that to me. A comfortable buddy sharing a lazy day.

Nothing else mattered then. Going someplace

42

or not. Arriving in New Orleans or shooting past and landing in Brazil. I didn't care about anything. The river kept me company and kept me satisfied. Nothing else mattered.

Then the river whispered, "Get ready. Get ready."

The day turned grey and strange. Clouds rolled overhead in wild swirls like batter in a bowl. I could see the rain storm forming off in the distance but swirling rapidly toward me like a dark grey avalanche. I felt the river dip down and up—a shallow dale in the water. I passed from the cool moisture surrounding me and into a pocket of thin air hot and dry. It was as though a gap had opened in the clouds and the sun streamed through to boil the water and heat up this isolated patch of river a scant thirty yards long. My first thought was to shed a shirt and stay cool, but when I passed through the far curtain of the insulated air, I knew I had better do just the opposite. I drifted and donned my yellow rain suit and hood. The sky above grew serious and advanced in my direction with the speed of a hurricane. Looking for a place to land I scanned the shore. There was no shore. Only trees. Because of the heavy rains and the high water, the shore had disappeared and the new shoreline of solid earth had been pushed back through the trees and beyond the woods. How far beyond, I couldn't tell. I looked across to the other side of the river half a mile away. No way could I have made it over there. Halfway across and the wind would have kicked up and trapped me in the middle.

The leading edge of the storm came and the first sprinkles passed over like army scouts. The wooded area lasted only another hundred yards or so and I thought I could easily get there before the rains arrived. I could then turn left and find ground to pull out and wait out the storm. But the voice of the river came out and spoke to me teasingly but with a chill of seriousness down my spine. I could have ignored it, but as if reading my thoughts and not wanting me to fight it, the river grabbed the end of the canoe and turned me toward the trees. I thought I was looking for land. I wasn't. I was looking for shelter.

The urge to get into the trees came on me quite suddenly and really without thought or effort on my part. Almost an instinct. No sooner had I ducked into the trees than the sky split open with a loud crash and a splintery crackle of lightning. I was not going to make it through the trees. The wind came in at hurricane strength. The tips of the trees bent way over and aimed toward the ground, like fishing rods hooked on a big one. Water flooded like the tide rushing upstream. The trees swooshed loudly as the leaves and branches brushed hard together. Branches fell. Rains came and poured down buckets-full.

The trees were tall and no more than three feet around. I maneuvered the canoe as best I could in the wind and rushing water, turned it to face upstream and kept my back to the rain which slanted in at a sharp angle. I reached out for the sturdiest tree I could get my arms around and I held on.

Water everywhere. The river sloshed over the side and into the canoe. I tried to keep the stern pointed right into the flow so the canoe could ride the waves, but it didn't work. The canoe was twisted about and water poured over the side. The rain was heavier than any I had ever been in or seen before. It really was more like a tropical storm. The heavy winds, the amount of water, the warmth of the air and the cold rain. Only my neck was exposed to the rain. When the rain hit my neck, it ran under the rain suit and very cold down my back.

The wind shifted as the storm came directly overhead. Water streamed straight down. I was drenched and the canoe was filling up quickly. Anything in the canoe that could float was floating. If the rain continued for long or if the wind kept up strong and the rain kept spilling into the canoe, I would sink. But I was not worried, hardly more than concerned. In fact I enjoyed the feeling of the water all around me and on me, enveloping me like a cocoon, and despite the drama I felt no real threat. I was more amazed than anything, trying to analyze the voice I had heard or whatever instinct or intuition it was that urged me to park in these trees. It had been something so very definite that I could feel it and yet so ethereal that I could not put my finger on it. So I stopped trying and just sat there patiently waiting and hugging my tree. I was one with this river and nothing could happen to me.

The storm slid forward and the rain slanted in on my face.

Then it moved on farther up river to drench someone else. It was gone as suddenly as it had arisen. Only the trailing edge was left, a light rain that lasted almost until I reached Natchez.

The sky remained grey but lightened and I paddled from my rainforest and down river to Natchez. My little boat lumbered through the water. The canoe carried six inches of water and was heavy and I could find no speed. But I didn't need any. I was relaxed and floating in the mist as thick as the mysteries of the river. It was evening when I reached Natchez.

Natchez, Mississippi, sits high above the river. Green trees and grassy hills rise up from the river to the city. Rising out of the hills and overhanging the river, huge white antebellum mansions guard the approach to the city like statues lining the wide corridor of some great cathedral. The homes stand beautiful and proud, reminders of gentler and nobler times.

The *Delta Queen*, another reminder, was moored at the foot of the old part of town. I went right up to get a closer look. A massive paddlewheeler that takes her voyagers back in time as she carries them up and down the river, stopping for brief glimpses of history at Natchez and St. Francisville and ancient plantations along the route. The captain told me she sails as far up as St. Paul and down to New Orleans with trips up the Ohio River to Cincinnati. They were on their way shortly to New Orleans and I asked for a ride.

"You don't want a ride," the captain said. "This is something you want to do all by yourself. You'll feel better if you do and you'd hate yourself if you didn't."

No I wouldn't. If he had said okay, I would have hopped quickly on board and ridden down with him. I had already found it, whatever this trip was for; I had done it, even if I didn't understand it yet, and probably wouldn't until years from now anyway.

A few great blasts from the steam whistle and she pushed away from shore and set out, lights on the big calliope playing merry music like a circus. It was 1836 all over again. The *Queen* paddled up river, turned around and slowly splashed south, the staterooms all lit up and gay. You couldn't see the boat at all in the darkness, only the lights. They seemed to float along with no structure holding them together. Too soon the lights were gone round the bend and the calliope faded into the night and the crowd that had gathered at the riverfront to watch as of old began to disperse.

I bailed out my canoe using a milk carton. It took a while. I had a few passing conversations and then walked up the hill. It was drizzling again and I must have looked lost.

This was the old town. A little park stretched off to the south—more a promenade than a park—and there were a few quaint shops for the tourists and a bar and a couple of nice looking restaurants. Three beautiful women were getting out of a car parked along the side of the road when I passed. The three prettiest women in Mississippi. They were going to eat in one of the cute little restaurants. They were all dressed up and hurried because of the rain. They wouldn't want to get their hair and clothes messed up. I asked them quickly if they knew the time and two of the three ignored me totally and kept walking. I felt like the invisible man. But the third woman had heard me. She looked toward her two friends. She wore a quizzical expression and it was plain that she was looking for the translation. She must have thought I was speaking a foreign language.

"I won't bite you," I said. "I just want the time."

Then she turned and the three of them walked purposefully on and I stood stunned for two seconds; I said nothing else. I chuckled to myself and silently wished for them to slip and fall in the mud. When they didn't, when they had crossed the little gravel parking lot and climbed up the three wooden steps and disappeared into the warmth and dryness of the cozy little eatery, leaving me standing out in the drizzle, I hoped they would order seafood and I hoped that each one would get a bad oyster or a tainted piece of catfish.

Two steps farther on, I passed a man sitting all alone in his pickup truck. He was killing time, watching the river and he turned to watch me walk by. When our eyes met, I tapped my wrist and gave the international symbol for what time is it. I don't know why I wanted to know; I had no place I had to be and nothing I had to do apart from finding a place to pitch my tent, which I couldn't do until all the shops had closed and everyone had gone home.

Bill invited me to warm up in his truck.

"Do you need to go to the store or anything?" He had a great Southern accent, heavy but cultured and easily understandable.

"Well, I guess I could use some milk and a few things."

He took me on a little tour of Natchez. He was proud of this little place, I could see, and he was happy to drive me around. He even tried to arrange a place for me to sleep for the night and later pointed out the Salvation Army shelter where I could at least be dry all night long. I half expected him to invite me home, put me up in the attic and then keep me over for Thanksgiving dinner tomorrow night, but that was asking too much. He already had relatives visiting for the holiday.

I told him I'd probably just pitch camp in the little park.

"I wouldn't build a fire or anything if I were you. The police will come down there and make you move. They might even want to lock you up for the night."

Then he fished in his wallet and pulled out a business card.

"If they do come along and throw you in jail, give me a call. You can sleep there for the night, and I can get you out in the morning. I'm the city attorney."

Actually, he was an attorney with a local practice and he was the acting city attorney whenever the regular city attorney was away, like now.

I had the feeling he wasn't too thrilled to be going home to his wife and the visiting in-laws, that he would rather have stayed down on the levee watching the river and the *Queen* or talking to me or driving me around showing me the beautiful homes of Natchez. Hope Farm. Stanton Hall. Longwood. D'Evereux. Ellicott Hill. Propinquity. Montaigne. Mount Repose. Homes as beautiful and stately and elegant as the names. But Bill had to get on home.

He drove away and I hung around killing time until late in the evening. When everything had closed and everyone had gone home—about nine o'clock, I'd guess—I pulled my canoe a few yards down river and put up the tent. It was in a little gully at the edge of the water with the blunt face of a muddy hill behind me. Not one of my more picturesque campsites. A rickety rowboat full of junk was tied up not far away and later on the owner of it staggered back drunk from town, climbed into the boat and slept there. I met him in the morning and was shocked to find out who he was—shocked and pleased.

Eleven hundred miles and I don't know how many days ago, Wally at Piasa Harbor had told me about a religious zealot rowing for Jesus down the river in a rickety rowboat of homemade construction. As James White talked the following morning, pieces fell into place and it hit me.

"Hey!" I shouted out of the blue. "I know you."

"You do?"

"I don't know you, but I heard about you. Back near Alton they were talking about this nut who had taken his bicycle apart and built a contraption for pedaling a boat down the river."

"That's me all right."

How strange to have caught up with him after all this time! I hadn't thought of him once since I left Wally.

We had breakfast together in a fancy hotel restaurant and they gave us a few funny looks, but served us without complaint. Smiles and good-humored politeness instead.

We took our good sweet time and sat there like millionaires chatting away the morning, talking about the two journeys. Jim had left Idaho on a bicycle pulling a little trailer that held his belongings. He had received the call directly, he said, from Jesus who had told him to go across the country on this bicycle and spread the good word, get a feeling for this nation, and set the place right. And, I presumed, to report back.

As a man who himself had heard the voice of God, I could not brush his calling aside as fanaticism or lunacy, but I looked askance just the same. The whispers I'd heard never told me directly what to do. Not in simple English, anyway.

When Jim got to Iowa and the river, he was instructed to change his course, get a boat and go down the river until further notice. He took to rowing down the river until his oars broke apart. He then dismantled the bicycle and set about sawing planks and hammering and putting together until finally he had constructed a paddlewheeler out of his rowboat. Now he could sit on his seat and pedal the crankset of the bicycle and the wooden planks fashioned into paddlewheels on each side of the boat would propel him.

It was slow, but a good idea, except that he got stuck in the rock dam just below Alton and Okie the salvage operator I had met had to tow him out. Then Jim had to rebuild and repair the damage.

Now, at Natchez, he actually prayed for the boat to fall apart. That would be a sign that his voyage was finished.

"I have to keep going until the voyage is done. Maybe in New Orleans, or maybe I'll have to keep going right on through to the Gulf of Mexico and South America."

"And then what?"

"I'll do whatever He tells me to do. But I'm sure sick of this river."

For a man spreading the good word, he hadn't met with much success, finding the land full of skeptics and godless people not willing to listen. So it would be disaster for them all, he said. Disaster and ruin will strike all those who refused him or who mocked him or who would not turn to God, and I made it a point not to say the wrong thing.

Jim had the look of a monk. Tall and lean, dishevelled grey hair and matching stubble on his chin, unconcerned about his appearance, a youthful face that lied about his age, and wild eyes. The eyes flared when he told me about the revolution.

"It's time," he said. "If the country won't turn to Jesus, it's up to me to make them, and if they still won't listen, I've been given the charge to destroy the country. I'm only letting them have one more chance."

When he started quoting from the Bible, I knew breakfast had lasted long enough.

"Maybe we could travel together," he offered. "Share Thanksgiving dinner, camp together, keep each other company. It gets lonely, you know."

His boat had everything in the world in it except a television. I don't know how I managed to fit inside and sleep. But

Vicksburg 49

he pushed junk aside and squeezed inside and showed me how he slid the plywood platform around that made his bed.

"You could ride inside with me," he said. "We could tie your canoe off and tow it and you could rest."

I declined, but did accept the offer for Thanksgiving dinner.

"You go on ahead. I need to fill up my water bag and take down my tent. I'll catch up with you."

Before he left he pulled a pair of pliers from his junk and repaired the zippers on my tent flaps. Now I wouldn't have to worry about mosquitoes sneaking into the tent at night.

"You learn to fix just about everything out here," he said.

He took off, pedaling down the river, and I watched him go. He looked very silly. Watching him, I felt the arrogance that towboat pilots feel, the contempt for lesser boats, and still the comraderie of sharers of the river—rivermen all of us.

I caught up with him after an hour or so and we built a fire on a sandbar. We boiled rice and heated a big can of beef stew and Jim prayed over it and we ate our Thanksgiving meal. It wasn't the finest holiday meal ever, but maybe this time I had so much to be thankful for and was really aware of it for once that this meal of all meals felt most like a Thanksgiving dinner.

*

I didn't find a place to camp until well after dark. The water had risen so high that what normally was dry land was under me now and I was canoeing right through forests with trees within easy reach on either side of me. These trees were up to their necks in the river.

I was searching for the short cuts, but there was no current and I had to work hard. The night was pleasant and I enjoyed the water rising up in mists around me, though I was startled from time to time by great plops in the water from some gigantic beast which I assumed to be granddaddy catfish, but which might have been alligators flopping in the river and snapping at passing meat. I was close enough to the Louisiana bayous and alligators were remotely possible.

In the morning the end was in sight. I came to a construction site where a dam was being built. A huge outflow canal was already there and great signs warned small boats to stay away. The heavy current would suck them into the canal like debris down a sink drain, and they'd never get out and might be chopped up by the gates of the dike there.

Near the construction site, David McKnight came down from his towboat to help me. He put me in his truck and drove me two miles to his office where I phoned home. I was preparing for arrival in New Orleans. It was Friday. I'd be there by Monday.

David, it turned out, was also from Missouri, from Hermann, the same little town where Robinovich grew up. He didn't know her, however, or her family. It didn't matter. He was still from close to home. He missed it as much as I was beginning to long for it, but he was stuck here.

Here was where the battle climaxed, the battle between the river and men. Here is where the Mississippi wants to swing west and link up with the Atchafalaya River. Here the engineers pull out all the stops to keep the river from taking its own route to the sea, the short straight route. They build outflow channels to divert the water, and dams to stop it and tame it and lessen the surge. They are winning, so far. A little farther on there is a lock and dam on the Old River which connects all these river systems, and revetments everywhere. It hardly seems a fair fight, but so far the river lets them win.

The river turns from the west, bends softly south and then makes a sharp corner to the east. Here the water slows and the river turns murky and gloomy. The water is wide and high. The trees stand waist deep in the river. The buffer of land has been swamped between the river and the Louisiana State Penitentiary. I get an eerie feeling as I pass through here. A discarded guard tower, the look of a concentration camp. Devil's Island. I wonder how many convicts try the river as an escape route and get lost in the trees or die in the swamps.

A little later on I'm called to shore by a couple of deer hunters. They have a beautiful shiny speedboat floating near their camp and a tent pitched big enough for a family. Chairs set up and a cooler full of beer and a gas stove. All the comforts. They've just finished dressing the deer they've killed and are relaxing before going out once more while they still have light. Robby Barry and Mike Hunt. Fine gentlemen from Baton Rouge. They start me off with beer and then switch to coffee.

"You ever have coon ass coffee?"

"Don't think so." I wonder if it's a brand name.

"You know what a coon ass is?"

I don't, but I could offer a few guesses.

"That's what we call Cajuns. And coon ass coffee is the best coffee there is."

"Why coon ass?"

"Cause they all talk so funny. Wait till you meet one. You won't be able to understand them."

And to demonstrate, while we talk about the river, canoe trips and fishing, the Atchafalaya flows into the conversation. But when they say it, I don't understand the word.

"Where's that?"

"What? Oh, I guess you call it the Atchafalaya." But when they say it, two or three syllables get chopped out or slurred together and the word becomes foreign.

"Did you pass the prison back up the river?"

"Is that what that was? I thought it was a death camp or something."

"Might as well be. I hear those guards like to shoot. They want you to try to escape just so they can shoot you down. I'm surprised they didn't shoot at you passing by."

The land around here belongs to hunting clubs. To shoot here you need to be a member. Unless, of course, you have a speedboat and are fairly enterprising. Mike and Robby intend to stay out until Sunday. By then, if they're lucky, they'll have enough meat to last a few months, even with deer steaks for gifts.

And so I slid out of their lives and on through Louisiana. This was the home stretch. Louisiana on both sides of the river now. Fewer than two hundred miles to New Orleans. Then I would be done. But first I had to get past St. Francisville.

The nearer the destination, it seems, the harder it is to arrive. Deep in the heart lurks the dread of a new uncertainty: what happens next? Will everything be completely new and wonderful and foreign, which is frightening, or, which is worse, will everything be just as it was? Will nothing be different? Will none of it have mattered? To finish is to find out.

Not to finish is to remain in limbo, a baby half born.

Luckily, St. Francisville provided one night's diversion from worrying about it all.

I could have passed it by. It was early enough in the evening to go on down and find a nice site for camping. Added to that was the high water, the trees and marsh all around the landing at St. Francisville that made camping on the river here impossible. I found one spot, but nearby was a big stagnant pool of water perfect for breeding starving mosquitoes. And trash all around dumped from cars waiting to cross the river on the ferry.

St. Francisville lay two miles from the river. The road to and from the town ended here at the water. A ferry carried the cars that needed to go farther, moving out every twenty minutes or so, with a loud blast of the horn and the engine roaring like a monster.

There was really no place to camp except a gravel parking lot, just to the north of the ferry and behind it, where an inlet was formed by a derelict towboat. Not the sweetest campsite, but what the heck! I had no choice.

I pitched the tent and ignored the cars that circled through the lot and in a little while I simply left everything there and walked the two miles into town to find a good spot to eat. I couldn't very well build a fire in that parking lot. The whole world would have come down to see what I was up to.

My mind strained toward the end of the river. I was fidgety and wanted to settle down, to stay in the present. The walk would help.

The road was narrow and the night black as ink. Not a light anywhere in sight unless a car passed. And then I would stray from one side of the road to the other to keep away from the cars zooming past going ninety. Past the little shack that housed the country tavern serving ice cold beer and hot food, across the railroad tracks and the little historical marker telling all about the old railroad, down through the valley and past the dingy shacks that housed poor people, past the string of shops selling bait for the fishermen, and up the hill to a small intersection.

The main road went on straight. A dog barked viciously in the darkness. I turned right and took the long way around to town.

I made it up into the heart of town and ate in a very unlikely restaurant—the St. Francisville Inn which is really an inn for staying overnight and yes, the thought crossed my mind. It also seemed the best place in town to get a real meal and the only place open unless I wanted chicken in a basket or fried fish with fries. That wouldn't have been bad, but I craved the touch of civility offered by the inn. I only wondered how they would receive me. I wasn't dressed for caviar and champagne dinners.

For some, the color of life is red. For others, black and white. I happen to know the color of life, at least in this country, is green. If you can pay, generally you can play.

James Kilgo

Actual Field Conditions

(GEORGIA)

As creatures of song and flight, birds suggest so powerfully the impulses of the mind and spirit that Adam himself must have made the connection. Even in ancient mythology and fairy tale, according to Marie Louise von Franz, birds stand for "a nearly bodiless entity, an inhabitant of the air, of the wind sphere, which has always been associated with the human psyche." Poets have persisted in the mythological view. Keats' nightingale, Shelley's skylark, Hopkins' kestrel, and Yeats' swans all correspond to something in our nature that refuses to accept mortality and dreams of the freedom of flying. The major weakness in this way of seeing, as any ornithologist will quickly tell you, is its failure to recognize the behavior of birds under actual field conditions.

When I was a boy there were men in my hometown who were respected for their knowledge of birds. They were not bird lovers in the usual sense of that term but farmers and foresters who spoke without self-consciousness about such things as declines in the redheaded woodpecker population or the rare occurrence in our area of a painted bunting.

Once, when we were fishing on the creek below our house, my father suddenly gripped me by the shoulder and whispered, "Look!" He put his hand on the back of my head and aimed my gaze toward a ferny spot on the far bank. There, flitting about among the sun-splotched leaves, was a small yellow bird I had never seen before. "That's a prothonotary warbler," he said. The conjunction of that improbable name with the brilliant flame color of its breast seemed marvelous to me.

The first bird I identified on my own was a black and white warbler. I was ten or eleven years old, sitting one morning on a log near the creek, when I spied it in the low canopy overhead. Although I was familiar with the species from an illustration by Louis Agassiz Fuertes in a set of cards I had ordered from Arm and Hammer Soda, I was not prepared for the precision of zebra striping on a bird so tiny. I ran all the way home, excited by a wild conviction that something had been settled.

What had been settled, I understood much later, was my experience of that particular species. The sight of the bird required a response—I had to do something about it. A camera would have worked—even a gun, I'm afraid, because I wanted to have the bird—but the name alone was enough. Armed only with that, I applied it, ratified the act of seeing, and appropriated the black and white warbler.

Perhaps the obvious way of seizing and holding such moments of delight, especially for one who is able to draw, is by painting the bird. For some reason, that possibility did not occur to me until I was grown. By the time it did, I had devoted several years to avid birding, naming every new species I could find until my fascination with birds was reduced to a mere game of listing, in which the checking off of a species amounts almost to a cancellation of it. As if that weren't bad enough, the game became for me a competition with other such binocular-visioned people.

Then one day on the beach of Sapelo, a barrier island off the coast of Georgia, something happened that changed my way of looking at birds. I was participating in a Christmas bird count with a small group of experienced birders and ornithologists. On Saturday night one of them reported having seen what he thought was a stilt sandpiper on the south end of the beach.

Because that species occurs rarely on the South Atlantic coast, most of us needed it for our lists, so early the next morning the whole crowd piled into a couple of vehicles and headed down the strand.

We must have presented quite a spectacle as we climbed from the jeeps—a brigade of birders, wrapped in heavy coats and armed with binoculars, some even with a 'scope and tripod, tramping down an empty winter beach to "get" a sandpiper. According to Roger Tory Peterson's description, the bird is almost indistinguishable at that time of year from dowitchers and lesser yellowlegs. Even the man who had reported seeing it had had trouble confirming identification because it was part of a mixed flock of small shorebirds.

The sun stood before us upon the water, its reflection blazing on the wet sand where the waves reached and retreated, and a cold salt wind was blowing off the ocean. I began to doubt that I would have the patience to sort out a stilt sandpiper from a large flock of sand-colored shorebirds, and I was bothered as well by the legitimacy of my recording it if someone else identified it first.

On the point at the end of the beach hundreds of birds were racing along the edge of the surf; hundreds more lay dozing in the dry sand, their feathers ruffled by the steady wind; and a few big, solitary willets stood here and there like unhappy schoolteachers watching children at recess. I took one look through my binoculars into the glare and realized that I didn't care enough about a stilt sandpiper to bother.

Looking for something to pick up—driftwood, bottle, or shell—I left the crowd and climbed the high dunes. On the other side, between me and the marsh, lay a long, shallow lagoon. It appeared to be connected to the sound at high tide, but now with the ebb it was an isolated pool. A flock of large birds, all of a kind, was wading in it, stretching, preening, and feeding. They were marbled godwits—a species I had seen before—but I grabbed my binoculars anyway and focused on one bird. From that angle the light upon its mottled brown plumage was ideal; I could even detect the flesh-colored base of its recurved bill. Then I lowered the glasses in favor of the whole choreography. There must be fifty of them, I thought, and I marveled at their obedience to the common will that moved them all in one direction, comprehending a dozen little sideshows of casual interaction. I delighted in the repetition of muted color and graceful form, reflected fifty times in blue water.

Suddenly, by a shared impulse the godwits rose crying from the pool and wheeled in an arc above me, their cinnamon wings flashing in the sun. I watched them fly south toward St. Simons, hearing their cries after I could no longer distinguish the flock in the shimmering air.

With the dying away of their cries I sat down on the dune. The other bird-watchers were scattered on the beach below me, still focused on the flock of sandpipers, but I was not ready yet to rejoin them. For I had seen godwits rising in the sun—a glory of godwits crying down upon the marshes—and I felt strangely abandoned. I wanted to grab hold of that moment with both hands, before it faded away with the birds, and keep it; and I wanted to tell my friends on the beach about it so they could see it too. If only I could paint it all, I thought—the strong winter light and the birds' insistent cries. I could at least try, I decided. I would paint it in watercolor, bathed in that light, and those who saw it would feel something of the loneliness I had felt.

Not long after the Christmas count on Sapelo I saw the illustrations by Robert Verity Clem for *The Shorebirds of North America*. They represented exactly the kind of thing I wanted to do. For the next year I studied them as well as the work of Fuertes and George Miksch Sutton, sketched hundreds of birds in the field, and often picked up road-kills to learn anatomy and plumage patterns. It was not mere illustration I sought but a representation of the experience of seeing a particular bird in its habitat, as I had seen the black and white warbler that day on the creek or those godwits rising above me in the sun.

The ornithologist who introduced me to the behavior of birds under actual field conditions was a south Georgia farmer named Calvin Hardy, one of the group on the Christmas count. When I met him on the dock, waiting for the boat to Sapelo, I could see right away that he was different from the rest of us. Big and sturdy, as though cut to a larger pattern than most men, he gave the impression that if something broke he could fix it.

I was not surprised to hear that Calvin was a farmer and a forester. In fact, he reminded me of those men whose interest in birds I had noticed when growing up. Before the weekend was over I learned, partly by talking to him but mostly from a mutual friend, that he was also an airplane pilot and a carpenter of better-than-average skill; that he had published papers on herpetology, mammalogy, and ornithology; that he photographed wildflowers and collected stamps and coins, antique turpentining equipment, and local folklore; and that he lived in an old railroad depot that he had moved two miles from its original site after cutting it in half with a chain saw.

Somehow Calvin and I discovered quickly that each of us had stories the other wanted to hear, so we spent the late night hours of that weekend drinking coffee and talking. By the time we left the island Sunday afternoon, I knew that he, like me, was one of those people who has to do something about birds. Painting, I had just realized, was the thing I would do; Calvin's was science. At that time he was working on the nesting habits of herons and egrets. "Come on down to south Georgia in June," he said, "and we'll go into a rookery."

Most wading birds are colonial nesters. The colony is called a rookery, or by some a heronry. In south Georgia the birds often select lime-sink ponds as nesting sites. As long as a colony site remains undisturbed the birds will return to it year after year until they eventually fill the capacity of the place; an established rookery may contain six different species of wading birds and as many as two thousand nests. Calvin had been going into the rookeries in his part of the state for several years, mainly for the purpose of determining and monitoring fluctuations in the populations of the predominant species—the little blue heron and the cattle egret, the latter an exotic that had made its way across the Atlantic from Africa at the end of the nineteenth century and has since worked its way north to our continent. Though the intruder does not compete for food with native species, Calvin suspected that it was taking over sites formerly held by the little blues.

In May he called to remind me of the invitation. The nesting season would be at its peak in a few weeks, he said; we might find as many as five or six species. I needed no encouragement. The rookery would afford a rare opportunity to photograph and sketch the wading birds in their own bedroom. I could hardly wait.

The morning was already hot when we climbed from the truck and started across a brushy field. Ahead of us stood the woods, quietly shimmering through the heat waves as though nothing remarkable were happening within its shadow. But presently we began to detect a commotion, a murmur of flaps and squawks. As we drew nearer, the trees before us seemed to bloom with white birds. Herons were ascending, reluctantly it appeared, to hover above the canopy, legs a-dangle, and complain at our intrusion. Still nearer, we caught a vague whiff of organic effluvium that grew stronger as we approached the trees.

Beneath the canopy we paused at the edge of what appeared to be not water but a pale green floor; through it rose a thin forest of tupelo gum, red maple, pond cypress, and pine. The flapping activity of the adult birds receded before us to the far reaches of the rookery, and for a moment I could neither see nor hear young birds. After the clamor that had greeted us, the silence seemed unnatural. I thought of alligators, prehistoric submarines cruising noiselessly beneath the green floor, and I felt some reluctance to enter the rookery. Calvin had not mentioned gators to me, but since we were entering their habitat I thought I might ask.

"I wouldn't worry about them," he said. Then he smiled, "But if you do get tangled up with one, remember now that his belly is the soft part."

His smile was no sure sign that he was kidding because he smiled most of the time—so I checked a bit furtively to see that my Randall skinning knife was still securely fastened on my hip. Then I followed him in.

A thick mat of vegetation, streaked and splashed with chalky excrement, lay upon the surface of the pond. Beneath this, the water was a warm chowder. Ten yards out we were waist-deep in it, pushing the surface before us like a buckling rug and releasing smells that engulfed us as we moved.

Calvin was already busy recording data with a pad and a mechanical counter as he moved confidently through the trees. I was dropping behind, still a little conscious of my legs but mainly marveling at the nests—frail platforms, four or five to a tree sometimes, lying in the forks of branches six to eight feet above the water. Looking up from underneath I could see the sky through them, and many of them held clutches of three eggs. By climbing onto the roots of a tree and holding on to the trunk I was able to look into several nests. The eggs were of the palest blue-green, as large as golf balls and oval in form. What astonished me most was the capacity of such slight nests to support their weight.

Many of the nests contained newly hatched chicks, nestled in damp clumps (sometimes around an addled egg), and looking back at me with yellow reptilian eyes. From the number of fledglings standing about on the edges of nests and neighboring branches, I figured that these birds, in their ravenous determination to receive food before their siblings, quickly developed the strong legs that enabled them to climb out of their flimsy quarters. Once out, however, they remained in the immediate vicinity, jostling each other in clumsy sidestep as they awaited the return of their parents with food. Most of the birds we saw were in this stage of development, ineffectual sentinels protesting our presence by gaping and squawking and, in their excitement, sometimes regurgitating or defecating as we passed by or paused to take pictures of them.

Most birds in the fledgling stage are ungainly—hence the tale of the ugly duckling—but few species present a greater contrast between the immature stages and the adult than wading birds. Crowned with ludicrous patches of hairy down, these tailless white creatures seemed badly put together—too much neck, too much leg, and none of it under control. They looked to be in constant danger of toppling from the branches, and occasionally a chick would lose its balance. We saw one hanging upside down, wings fallen open so that the light shone through the membranes, and clutching its perch with the toes of one desperate foot.

I wondered how long the bird could last in that position and how long a gator would take to find it once it had let go. Calvin said he doubted that alligator predation was a significant factor in the mortality of immature birds, though he was sure that the reptiles took an occasional victim as they scavenged the rookery. Just then he pointed out a young bird crawling from the thick gravy at the base of a tree and clambering laboriously up its trunk, using beak, claws, and even wings like some prehistoric creature moving from the amphibian stage through the reptilian to the avian in one heroic action. But I was not moved to admiration. In its mindless determination to survive, the creature seemed hideous to me—but I was hot and filthy, and I had already seen too many birds, too many eggs.

On our way out of the rookery Calvin spied a pair of anhinga chicks perched in their nest about ten feet up and had me stand on his shoulders to photograph them. Their buff down looked as thick as the nap on a baby harp seal, and I had to restrain an impulse to stroke them. After snapping several pictures I lowered the camera to Calvin and embraced the tree to shinny down the trunk. As I glanced over my shoulder at the green surface beneath me, I felt suddenly that I was suspended above the primal generative slime itself, composite of earth, air, fire, and water, secreted from the earth by what Annie Dillard has called "the pressure of fecundity." I clung to the tree, appalled by the terrific energy that digested sticks, eggs, leaves, excrement, even baby birds, and bubbled up a scum of duckweed, releasing in the process a blast of heat and odor. God knows, I thought, what it might produce if it had the time.

"You need some help?" Calvin asked. The question restored my equilibrium. This was after all only a rookery. So I climbed down and followed in his wake toward dry land. As we approached the edge, adult herons and egrets with a clapping and beating of wings began to reclaim the area we had deserted, young birds commenced to clamor again for food, and the rookery resumed its normal business. Give them a wooded lime-sink pond, I thought, and they would do the rest—these ethereal white creatures—by dropping sticks and laying eggs and regurgitating a mash of protein and defecating thousands of times a day. And the result? New egrets, hundreds of them, emerging from the rank miasma to glide like angels upon fields of summer hay or to float upon their individual images in quiet ponds.

Near the edge of the rookery a white egret rose up from a low nest ahead of us and flapped off through the trees. Calvin sensed it was something different, but he resisted a conclusion. In the nest we found a wet, new chick and two eggs, one cracking even as we looked into it. "Snowy egret," he guessed, but the scientist in him required confirmation so we hid and waited for the parent to return.

The most elegant of American wading birds, the snowy is a predominantly coastal species, and we were over a hundred miles inland. Calvin suspected that this might be a nesting record for the interior of the state—he had never found snowies in a rookery before. I shared a little of his excitement, but my thoughts were of a different nature. As wading birds go, the stumpy little cattle egrets we had been observing occupy the lower end of the aesthetic yardstick. Somehow, it seemed to me, that fact had something to do with the evidence we had just seen of the birds' appetite for breeding. I had no trouble envisioning a field of cattle egrets shamelessly engaged in the business of reproduction, but the image of snowy egrets copulating had never before occurred to me.

When the adult returned to the nest we spotted instantly the bright yellow toes on black feet that confirmed Calvin's impression. Grasping a thin branch, the egret seemed to reverse the direction of its wing beats in a frantic effort to balance itself. I couldn't tell which parent this was, but the bird's white flurry in that shadowed place startled me into a vision of a gorgeous male, nuptial plumes aquiver as he climbed the back of a crouching female and held her neck in his beak.

I didn't give much thought to painting that night. As we sat in front of his house, watching purple martins in the heavy twilight, Calvin interpreted the statistics we had gathered, and his eyes sparkled as he recalled various details of our trip. But my skull was filled with a green stew that sloshed when I lay down to sleep, and my imagination struggled with wet wings to climb out of it. If I was praying to the same God who charged egrets with the procreative urge, I didn't see how I could expect much of an audience.

The next morning Calvin took me up in his Taylorcraft, a flying machine of uncertain vintage that reminded me more of a kite than an airplane. He thought he had discovered the general location of a new rookery in the next county and wanted to see if he could verify it from the air. About ten miles west of town, at fifteen hundred feet, he pointed out a cool green spot on the ground that looked exactly like a mint, dropped down onto the patchwork of fields and woods. "Recognize that?" he asked. White specks, brilliant particles against the dark ground, were converging upon the spot and radiating from it in slow, deliberate flight. I felt as though I were looking down through clear water at something going on in another world. The effects of the day before were already beginning to diminish; nothing about the mint-green spot prompted memory of the rookery's reek and clamor. I began to understand the lofty point of view. It was easy up here to ignore rookeries, even to deny the fall of baby birds, and I saw that there might be some chance for the imagination in the clean, cold, blue air.

Then came the hawks. They appeared at first as a dark shape out in front of us. We didn't recognize it immediately, the thing not in flight but falling, and hurtling not away but toward us. Then, for a single instant, we saw clearly *two* birds in clasped union; for that frozen moment they seemed suspended in the force of their own energy. Almost into the prop, they split apart, one blown past the windshield, the other peeling away below. If I had been standing up, my knees would have buckled.

"What was that?" I shouted above the engine.

"Red-tails, weren't they?"

"I mean, what were they doing?"

"What did it look like?"

"You mean they really do it in the air like that?"

"What do you think?" he asked.

But I couldn't answer. I was so exhilarated by that incredible intersection, thinking was out of the question.

On the ground again, I remembered Walt Whitman's poem about the free fall of copulating eagles: "A swirling mass tight grappling,/In tumbling turning clustering loops, straight downward falling." A single, graphic image of what he calls their dalliance, it risks no statement of meaning, evidently because Whitman thought the image was message enough. I agree with his judgment, but I had made closer contact with the birds I saw. Their attractive force clapped me to them. And though the roar of the plane had interrupted their long tumble and blasted them apart, I continue to fall with them, convinced that the whole green earth below was one damned rookery, its power as strong as gravity.

Janet Lembke

River Time

(NORTH CAROLINA)

"You won't be a real river rat till you throw your watch away," says Mo, looking at my manacled wrist.

We've been talking about time, how it's told on the river in ways ancestral to the clocks of human devising. Life here is not timeless or without change, but it moves like a rolling hoop to aboriginal rhythms. On the river Neuse in coastal North Carolina, days and nights tick for us the way they must have for the people here long before we arrived in our automobiles and blue jeans—the colonists who did have clocks, the Indians who didn't. River time depends upon the circlings of sun and moon and the sweep of the constellations. The seasons make their rounds, directing the migrations of fish and birds, orchestrating the birth, death, and resurrection of the green world. Now from the northeast, now from the southwest, the winds blow constantly; they, far more than the tides, affect the river's rise and fall. Weather plays daily improvisations on a grand theme: brilliant blue calm, overcast, frog-drowning rain, waterspout, hurricane, and back to calm. The river burbles contentedly along the bulkheads or ripples with the gleam of hammered brass or rolls white-capped to crash on seawalls with slap-cracking explosions that hurl white shards of spray high into the air and push dark waves of leaf-burning, grass-killing, soil-robbing salt water over the land.

We read our instructions. Time to plant beans and squash because the moon waxes and the leaves on the sweet-gum trees are new-minted green. Time to fish because the wind blows steady out of the northeast, the bluefish are running, the spotted seatrout are in. Time to put heavy-gauge plastic on the trailer's windows because Orion is rising, the ducks begin to raft on the river, and loons wake us daily with their yodels as they fish our nets. Time to stay inside, heat on, and catch up with reading because the pier pilings wear petticoats of ice and the ice itself catches fire when the sun goes down in a blaze that stains the whole sky before it turns to soot.

Conventional terminology is supplanted by days named for immediately significant events—The Day of the Five-Pound Puppy Drum, the Day of Harvesting the First Homegrown, Non-Cardboard Tomato, The Day of the Rescued Doe. Larger periods of time also bear the names they've earned—The Moon of Deer in the Soy Fields, when dawn brings the dull thump of hunters' guns; the Moon of Wild Cherries, when nineteen species of birds, including the feisty mocker, coexist in close, harmonious proximity as they gorge on the small black drupes.

Forgetting workaday time can, of course, be perilous. The Day of the Flounder Jubilee turned out, a week later, to have been Thursday the 12th, when I was supposed to have been subject to the ministrations of a dental hygienist at nine A.M. But my husband and I were too busy carting away and cleaning self-beached summer flounder to pay any attention to such mundane matters. Dentists will wait; flounder, under pain of spoilage, will not.

We have television, three networks and a PBS channel, with more for those who have satellite dishes. The easily accessible stations devote little time to coverage of national news, and the regional newscasts tend to feature murder trials and sports. We watch because of the weather forecasts. It's important to know if the wind will switch from southwest to northeast because a change in direction affects the fishing conditions in our front yards. And it's important for me to know, especially in spring and fall, if a cold front is coming through because off-beat species of migrating birds are often blown our way by the passage of such a front. We have radio; rock, country music, and ballyhoo for the best car deals ever overwhelm the three-minute news breaks. We have newspapers. Those of national stature, such as *The Washington Post* and *The New York Times,* arrive in the mailboxes a day or two after publication. Local papers are delivered promptly—when there's a carrier willing to brave our labyrinth of rural roads. One of the biggest sources of information is the traffic over Cherry Point Marine Air Station, visible catty-corner across the river; a rise in the numbers of certain types of aircraft coming into or leaving the base often signals an international crisis before it makes the news.

The quality of river life is enhanced because geography and circumstance spare us from a cannonade of news and non-news dealing with matters we cannot influence. To say this does not mean that river-dwellers are lackadaisical. Far from it. Folks here vote regularly, volunteer their services to the fire department, take courses in CPR, and fly the flag on the Fourth of July. We read, discuss, argue, and gossip. The grapevine is the most vital source of information, letting all of us know quickly about policies and legislation—national, state, local— that affect our daily lives. The fire department entertains notions of building a substation close to the Point. The volunteers hold a fish-fry fundraiser. The state's Division of Marine Fisheries will change the rule about marking gill nets, from using one float of any kind at either end, to attaching two yellow floats for greater visibility. We avoid confiscation of our nets by tying on the requisite double lemons fore and aft. Washington debates taxation or the disposal of nuclear wastes. Off go the letters and telegrams to Congress.

We're fortunate, my husband and I, to be able to live almost solely on river time. We give partial credit for that to his years of service to the U.S. Navy; he's a retired chief petty officer—I call him Chief—who specialized in photography during his career. Some small credit goes to the work I do when not living on river time; I write and teach, translating Aeschylus and Euripides. But the river and Great Neck Point receive the most sweeping bows for enabling us to survive on a shoestring. Water gives us fish and crabs. Earth provides summer feasting and bounty for the winter—tomatoes in dozens of mason jars, Blue Lake green beans packaged and frozen pint after pint, butternut squash laid in plump, tan rows out in the shed, popcorn for winter nights. Neighbors who keep chickens trade eggs for our fish. Hunting friends bring deer hams big enough to feed fifteen people at Thanksgiving and still leave sufficient leftovers for two small meals. All of us at the Point long ago joined the barter economy. The Chief has traded his woodworking talents for haircuts, and his services as a photographer for the labor needed to sink our pier pilings into the riverbed. We beachcomb, too—scavenging, some might call it—to bring home everything from crabpot floats to solid boards washed up the creek after a particularly savage nor'easter has torn down docks and piers. Once the river gave us a set of wooden steps to replace those stolen by Hurricane Gloria.

Deer for Thanksgiving—every day on the river is Thanksgiving, a source of something to be grateful for. And every morning is Christmas morning, wrapped in sun or pearly haze, rain or rare snow, a young day waiting to be opened. The gifts heap high. We discover that stingray meat is delectable. I see the hundred-and-eighty-first bird for the grand list of species seen in our environs. Mo's granddaughter K. D. brings me a snake I haven't seen before; I can't identify it till, a day later, the book describing reptiles falls open by accident to the section immediately preceding that on snakes: it's not a snake at all but a lizard, a legless Eastern glass lizard. Dorothy, who knows how overdosed on tomatoes I've become after canning or stewing seven five-gallon buckets full, gives me a recipe that revives my enthusiasm; I make half a dozen pints of spicy tomato relish. The Chief shows his latest photographs; the hungry splash of the brown pelican diving for its dinner, the trepidation of the newly-fledged pileated woodpecker leaning from its nest cavity in the half-dead loblolly. The beach presents Indian potsherds; the woods, a swarm of bees. Or the river sends us a creature not usually found in its waters:

Yesterday, two days after Christmas: seven degrees above zero, and the river was frozen fifty feet out from shore. Ring-billed gulls perched on the ice; scaup and buffleheads swam at its ragged edges. Today, near noon: the temperature has climbed to seventy, wide skirts of melting ice drop from the pilings, and the frozen water breaks, separates into small floes, and turns to slush. The Chief stands at a window to observe this easing of winter's fist and remarks offhandedly, "Funny-looking duck out there."

Wings upraised, it's moving rapidly away from shore but somehow fails to become airborne. I get the binoculars: not wings but long ears! It's a deer swimming full-speed ahead. It must have entered the water from the sandy beach just up-river. We watch it for fifteen minutes, half an hour heading all-out for the far, far shore before it turns and swims this way again. It reaches the soft edge of the ice and barges through, making not for easy-exit beach but a stretch of wooden sea-wall rising vertically four feet above the river. Ten yards out its hooves touch bottom, and it wants to leap, hindlegs planted on the riverbed, forelegs lashing upward to gain purchase on the higher ground of ice but plunging through again and again.

We're outside on the bulkhead now. Bonnie has joined us. The animal is tired, cold, and scared. Driven to the desperate swim by duck-hunters' dogs? Who knows. The Chief fetches a length of rope. Bonnie puts on rubber boots and descends into the river. Tying the rope around the deer's belly, she tugs it gently toward the wooden wall and hands rope's end to the Chief. While she pushes, he pulls, and the animal is landed— a half-grown doe. She screams hideously once, then is silent, docile, as the Chief carries her to Bonnie's house, to the warm laundry room by the back door. The little doe is wrapped in a quilt and placed on the floor, where she lies without struggle. Bonnie's daughters come to look and stroke her nose. After twenty minutes she rises. The back door is opened. She bounds down the steps and into the back fields. Bonnie pulls off her boots and empties them of now-warm ice water.

Sometimes the surprises are terrifying: the Chief, cutting grass along our back property line, stirs up a monstrous timber rattler. Sometimes they strain our slender means: low water reveals that a section of our bulkhead is rotting out; what can we exchange for the costly, necessary repairs? Sometimes they're merely unpleasant: the first vine-red tomatoes show blossom-end rot. Or looking up at a kingbird's nest, I edge close to the base of the pine in which it's built and find, too late, that I'm standing on a hill of fire ants. My shins are peppered with the buckshot of sharp bites. Longer-lasting was the surprise brought by a summer-day traipse through the woods on the eroded property just upriver. That evening I began to itch. The next morning, at least a hundred and fifty oozing bumps polka-dotted my feet, shins, thighs, crotch, belly, and arms.

"Mo," I say, "there's another reason not to wear a watch. Chiggers love to snuggle underneath the band."

"You won't be a real river rat," he retorts, "till you learn to call those things red bugs the way we do."

*

The lower Neuse—the name rhymes with *Zeus*—the lower Neuse and Great Neck Point are not among North Carolina's famed attractions. The Point is not tourist- or condo-country offering haven to fast-food strips, bars, and other manmade accoutrements of beach life. It's tucked away twelve miles upstream in a near-wilderness, little changed from that seen by the colonists and, long before them, the Indians.

The Point extends into the lower Neuse in a slow, three-mile curve of bulkheads and untamed beaches. Downriver the Great Neck peninsula is bounded by Adams Creek, now a portion of the Atlantic Intracoastal Waterway; upriver by Clubfoot Creek, one of the countless streams that wander through black needlerush and giant cordgrass to drain the coastal wetlands. Adams Creek and Clubfoot—the names figure on pre-revolutionary maps. The nearest towns are Beaufort to the south on Bogue

Sound, twenty-five miles by road, about eighteen by the Waterway, and Havelock–Cherry Point, five miles across the water but twenty-two by land.

Close to the water, pines, sweetgums, baldy cypress, live oaks festooned with Spanish moss, and wax myrtle flourish in the sandy soil: typical maritime forest but tall and straight, unlike the oceanside version that's stunted and blown into bonsai shapes by salt-bearing wind. Trumpet vines, honeysuckle and snakehead greenbriar, Virginia creeper and poison ivy wind around the tree trunks and tangle high in the branches. It's a job to keep wilderness at bay, to grow green lawns of centipede or Bermuda grass, varieties that can survive drenching by saline water. A little farther inland, the earth is rich, dark humus over clay. Bordering the fields cleared long ago, hardwoods like maples, hickories, and pin oaks thrive amid the ever-present pines and gums. In the fields, we cultivate our garden plots, protected from the salt-bearing winds by woods and hedgerows. Joe has devoted half an acre to the melons that he shares with everyone; Al's made a forest of speckled butterbeans climbing green and heavy-laden around poles eight feet tall. Not all of us are so ambitious; our smaller vegetable patches, bright with zinnias and marigolds, yield just enough produce, including good old southern collards and okra, for our own use. It's reliably reported that another crop is cultivated up Courts Creek, the Point's small waterway, where the feds and state troopers aren't likely to find it.

Water, brackish marsh, fields, hedgerows, woods, and gardens offer shelter to an array of aquatic and terrestrial wildlife whose diversity is increased by the Point's location at a latitude, just south of 35°, where southern and northern species overlap. They—and we who live here—have been protected from onrushing urbanization by the marshes and the forested wilderness that embrace the Point's fields and woods; landward, much of the Point is closed off by miles of pine plantations owned by timber companies.

The human community here is comprised of permanent residents and people who live within a small radius and come down regularly for weekend river time. Unlike some waterfront communities we have elbow room and more. The places on the waterfront sprawl out eighty-five to eight hundred feet wide, with occasional second and third tiers directly, discretely inland. One small brown-painted house rises on stilts in the third tier, out of a one-time tobacco field; the stilts lift it high enough to afford the young occupants a view of the river over hedgerows and rooftops. Away from any sight of water, other houses sit in shadowed clearings amid pine straw and oak leaves.

On the riverfront, *house* is a word that can be appropriately applied to only a few dwellings: Bonnie and Al's brick ranch that can weather almost any gale; the two-story cedar house that Dorothy and Kent built with their own hands. Tom and Merle's place, just downriver from ours, had its 1950's genesis in a superannuated school bus. The decades since have seen the slow accretion of a bedroom, a room containing a real commode, and an attached storage shed for gill nets, a boat motor, and all the other paraphernalia needed for heavy-duty fishing. Most recently, Merle has been able to stop taking what she calls "bird baths;" after twenty years without, the place now boasts hot water and a stall shower.

Other people live in cinderblock cottages, double-wides (some luxurious), and the tied-down house trailers that manufacturers call mobile homes. The Chief and I, with Sally our flop-eared black-and-rust Doberman, live in just such an immobile home, an elderly 12 × 60 three-bedroom model.

Sally Doberdog has lots of company. Everyone keeps dogs, more or less. Some are pen dogs, black Labrador retrievers or reasonable facsimiles thereof for duck hunting and beagles or larger, rangy hounds for work in deer season. Most are strictly yard dogs that spend little time in their own yards and much in everyone else's. There's always a bitch in season, and a traveling gang-bang. Puppies are always tumbling at the heels of droopy-dugged mothers. Some could be registered with the AKC—a shepherd, a chow—but others mix the common with the exotic, Heinz 57 crossed with rottweiler. I know of only four house dogs in the neighborhood; one is obedience-trained Sal, the others are toy poodles.

Several yards contain chicken coops, and Eva also pens geese. Mo has stabled horses in his barn, and Jake the Dog-Killer used to tie out close to a dozen goats on his lot of less than half an acre. Caged mallards quack in another neighbor's back yard, while still another farms pigs, all of them named Dinner, in a wooden enclosure thirty yards from his house. Al specializes in California rabbits, a white breed with sooty ears and noses; most of them are also named Dinner.

Inland or on the water, almost every yard sports a pickup truck and a boat. The pickups are often embellished with a gun-rack across the rear window of the cab and a dog-box in the truckbed—testimony to the local fondness for hunting. There's always a mess of hauling to be done—brush, storm debris, aluminum cans for the recycling stations. Bringing home the new appliance in the truck saves the fifty-dollar delivery charge imposed by the stores in town. These trucks are not expressions of machismo but modern-day workhorses. The Chief and I manage without a truck (we borrow on occasion), but we do have a boat, a modest fourteen-foot fiberglass Minnow that's propelled by an electric motor. A few of the local boats are play toys: some the sleek and superpowered hulls that can kick up long white rooster-tails as they're driven through the water at sixty knots an hour; others canopied platforms on pontoons that cruise the river sedately on calm days. One grizzled owner has christened his pontoon boat *HUCK FINN;* the letters are writ so nostalgically large that the naked eye can read them as the boat chugs by five hundred yards out. Almost no one sails. Benign wind and water do bring out a Sunfish or two and a solitary wind-surfer. But there's nothing here, not a blow-boat nor a stink-pot, that can be legitimately called a yacht. The large ketches and yawls, genoas billowing, and the blinding white cruisers with flying bridges stick to the channel on the river's far side. Utility characterizes our boats. They're small vessels for fishing, shrimping, and scavenging—shallow-draft johnboats squared off bow and stern, Boston Whalers for stability on choppy seas, sturdy aluminum rowboats like the dented sixteen-footer that Tom keeps next door. Al's yard holds a would-be boat, a beat-up fiberglass shell that he picked up at auction for fifty bucks. One of these days he'll get around to fixing it. The river is patient when it comes to boat-repairs.

Nobody seems to know much about the lower Neuse except the people who live and make their livings here. Yet, it's not a small river. What we see from our front yards is the more southerly of the two great rivers—the other is the Pamlico—that pour into Pamlico Sound. Way upstream, the Neuse is not a river but a creek, narrow and stained coppery brown by the humic acid of decaying bark and leaves. Much farther downstream, past the towns of New Bern and Havelock-Cherry Point, the mature Neuse bends like a giant's elbow and turns northward to make its final twelve-mile rush to the Sound. Oldtimers call the bend the Rounding of the River, and it's the place at which fresh water becomes saline, mainly because of the nor'easters that funnel water and salt-loving fish from the Sound into the river's gaping mouth and down its gradually narrowing gullet. Under a hard wind from the north, the river can rise a foot in an hour.

The Chief and I are the Great Neck Pointers who live farthest upstream, 861 feet from Courts Creek and the beginning of the Rounding. From our front yard, the far shore of the Neuse is nearly five miles away. Of all the wide rivers in the United States, our river, at this point in its course, is the widest of them all. Sometimes fog or haze closes in, the far shore disappears, and the river rolls across the world without a perceptible horizon.

Great Neck Pointers are isolated, inhabiting a peninsula that might as well be an island, cut off by water on one side, by a sea of green pines on the other. Nor is it just water and wilderness that separate us from the rest of the world, but the intangible barrier of distance from the services and amenities of urban life. On winter days, youngsters board the school bus before dawn and come home at dusk; the stop-and-start ride to the Havelock schools takes well over an hour each way. The providers of necessities—doctors and dentists, police and firefighters, supermarkets, banks, fuel suppliers, and more—are all out there twenty-two miles and thirty long minutes beyond the water, marshes, and pine plantations.

The river makes two stringent demands. One, given special force by our isolation, is for neighborliness in all matters from the borrowing of eggs and tools to rescuing the injured and comforting the bereaved. People survive at the Point because someone has a saving skill; people have died here because town is too far away to send help in time. The other demand is to honor the river with heart and soul. It must be respected both for the bounty it yields and for its power to devastate and kill. These commandments aren't always obeyed. We can be down-right navel-gazing and nasty. But most of the people who have settled here have packed skills and a taste for isolation along with their household goods. Ralph Waldo Emerson would have approved the flourishing of self-reliance at the Point and of the way in which it's daily honed. He made the pertinent comment in his essay "Self-Reliance": "Your goodness must have some edge to it—else it is none." Isolation makes a fine whetstone.

As for my watch, it's still attached to my left wrist, more as a precaution against losing it than as a device needed to regulate the course of my days. Occasionally it comes in handy. But I consult it infrequently, and I stay out of the woods in red-bug weather unless I'm well-greased with insect repellent.

Right now no watch is needed to tell me the time. It's time to stop writing in favor of fishing our seven crabpots. With a hot-season moon bulging toward the full, the blue crabs come scuttling inshore to molt and mate. Last evening at sundown, I baited the pots with gizzard shad and set them off the bulkhead. The sun's now close to meridian. If the river has been generous, those pots will hold several dozen beautiful and tasty swimmers. The jennies will go back into the river to lay their eggs and make more crabs for next summer's catch, but I should harvest at least half a bucket of claw-clacking, yellow-bellied jimmies. Yum, crabcakes for supper.

Archie Carr

Living with an Alligator

(FLORIDA)

Until recently I have been very intolerant of people's intolerance of alligators on their property. It seemed to me that one hope for keeping free alligators in the land was their willingness to live in urban and suburban lakes and ponds. Anyway, it has always appeared to me that anybody lucky enough to have a personal or neighborhood wild alligator ought to be so gratified that he would gladly put up with inconveniences in order to perpetuate his happy state. I still hold that belief, to some extent. But now our own alligator—the oldest of the three alligators that we seem now to have in our own pond—has grown big, and I can understand the problem a little better. I am attached to our alligator, deeply so, but she has made me see that a three-hundred-pound predator in the front yard is simply bound to be a mixed blessing at best. In fact, the plight of people vis-à-vis alligators is sort of summarized in my own family's experiences with the alligator in our pond.

Living with little alligators is no problem. It is when they get to be five or six feet long and then grow on up to ten, twelve, or even more intemperate lengths that trouble may come in the yard pond or urban lake. The alligator in our pond is going on eleven years old. We have known him since he was small. He really is a female, but it is a family custom to call her "him." Anyway, this alligator is pretty close to us, really, except during the coldest weather, when he sinks morosely into the muck and is close to no one for days at a time. Shortly after he bellowed for the first time another big alligator turned up from somewhere, and for a while the two of them circled and dashed about the pond, making waves and white water that hid whatever they were doing out there together. A little later we discovered that our alligator was a female. We found a nest that she had made on the far shore of the pond, and not long afterward forty-two little gators came out of the nest. She herded them into the deep sinkhole in the corner of the pond, and for a while they all lived there together.

Our alligator kept growing in size and appetite and began eating things she had not been able to eat before. If our eight-acre pond had stayed that size it might have supported the alligator, but during dry spells it shrank, and then she would gorge herself with distressing abandon. You could hear her cracking turtles clear up in our living room. Then, after a while the pond would flood again and dilute the reduced remnants of turtles, bullfrogs, rice rats, and swamp rabbits. Hard times came for the alligator, and she stayed hungry all the time. The sulfur-bellied frogs disappeared from the open pools, and the big bullfrogs that bellow under the buttonbushes around the edge grew few and quiet before each season ended. We had six mallards on the lake, and the alligator ate them all. We got four more mallards and built a strong cage for them, half in the water and half out. On the second night it was there the alligator ripped a hole in the wire and ate two ducks and then tore another hole to get out.

After a while we seemed to have reached the point at which we must choose between having a big alligator and having a pond with other animals in it. The alligator seemed to be consuming everything, and one day we shamefacedly reached the decision that she had to go. Not killed, of course—we still felt affection for her, and anyway killing even your own alligator is against the law. She would have to be caught and hauled away somewhere to an ampler, wilder place. My wife called Sheriff Joe Crevasse and explained the problem, and he seemed not to be surprised to hear about it. It was May, the month when all through the county alligators were walking, and Joe had already had thirty calls about them being on the road or in people's yards, and he was expecting more in June. He said his staff was busy, but that they'd try to move our alligator if it was really important. My wife said it was.

The next night Deputy Shelly Downs came out to the house. Shelly was pound master for alligators and rattlesnakes in the sheriff's department. He came in a truck and brought his regular gator-catching equipment: a canoe, a long pole, a heavy nylon line, and an assortment of nooses made of different gauges of stainless steel cable, each with a shackle at one end for the noose to run in and a ring to fasten the line to at the other end. To catch an alligator, you open one of these loops out and fasten it to the line, then suspend it from the end of the pole. The idea is to get close enough to the gator to slip the noose over his head, then tighten the springy loop by a sudden heave, jerk the pole loose, and play the alligator on the line.

A big soft-spoken deputy named Jenkins came with Shelly to paddle the canoe. The two of them got out of the truck and we walked down to the shore to get the lay of the pond. Shelly played his spotlight out over the water, and at once picked up the alligator's eye shining on the far side of the pond, like a hot blown ember about to blaze. He snapped off the light and the two of them went back to the truck, put the tackle in the canoe, took it down to the shore and slid it into the water. Deputy Jenkins got in the stern and Shelly told me to sit on the bottom amidships. He pushed the canoe out into deep water and took his place in the bow, crouching low there and holding the long pole with the loop hanging from the end. Then he turned on his light and quickly picked up the blazing eyes again.

Jenkins was a good hand with a paddle. He drove the thin canoe through the floating mat of duckweed with only a whisper of a sound. The eyes of the alligator burned on unblinking in the spot of light, and it seemed no time at all till only a pole's length lay between them and Shelly's noose. We slipped over a school of bream, and they flipped and churned away in every direction, two of them jumping into the boat and clattering noisily on the bottom. Jenkins and I groped about after them, uneasy over the noise they were making, and finally found them and slid them back into the pond as quietly as we could. In spite of even this disturbance, the gator stayed there steady in the tight beam of Shelly's light, unalarmed, floating high, with most of her back and the keel of her tail above the surface of the water. It seemed sure we were about to make fast to her. She looked very big, maybe eight feet long, and I wondered belatedly how exciting it would turn out to be to play her from a canoe. I recalled how an alligator that Ross Allen and his wife Celeste had noosed had grabbed the bow of their canoe in its jaws, crumpling the aluminum hull and breaking Celeste's ankle inside it.

But Shelly seemed to have no misgivings. As we got closer he gently dipped the noose in the water and the glide of the canoe slid it toward the alligator, toward the long smile of her face, now clearly visible down there under the clear tan of ten inches of pond water. It seemed sure that our alligator was about to have the first bad time of the ten years of her unmolested life.

But just as the circle of cable slid up past the two humps at the end of the broad snout, it touched a strand of coontail moss, shifted sideways, and brushed the side of the smiling face. Instantly the pond erupted, the gator was gone, and Shelly was sitting there swearing.

"You nearly had her, Shelly," Jenkins said.

That stirred Shelly to more rough language, but he soon got quiet again and started shining his light around to see where the alligator had made off to. Fifty yards over at the edge of the pond we picked up the blaze of the eyes again. Again Jenkins began shoving us across the solid-looking deck of duckweed. Quiet as a blown leaf, the canoe slid up to where the gator lay like a log facing directly toward us and unblinking in the light. Once more Shelly pushed the pole out and let the noose come down, and it made only the tiniest of ripples as it slipped cleanly over the snout, past the bulging jowls, and back to the neck of the unsuspecting alligator. When it got past the shoulders, Shelly heaved hard on the pole and the noose tightened solidly in place just behind the short front legs. The cold steel squeezed, and it scared the alligator badly, and she dived for the bottom. Her dive slanted in under the canoe so fast that Shelly was not able to keep the pole up, and it slapped down on the gunnel and snapped and splintered there. Shelly dropped it and grabbed for the line but he missed the first grab, and the moment of slack let the steel noose loosen. The alligator streaked out free of the loop, roiling a trail across to the farthest side of the pond.

After that we stayed out in the lake for quite a while, swearing and trying to pick up the alligator's eyes, but we never found them again.

"She's on the bottom thinking about that cold steel that squeezed her," Jenkins said. "She'll be down there a week."

After a while the green tree frogs in the buttonbush trees on the floating islands again took up the chorus that our noise had interrupted, slowly building back up its curious cadence, one by one joining in, all around the pond, until a thousand of them again were shouting together—"*fried-bacon, fried-bacon*"—in the strange unison they work into. Shelly played his light around once more, and still there were only bullfrog eyes to see; so we went in and had some cake and coffee my wife had made to celebrate or to console us with. After that Shelly and Jenkins stowed their gear, got into the truck, and started the engine.

"We can try it again in three days," Shelly said. "No use any sooner. She'll only be wanting to hide."

Three nights later they came back again. I was away, but the two of them went out on the pond and made two good approaches to the alligator. Both times the noose snagged in the coontail just before it slipped into place, and after the second miss the alligator refused to hold for the light. Shelly said the gator was getting prejudiced against them and that a trap would be the only way to get the gator now. They went away to let her calm down before we built the trap. Early the next morning the alligator broke into the pen and ate three more mallards.

So, after all the soul-searching we did, after painfully concluding that we had to banish our alligator, we still have her out there in the pond. The water has stayed at high level for three years, and her depredations have been less obtrusive than before. I don't know what she eats, really. Snakebirds fish out there with her, and Florida gallinules each year tend small bands of utterly helpless and no doubt succulent chicks. Each fall flocks of teal, widgeons, and ring-necks come down, and on the warm days when the gator is out they swim all around her, opening in only the most inadequate-looking circle of emptiness about where she lies. The ducks seem foolhardy, but they obviously know what they are doing. In fact, they and the gallinules and herons all know so much of alligator psychology that they use her as a foraging aid. If they are nearby when the alligator starts moving through the floating vegetation, they often swim in close to her—just as a cattle egret walks up close to a grazing ungulate—and move discreetly alongside, snatching at the small creatures stirred up by the advance of the gator's bulk.

I ought not fail to mention that one of our flock of tame mallards, a big shiny drake named Sam, escaped the fate of his fellows and lived on in the pond for a couple of years, joyfully joining the flocks of widgeons in the winters and perhaps from them learning how a duck can live with an alligator. One spring Sam disappeared. Maybe he flew away with the wild ducks, or possibly the alligator ate him. But in any case he showed clearly that a fat, slow-moving, tame mallard can adjust to coexistence with a ravening predator, and this is a good thing to know. Knowing it has brought new tolerance to our attitude toward the family alligator and has steeled us to stand her misdemeanors and try to learn from her a necessary protocol for future vital relations between her species and our own.

Harry Middleton

Bagpipes on Hazel Creek

(NORTH CAROLINA)

Exie Sopwith was right about Hazel Creek —about its trout, its beauty, even about the voices. About everything. I traveled to the creek more than twenty times before I came across another angler camped along its cool, fast water. That doesn't include the shadowy, mysterious person who moved up and down the creek's narrow valley during every season, playing the bagpipes.

When I heard the bagpipes for the first time, I thought nothing of it, dismissed the music as some enchanting combination of wind and rushing water that produced a soothing litany of liquid notes up along the higher reaches of the creek where the valley narrowed and the creek moved through membrane-thin shadows.

I heard the bagpipes again the next morning. A truly Great Awakening, more startling and invigorating than frightening, as though the notes were attempting a musical interpretation of a chicken coop caught up in turmoil and rebellion.

I sat at the open flap of the blue tent and listened. This much was certain: whoever the hidden troubadour was he believed strongly in vigorous and uplifting streamside music, something that mingled with the creek's tricky rhythms. At first I thought the sound came from above my campsite, up on the worn, rounded ridge along the trail that led up from Fontana Lake. A half hour later, though, like a fickle wind, the music had shifted and now seemed to seep out from a huge gallery of lichen-mottled stones the size of bank vaults just where the creek bent in a gradual arch to the left and fell into the silky light of early morning.

Whoever filled the dawn with music kept it up until well after first light, fitting the morning with a cycle of haunting music, a humble painting of notes and harmonics: images of tone. Like the creek, both the musician and his music were ever changing, mixed cadences of tremor and the unlikely hurdy-gurdy sound of bagpipe jazz.

Exie Sopwith had promised voices, but nothing so grand as some lunatic mountain balladeer who greeted each day along the creek, each renewal of light glowing off the water, with a celebration of rough-edged music.

I ate cold cereal and made hot tea over the camp stove and the elusive bagpipe virtuoso played on. The smooth gray morning light broke up, dissolved like thin clouds rising in warm air, and the music took on a stronger beat, sounding suddenly like a chorus of pipe organs playing madly, wildly, all stops open wide. I washed out my bowl, stowed my few belongings inside the tent, and did not bother to tie the tent flaps closed, and went about easing into my pair of old waders. The thick rubber still held the night's deep chill. And the music came now from the far side of the creek, from among wild dogwoods and stands of oaks and maples. The change in location brought a change in sound—softer, the low, reedy, melancholy sounds of wind high among the trees, notes as solemn as prayer. I thought how easy, how nice it would be just to crawl back into the tent, roll back into the wrinkled comfort of the sleeping bag, and slip into dreams as I listened to the sound of the music drifting down the narrow valley toward the lake, toward open skies.

The chilly night air left the 4-weight line stiff. It felt as tense as cramped muscle as I threaded it through the little R. L. Winston rod's ferrules and worked out about thirty-five feet of it, massaging each inch of it thoroughly, stripping it hard and fast through my fingertips as though trying to rub off the night's cold. I worked it until I felt it pinch, bend gracefully, take on the physical characteristics of good tooth twine: supple yet strong, unobtrusive yet enduring.

The day I set up camp I purposely ignored a wide pool of alluring water just downstream from the small rise above the creek bank where I put up the blue tent. It was good water, a good place to play a hunch, cast line and hope for the unexpected—wide and smooth and deep water, the kind of creek water where a streak of good fortune might fill an angler's creel with as much solitude as brilliantly colored, hard-muscled, belligerent mountain trout. It was a stretch of water worth saving, for tomorrow or the next day, or a morning such as this.

I sat on the big stone by the tent. The rod was ready, as was the angler, and the creek ran fast and cold. Daylight widened along the creek, giving a flat shine to the stones and the damp ground littered with a chaos of fallen leaves heaped by the wind into low swales, against outcrops of stone, in weathered coverts, ravines, and cuts, scattered like winnowed duff about the deep shadows of the forest floor. With each breath of wind the landscape shuddered, became almost liquid, a geography of colors rather than of fixed landmarks and boundaries, colors endlessly mingling one with the other. On the far west ridge, damask reds and vermilion giving way to softer Chinese reds and the blunt reds of aged wine, and these, in turn, mixed with leaves of moody sallow and the dull yellow of sulfur and raw cream, and among these were newly fallen leaves still bright as jonquils. Lower down the slope, down among the sturdy oaks, amid the random sprawl of reds and yellows, were scattered leaves of pumpkin-orange, trees looking like daring blotches of apricot, and now and then the wrinkled browns of the oaks with leaves the color of tarnished copper and well-worn leather. All along the upper ridges, the thick deciduous forest glowed in the hazy autumn light. Under a press of wind, the trees and their fashion of dead, brightly colored leaves bent and swayed like great coils of undulating ribbon, bolts of warm, rich color.

Sitting on a large, flat, comfortable stone, I took a No. 18

Royal Wulff from my small metal fly box, examined it carefully, decided it looked too well kept, too tidy, too much the imposter to entice a fish as suspicious as trout, especially at this time of the morning. Instead of putting the fly through the expected routine of preening, making it presentable, I intentionally mussed it up, giving it a rumpled, tacky, almost ruinous look, like an insect truly fallen on hard times and in deep trouble, a morsel ready for the taking, a temptation tied invitingly about a fine, well-sharpened hook and knotted securely to nine feet of 6X leader and tippet. A tippet's thickness is measured down to the thousandth of an inch. The end of a 6X is like spun gossamer, yet it is strong enough to stay with and haul in two to three pounds of wild-eyed, twisting, flailing, unrelenting trout. I remember confessing then, in a delicate whisper, as I have often confessed in such private moments, "Okay, okay. So technology can sometimes be a wonderful thing."

Rod in hand I walked up the creek. Brittle leaves crumbled underfoot. At the instant of my first cast above and across the deep pool's smooth dark surface, the bagpipes fell silent and a kingfisher across the creek squawked harshly.

Two days before, I had taken a small boat from the boat dock at Fontana Village (now the Peppertree Fontana Resort) and crossed Fontana Lake to the mouth of Hazel Creek. The only other convenient way of reaching Hazel Creek is the hike down from the summit of Clingman's Dome.

It was October and the brown trout were on the move and I was anxious. Brown trout have an unsettling effect on me. Despite the calendar, the weather was mild and had been for a week. I had fished the creek before in such pleasant weather and taken some nice trout both near the mouth of the creek and high up near Bone Valley. On a Friday the weather began to turn: the temperature dropped and the wind blew cold out of the northeast, and I knew the browns would be moving. By Friday evening I had rented a small boat and loaded it with tent, sleeping bag, fly rods and reels, and enough food for two days along the creek.

The boat's motor cranked on the first pull. Moving away

from the floating dock, I drew my collar up high over my ears. The cold left my fingertips numb, feeling heavy and useless, as though they had been injected with Novocain. As I nursed the motor's throttle easily, the boat eased through shredded wisps of wet fog. The mountains rose up and in the sunset's faded light, fall's colors burned like thick tongues of flame across the high wooded peaks. I remembered how dead leaves had scuttled about the wooden dock giving off a low, raspy sound. Death's tune, one of them, at least, and the sound, sure and true, of winter's approach, of life burrowing in, settling down, conserving itself in seed and warm ground, in hidden warrens and in cloisters of stone, wherever it might hold out, hold on, wait. In the mountains come autumn and winter there is an overwhelming sense of waiting, waiting out the cold, even though the life that waits cannot know that the cold will end, that the sunlight will again warm the land. Instead of assurance, in place of certainty, there is only the silence of the cold, the long, emotionless waiting.

Along the creek, dropping temperatures put a shiver into already cold water and brought the moody, rapacious brown trout out of their dark watery holes and into flat shadows that spread across the creek like opaque planking. Autumn's sober light, the livid light of morgues and funeral homes, a light that is abstract and tender, just the right light to shield the fickle, often mysterious movements of the brown trout. The brown trout is a brutish fish, the great piscine carnivore of cold mountain trout streams. As a predator it is deadly yet fair, eating everything with equal resolution and enthusiasm.

Despite the wind, the surface of Fontana Lake the day I crossed over to the creek was flat and smooth and looked of old, unpolished glass. I put my left hand in my coat pocket, maneuvered the small motor with my right, and with my head tucked in turtle fashion, I leaned my shoulders forward into the wind. The bow rose up and moved ahead, bouncing only slightly, and I remember settling down onto the cold plastic cushion and thinking how time in the mountains seems thicker, heavier, slower, insulated. The cold holds its own fascinations, its own delights. For one thing, it tends to thin out the traffic that can sometimes clog the narrow winding roads that snake through these mountains. It sends the tourist packing, heading for home, comfort, and warmth. Meanwhile, the brown trout stir and I stir with them, eager to move in that same pale gray light and watch for them in the creek's cold, deep pools, wade in the icy water and feel winter hard against my skin, and, if my luck holds, feel a good trout's great weight on my line, bending the little Winston rod even before I have fully set the hook.

So I put on extra clothes, filling the old rubber waders with layered warmth, and tried not to think too much of the cold hours because there is that chance, no matter how remote, of being among or near trout, a fish whose company has never failed to thrill and astonish me. Trout never cease to surprise, to fill the blood with great soaking doses of adrenaline. For a moment, as they rise, they seem, all at once, fish, image, illusion, symbol, wildness suddenly fleshed in substance: color, character, the power of sleek, raw muscle and undiluted energy.

The trip across Fontana Lake to Hazel Creek is several miles. Each time I pull into the slender cove where the creek empties into the lake, I shut the boat's motor off, drift slowly into the shallow water listening to the sound of the creek hissing and percolating over jumbled piles of stones. Rocks completely submerged in the swift water look almost alive, like something desperately attempting to shed a thoroughly worn-out skin, something sloughing off an ancient burden, grasping for release. Above the sound of the water is the sound of the wind rattling in the trees and the trill of birdsong. Over my shoulder, out over the spreading lake and rising mountains, only a deep and abiding silence, the kind in which a child imagines hearing the sea's roar in the hollow, dry chambers of a spent seashell or the kind in which an angler imagines seeing the shimmering shadow of a trout moving in clear, cold water, rising to strike violently, relentlessly, at insects hatching off the surface of the creek.

I pulled the boat up past the big rocks, up past the mud, up onto dry, hard ground, tied it firmly to a chunk of granite the size of a VW, grabbed the backpack and fly rods, walked up to the trail that shadows the creek, follows its rock-strewn twists and turns. The relationship between trail and creek is conventional, traditional, one of cordial, even-tempered tolerance rather than intimacy or some essential symbiosis. I walk the trail as I do most mountain trails, in some mild, harmless trance, pleasant and lucid, brought on by the rattling sound of the creek just down the ridge, just beyond the trees and tangles of creeper and greenbrier, honeysuckle and deer laurel.

High up beyond the ridgeline, the day's light was fading. Only a gauzy pale light lingered among the branches of the trees, high up on the humped and swollen summits whose silhouettes are pressed hard against the horizon. Once, from high up in the Blue Ridge Mountains looking south and east, I saw just the charcoal shadows of the Smokies, a ridgeline that looked at that distance like a diseased backbone, a long, ragged scar of violent breaks and fractures worn smooth by time.

The trail following Hazel Creek up the mountain from the lake is good, hard-packed, easy to follow. I know it well, so well that I walk it measuring not its mood but mine. The trail is not bothered with destinations; it goes on and so do I. I walk until there is reason to stop, and in these mountains almost every footfall kicks up a dozen reasons sane and sound enough for stopping. No imperative manipulates these harmless trout journeys of mine except the desire to be where trout are. Too, there is something in me, something deep and inescapable that needs the rush of mountain streams, the nearness of trout, the possibilities of both, the honest feel of root and stone and mountain wind.

Trout are excellent company, creatures of noble and admirable and perplexing qualities, much like human beings only more honest and sincere. They are totally unpredictable and therefore totally bewitching, at once brutal, beautiful, suspicious, graceful, and powerful, fastidious and wary, cautious and aggressive. Raw instinct burns like electric current through their cold, wild flesh. There is a charming snobbery about mountain trout, a stubbornness that is absolutely unbending. Their needs are specific rather than arbitrary and capricious. They know nothing of compromise. Life means moving water, fast water, clean water, water rich in prey and with at least a measure of wildness, meaning a solitude free of the whirl of cities and civilization. These are not luxuries or whims. To the trout they are necessities, the basic elements of life—a life worth living, struggling after. It's wildness or nothing. Some things are worse than death, at least to a trout. Clear-cut the forest up the valley from their stream and they die. No compromise. Pump toxins into a stream's watershed miles away and the trout go belly-up. No compromise. Dilute the balance of their streams with acid rain and they bloat and float to the surface. No compromise. Among mountain trout, wildness is more than a notion, a principle, or an attribute; it's a matter of blood and bone, the instinct of cold, hard, inexorable refusal to accept less of life than what they need.

Night on the creek came easily and smoothly, like a dark silk shirt slipping down slowly over the hands, arms, head, shoulders until there was a complete and comfortable soft darkness covering everything. In the hour since anchoring the boat, I hadn't walked half a mile up the trail. I stopped, put up the blue tent quickly near the Proctor campsite, one of the handful of designated primitive campsites along Hazel Creek, tied my backcountry permit to the tent flap. Permits are required for backcountry camping in the park. Park rangers issue the permits to keep track of who is wandering about the mountains, off the main roads, off the well-used trails. There is no fee, yet. It's all done by way of the honor system. The rangers let you go and you promise to use only designated trails and campsites and generally leave the backcountry as you found it. Just in case you don't make it, in case you end up facedown in some deep pool along a creek, in case you lose your footing along a ridge, in case some irascible trout gives you heart failure, the permits also come in handy as body tags, with two thin strips of wire easily twisted about a naked big toe or through the black zipper of a body bag.

As the light retreated it seemed to leave a slight warmth against the skin. Just enough daylight to rig up the little rod, attempt a cast or two. Fall trout fishing on Hazel Creek calls for daring among fish and angler alike. The cold urges the experimental, the unexpected, the improbable, even the provocative. No need to match flies with nonexistent insect hatches. For the trout, the cold means a lean diet. Anything goes. The idea is to tie on a fly that is both alluring and believable, something that might strike incorrigible trout as honest, something that will stir their blood, pinch their deep winter hunger. My autumn collection of flies is modest, but bold: some dry flies, sizes 12 to 20 and a handful of nymphs and wet flies, all tucked safely away in empty film canisters. I tied on a slightly frazzled McGinty, forgot the waders, walked up the trail to just below the Proctor Bridge, then walked into the river, wide and cold, a glacial cold, deep and numbing. Below the bridge, on the far side of the creek where the bank curves sharply, small oaks bent gracefully out over a large pool of quiet water. My line, leader, tippet, and the old McGinty fly unfolded inches above the pool's surface. It was so flat and calm that the water had the dull, thick shine of quicksilver.

For two years, through every season, there was a fine trout that lived in this big pool. An old fish, I imagined, fat with experience. Not wise, just knowing. Just the sudden ripple of its great charcoal shadow across the pool would raise atavistic hairs on the back of my neck and put a shiver on my skin. That undulating shadow got to me, obsessed me, possessed me. All I wanted was to somehow get to that trout, tempt it, get it to not just take my fly, but swallow it, hook and all, so that I might haul its massive shadow into the light, feel its great weight on my line, watch it jump in pure desperation twisting violently in midair, the wide stripe along its flanks as pink as flesh laid bare by a sudden wound. If even for an instant, I wanted to see the glint of daylight in its limpid black eyes. I wanted that trout, not to keep, not to hang on the wall, not even to eat, but only for the assurance of its reality. I dreamed of it, lit candles for it, courted fortune for it, even took a chance on Ambrose Noel's prayer wheel for it.

*

Ambrose Noel wore simple brown shorts and a red flannel shirt, worn leather hiking boots, and a permanent smile. He had the features of a small-town police blotter description —

cheerfully nondescript. He was a man of average height, average weight, average looks, abiding concerns and convictions, and a Thomistic belief in a divine logic lurking just under life's chaotic skin.

I heard him before I saw him. He was up near the headwaters of Hazel Creek where he had stopped for lunch and was singing a single line of lyrics from an old Doors' song. "When you're strange, faces come out of the rain, when you're strange." The words never varied, although his style and delivery did as he crooned, yodeled, screamed, even hummed the lyric as ballad, anthem, lullaby, psalm, requiem, and rhythm and blues.

I walked down along the creek to where Ambrose Noel kneeled patiently over a pot of simmering butter beans, pinto beans, field peas, kidney beans, shallots, and squash, all of it covered with a hash of bean sprouts.

Introductions were made.

"Sit," said Ambrose Noel. "Let's break bread together."

I cringed at the notion of some kind of hideous bean bread, but it turned out to be harmless whole wheat.

We talked and ate beans and bread and divided a ripe tomato that sat temptingly on a bright blue bandanna. Ambrose Noel told me he was on a mission to bring hope to these hard-luck mountains.

"God came to me at 1:03 P.M. in the parking lot of the Mc-Donald's in Pigeon Forge and told me to pack up and get into the mountains," said Ambrose Noel severely, with absolute sincerity. "God is invisible, in case you're wondering. He's just a voice. But, man, what a voice!"

I helped myself to seconds on the beans.

"No trumpets," said Ambrose Noel, "not even electric violins. Just a voice, as unemotional and flat as an insurance salesman or the midsummer drone of an irritating insect. I kept hoping it would just go away. It didn't. In fact, it kept coming back, always to the parking lot at McDonald's. Some recruiting station, huh? God has one lousy memory, man. He had to keep coming back because He couldn't recall what He'd told me. Hell, He wasn't even sure I was the guy He had let hear His voice. We met in the McDonald's parking lot four times, then He stopped coming. Believe me, man, I stumbled onto this gig.

"Glad I did, though, ya know. Great job, having a mission and all, and these mountains are way beyond mellow."

"Why the wheel?" I asked as I imagined God and Ambrose Noel exchanging small talk outside McDonald's over hamburgers and Diet Cokes.

"To make things fair and to make sure that everyone has a chance," said Ambrose Noel. "The Man told me to peddle hope, not assurances or guarantees. The wheel gives everybody a spin, a chance at hope. This is what God said to me: 'I have given hope some thought and have nothing against it, though My principal means of employment is Life and Death. Life is the root, Death the leaf.' That's what He said to me. You go and figure it. Mostly, the whole thing's a gamble. Everybody likes to gamble, man, take a chance, risk something for something more. Hope is the something more."

It was well after noon and the May sun was warm against my face. I leaned back against the cool, smooth surface of a huge outcrop of granite.

"How about the odds?" I asked. "What are the odds these days for hope?"

"Lousy," said Ambrose Noel, the smile on his cherub face growing wider, a perfect slim upturning curve of lip and cheek. "But the wheel's bound to hit it sometime, bring some lucky soul more hope than he's bargained for. Meanwhile, brother, everybody can spin, turn the wheel."

Like Johnny Appleseed sowing seeds, Ambrose Noel walked about the Smoky Mountains offering hope, a chance to spin the wheel. Just a spin of the prayer wheel and your luck might change. In these mountains stranger things happen all the time.

I sat up, brushed off my hands, put my lucky worn-out bush hat back on.

"Okay, Noel, set the thing up, I'll spin."

"Dollar first." He said the two words crisply, evenly, as he took up the prayer wheel, set it firmly on his crossed knees.

"What dollar?" I asked, suddenly realizing the source of Ambrose Noel's permanent smile. "What was all the talk about everybody getting a free spin?"

"Truth," said Ambrose Noel. His eyes were closed now as he rattled the thick wooden wheels stacked on the wide wooden cylinder that made up the prayer wheel. Each of the wheels on the long center peg were heavily engraved with strange symbols, characters, it seemed, of some alien alphabet, rubbed smooth by legions of chance takers, crowds of the hopeful and hopeless.

"Everyone spins for free as long as they're willing to make a dollar contribution to my Mission of Hope. Just a dollar to keep one of God's pilgrims alive and in the pink."

Using his left hand, Ambrose Noel spun the wheels which turned noisily, making an unsettling heavy clacking sound. Above the noise of the rotating wheels was Ambrose Noel's voice, suddenly like that of a heroic tenor giving a pained and somber importance to the Doors' Lyric, "When you're strange, faces come out of the rain . . ."

Just one chorus.

"Hope's worth something, isn't it?" he said. His speaking voice, like his features, was featureless—smooth, lackluster terrain. "And the dollar goes toward the work of the mission, toward keeping hope alive. And the spin's for free, as long as you believe enough to contribute to the mission."

While he talked, I kept looking down at the tin bowl of beans and sprouts, what was left of the single tomato. A dollar for the mission: a fresh sack of beans and a prayer wheel of hope.

I put my dollar down by his knee, spun all of the wheels at once, prayed for enough hope and fortune to hook the big rainbow trout in Proctor Pool, bring that hulking shadow up through the deep olive-green water and see how the mountain sunlight and its deep-water wildness mixed, how the light might come off its body like electricity and ripple in blue waves across the smooth surface of the pool.

But the prayer wheel fell short. While my luck stayed sour, I went on hoping that I would somehow connect with that trout. It was some fish. Often I dreamed of the worlds of sensation, of reality and image, through which its muscled weight might pull me, set me to wandering.

I saw the shadow of the big trout that moved warily about the edges of Proctor Pool off and on for almost two years, then it vanished. Even in that deep green water the trout's shadow had a dark blue cast, as all shadows do on cloudless mountain days. Shadows gather the sky's reflected light, an array of blues, rather than the sun's stark golds, hard yellows. Light—every man's magic show—the extraordinary swaddled in the common. It warms life, feeds life, sustains life, fuels life, seems a sea of inestimable size, a sea choking with particles and waves that considered separately are of almost no consequence or importance. The magic is not in the pretty cold colors, but in the warmth. Wherever light is denied, even partially, there are shadows and every shadow is a mystery, whole and true, because it portends the unrevealed, not only undiluted beauty but, as well, unspeakable brutality.

Other shadows, other fish, other mysteries, have moved in and out of the pool's rich water and soft light. But the old trout is gone. Dead, surely, rather than caught, because that is the way I want to think of it, a natural end: water to fish, fish to water. Death and life are the energy of the same process, one preoccupied neither with beginnings or endings. The first breath of life is also the first step toward death. Time flies on death's wings.

The big trout's shadow is gone, but its energy is here yet, moving in the creek, in this rush of fast mountain water mingling with the day's moody light.

Like the big trout in Proctor Pool, Ambrose Noel disappeared. For a long time I would stop along mountain trails, rest along stream banks, listen deep in the mountain nights for the telltale wooden clacking of his Himalayan prayer wheel and his voice rising above its spinning wheels singing the Doors' lyric as though it were part doxology, part canticle. But he never comes, Ambrose Noel, peddler of hope. Nevertheless, I always carry a wrinkled dollar bill, a humble contribution to keep his mission alive, just in case. The spin for hope, of course, should I ever get another chance, is free.

It seemed that I had only just allowed myself to think of the trout's big shadow and Ambrose Noel and the day's light went dull, lost tone and texture as night rose with the moon and eased over the mountains and onto every leaf and stone. I stood at the edge of Proctor Pool for a long time watching the widening night and the first smudges of starlight on the surface of the creek, light thin and cold. I reeled in my line, walked back to the tent, and the darkness was like an artery in which I felt, at once, safe and secure and yet, too, poised on the cusp of unimaginable wonder and adventure.

Dinner: cheese and crackers, hot chili, and lots of water. Dinner music compliments of Hazel Creek, barred owls up on the far ridge, and what sounded like a coyote to the east. In all, a heady blend of mountain chamber music, the coyote's melancholy yowl balanced by the endless syncopation of rushing creek water. I closed my eyes and featured an ensemble of oboes and jazz piano.

Clouds drifted over the mountains from the west, hid the moon, diffused the night's deep blue light, and I crawled into the tent and lay still on the sleeping bag listening to the night stirring. Predictably, since I am a member of the Information Age, a fact broke loose from my brain, swung loose as a hammock in my mind. It was this: the average person sleeps 220,000 hours during his lifetime. Time flies, it seems, not only on death's wings, but on sleep's as well. I decided to stay up and enjoy the mountain night, put a wrinkle in at least one average man's lifetime statistics. I spread the sleeping bag on the cold ground outside the tent, crawled in, watched the night sky until it seemed to press on my chest, overwhelming every thought, every feeling, until my only connection to the earth was the sound of the night's cold wind high among the trees and the hiss of the creek's waters over wide beds of smooth stones.

Over the last decade, I have discovered, to my pleasure, that the Smoky Mountains delight in paradox.

Irony and the waters of Hazel Creek surely mingle, at least in my experience. When it comes to reputation and popularity, Hazel Creek is one of the most famous Smoky Mountain streams. Although the Smokies are marked by hundreds of miles of prime trout streams, few are as loudly heralded, frequently praised, or widely loved as Hazel Creek.

But here's the good part. There is rarely anyone along the creek, much less actually fishing in it. Some years ago, as I walked down the creek from Clingman's Dome, I came across two other fly fishermen and immediately grew sullen, morose, disillusioned. Here were two other anglers on a creek I had more or less fished alone for years. In trout fishing, and especially in mountain trout fishing, one angler and trout borders on the idyllic, or some version thereof. Two anglers and trout is a crowd, claustrophobic and unbearable.

I hiked on down the mountain, well beyond the second angler, who tipped his hat and sent me on with a cold stare. And when I had walked a mile and had not seen another human being, I shed my pack, took up the Winston rod, and waded out into the creek's cold, fast water. The sun was high in a clear sky and its warmth felt good against my face and eased my building sense of doom, the lurking, dreadful thought that tomorrow there might be four anglers on the creek or five. Not just a mere crowd, but a chaotic, jarring horde.

I fished until well in the afternoon, then shed my waders, put up my rod, and stretched out in the cool shade of the tall trees along the bank, eating a firm apple, mostly not concentrating on a book I had brought along, and just thinking about the creek. The afternoon hours are as good as any for taking stock, massaging memory and experience.

From where the creek empties into Fontana Lake, the main Hazel Creek Trail climbs toward Siler's Bald and Clingman's Dome, a rise in altitude of 3,500 feet. It's a pleasant walk, especially with frequent stops for fishing, enjoying the creek's great beauty and tranquillity. The creek can also be reached by hiking down the valley from Clingman's Dome, which is an easier proposition: mostly downhill. The cold mountain springs that make up the creek's headwaters are up on Siler's Bald. From there, Hazel Creek meanders generally southwest down the mountains toward the lake. The creek's beauty and intrigue are deepened and increased by its many branches, especially up around Sugar Fork and Bone Valley Creek where a side trail goes to Pickens Gap, crosses the Appalachian Trail, and continues on to Eagle Creek, another fine trout stream.

Bone Valley is memorably quiet. The valley supposedly got its name after a late and especially cruel winter storm hit the mountains killing cattle already put to pasture in the high country. The spring thaw exposed their bones. Death of any kind has a way of marking a place, giving it a name soaked in memory and meaning. Bone Valley. Too, last year, not far down the valley, an angler took a brown trout that weighed in at more than six pounds, not the biggest brown ever taken from the creek, but quite a fish to be found so high up the valley.

It was here along the creek, up around Bone Valley, that whoever had been playing the bagpipes along the creek for so many seasons stopped for good. Maybe it was the crowd, the two other anglers, the sudden appearance of so many people at once, the startling, but undeniable press of civilization. Whatever it was, like the big trout down in Proctor Pool, the bagpipe player along Hazel Creek simply vanished. The music stopped.

I heard it for the last time not far from where Cold Spring Branch enters the creek. It was early morning, the pale blue light easing down through the valley like a low-hanging fog. There was tea warming on the camp stove and fresh apples and dry cereal for breakfast.

I had started hiking down the creek some days before and was in no hurry. The day before I had taken two fine rainbow trout. Both fish hung high in the water at the edge of a wide, fast section of shoals. The trout fought hard, betting all of their power and energy against the hook and line, and I set them loose in the calm water below the shoal where they regained their strength and moved off quickly into deeper, darker water. How slowly that absorbing hour on the creek passed, like a glacier over hard ground. I wore that hour of thin sunlight and widening shadows, of water and the two good fish, as though it were my skin.

I had that same sensation sitting up on the old railroad grade in dripping clouds of fog, waiting for the tea to warm. Rivers flowed all about me, through me: rivers of water and air tinged with the smell of wild onions, rivers of sky and changing light, moving water, rushing time. The creek raced by giving up so much more than fish—a morning of revelations and sounds, and, finally, a river of music. The bagpipes pouring out mountain folk songs, bluegrass bagpipe tunes coming from down the creek, down where the Sugar Fork Trail split off, goes up Sugar Fork. Like Bone Valley, Sugar Fork and the Little Fork of Sugar Fork have their own fascinations, most of them bound up as much in one man as in the delicate beauty of the small creek and the mountain country it moves through.

The man was Horace Kephart.

Among those whose lives have been entangled completely with these mountains, Kephart remains an intriguing and haunting figure, as much legend and myth as fact, mere crumbled bone. Although a great many writers have tried to figure him out, Kephart, so far, has mostly eluded every writer who has tried to interpret not only his dreams, but what fueled them.

The music along the creek lasted until the warm May sun rose above the mountains, until the fog had lifted, dissolved, except from the low places along the creek where it hung like lacy clouds of bone-colored mist fringed in yellow sunlight.

While the music went on, changed from country swing to down-and-out blues, I walked down the creek and the cool morning wind pressed gently against my face. And I thought I saw him, finally, the bagpipe player, well back in the shadows of the trees, tall, thin, leaning against a big sycamore tree. He was wearing a red baseball cap.

I sat by the creek, watched, listened, and stayed quiet, as though I were watching some wild animal as yet unaware of my presence. I studied the man's every move, his manner. Like the big trout in Proctor Pool, here was yet another beguiling mixture of water and light, mountain and shadows, something obviously real and yet compellingly incomplete. He stopped playing and the disembodied notes of the last song hung on the air for a long instant, drifted on the wind. The man in the green shadows of the sycamore tree took up his instrument again, began playing an old gospel hymn, a tune that was familiar to me, a melody out of the shipwreck of memory, and yet its name escaped me. The bagpipe player turned and walked back toward the thick woods along the creek, never missing a note, and I kept on listening until the only music was that of the creek, the slap of water against flat stones. All that day I fished the creek and mindlessly hummed that half-forgotten gospel hymn whose name I still can't remember, though I flip through church hymnals when I can hoping to find it. It is important. It was the last song the bagpipe player along Hazel Creek ever played. It is fitting, perhaps, that the bagpipe music stopped in May, the mountains newly green and wrinkling with the wild energy of renewal, both the anticipated and unexpected.

There is a mountain story I first heard in Robbinsville that goes like this—when Horace Kephart showed up in these mountains he had reached the interesting and vexing point of intoxication where the body goes happily numb while the mind hungers for immediate adventure, anything that smacks of lawlessness and daring. Since he was well past the point of navigating with his legs, so the story goes, someone managed to slump Kephart over a mule. A sudden surge of energy supposedly rippled through Kephart and he raised his head, took off his rumpled hat, bent close to the mule's ears, and said loudly, "Take me to paradise, you ass, and quickly." Eventually, the good-natured mule deposited Kephart near Dillsboro. From here he would later move up Hazel Creek. The remains of his old cabin are still there, off the Sugar Fork Trail along the Little Fork of Sugar Fork up toward Pickens Gap.

True or embroidered, the man who ended up on Hazel Creek had been all but unhinged by city life. He came to the mountains both to be healed and fulfilled, to celebrate in his own way these mountains and those who lived in harmony with them.

Kephart wanted resolution and balance more than escape or complete solitude, refuge. He did not come to the Smoky Mountains to hide, sink away into the cool shadows, but to sing their praise. Like Muir, Kephart wanted to call his fellowman's attention to what he considered the greatest of temples, the world's richest cathedral: the mountains, where God was not over the earth, apart from it, but of it, inexorably—in all the dispassionate beauty and power and process of water and stone, wind and forest.

Kephart, the often bitter old drunk up on Hazel Creek, was a man of firm beliefs, unshakable principles, and opinions concerning man and wilderness, ideas that finally cost him everything, one way of life lost and another gained.

Kephart was born in East Salem, Pennsylvania, in 1862, the son of a stern God-fearing father. The Kepharts moved from Pennsylvania to the back-country of Iowa, where wildness and wilderness became the young Kephart's passion, one he was never able to kick. The still rough-edged Iowa countryside filled young Kephart's every need, his every wish. As he grew, he had two great passions—books and the outdoors. These loves stayed with him always, even though his father took a position with the United Brethren Mutual Aid Society and moved the family back to Pennsylvania. More and more, Kephart turned his great energies to scholarship, attending Lebanon Valley College, Boston University, and Cornell. Horace Kephart quickly became one of the most respected young librarians in the nation. He studied and worked in Italy, worked at Rutgers, then accepted a position at Yale, and married.

A life greatly blessed, or so it seemed. His good fortune continued until his deep interest in the American West landed him the position as librarian at St. Louis's much respected Mercantile Library. By 1897, he had a prestigious position, the respect of his academic peers, a growing academic reputation, a successful career, a social position of importance in St. Louis, a wife and a family of six children. Horace Kephart had it all, save what he wanted: to live the life he spent his days and nights reading about, a life in the wilderness, a life devoted entirely to the outdoors. He began, more and more, to shun his duties and responsibilities at the library and ignore his family as he slipped off into the Ozark Mountains, often for days at a time.

Instead of scholarly works, he began writing articles on woodcraft and hunting for the popular outdoor magazines. He drank and went off into the mountains. And when he came back to town, he drank more and more until he could go into the mountains again. There was talk of his wife having an affair, of Horace finding her with the other man. Whatever happened, his need for drink and wilderness increased dramatically.

Wilderness absorbed Kephart's anger, eased his bitterness, took the edge off his rage. Finally, he decided to leave the Mercantile Library, St. Louis, even his wife and family, live the life that threatened to suffocate him if he did not embrace it—a life in the mountains, a life lived for the most part alone. Depending on who you read about Kephart, his last days in St. Louis were either marked by a nervous breakdown or complete alcoholic exhaustion. Whatever the condition or the reason, Horace Kephart was in bad shape when in 1904 his father showed up to carry him home. The next anyone heard of him he came falling off a train near Dillsboro, North Carolina, in the Smoky Mountains. Drunk again, but happy. Actually, his first camp in these mountains was on Dick's Creek and from there later in 1904 he moved up Hazel Creek. Of this new journey into the Smoky Mountains, Kephart wrote: "When I went south into the mountains I was seeking a Back of Beyond."

The "Back of Beyond" he found was among mountains that knew man's presence and touch, mountains heavily logged and mined, mountains whose summits looked out not over great wild lands stretching to the horizon but over some of the most populated and polluted cities of the Southeast. Here, Kephart came in search of his wilderness and here he found it.

Another intriguing Smoky Mountain paradox. A man consumed by wilderness ending up not among the sprawling open lands and great mountains of the West or Alaska, but in the Smoky Mountains, lands that had stood up to nearly everything man and civilization had thrown at them and still hung on to their wildness. Kephart admired these mountains and the people who lived in them for their tenacity, self-reliance, and resolve. Here, deep in Southern Appalachia, Kephart lived, worked, and died. Sometimes he would spend days, even weeks, in the mountains, hiking, hunting, writing, living the life he loved.

In the end, another Smoky Mountain irony: Horace Kephart

died in an automobile accident on a mountain highway. It was the spring of 1931. He died pretty much the way he came into the mountains: happily drunk. He and a visiting writer were on their way back to Bryson City from a local bootlegger's place outside town. Both died instantly. Only the car's driver survived.

Kephart was buried on April 5, 1931, up on School House Hill in Bryson City, North Carolina. His grave is marked by a huge piece of Appalachian greenstone. There is a simple plaque fixed to the face of the stone with this inscription: HORACE KEPHART 1862–1931. SCHOLAR, AUTHOR, OUTDOORSMAN. HE LOVED HIS NEIGHBORS AND PICTURED THEM IN "OUR SOUTHERN HIGHLANDERS." HIS VISION HELPED CREATE THE GREAT SMOKY MOUNTAINS NATIONAL PARK.

The cemetery on top of School House Hill is a fine place to wait for the Hereafter. It is a hill with a clear view out over town toward where Deep Creek joins the Tuckaseigee River. Kephart had his last camp along Deep Creek. In the far distance are some of the high peaks of the Smokies, including Mount Kephart, named in Kephart's honor just weeks before his death, and dominated by Clingman's Dome.

Kephart's great love for these mountains and their people produced two books that have measured well against the passing years—his *Camping and Woodcraft*, a classic among a dull crowd of often bland and useless outdoor field guides, and *Our Southern Highlanders*, Kephart's personal paean to the Appalachian Mountains and the Appalachian way of life, both of which he not only celebrated but struggled to preserve and protect. At the time of his death, Kephart had turned from his writing to fighting for the establishment of a national park in the Smoky Mountains. He also championed what later became the Appalachian Trail.

I go up to the School House Hill Cemetery often. It is well tended and crowded with silence and people joined even in death by their sincerity, their fierce determination and spirit. Most of the extinguished lives in the School House Hill Cemetery are marked by hard luck or no luck at all. They were and are a people of hard, unflinching faith, a faith that allows for humor and lets them love the mountains while praying for a way out of them into some kinder fate, gentler heaven, higher glory. Whatever their fate, though, they are, like Kephart, still here, of this ground, these thankless mountains, bones blended back into the rocky dark soil, the pungent loam, deep down among the roots, home at last.

My first visit to School House Hill came a year after meeting Exie Sopwith down near Newfound Gap along the Oconaluftee River. I had fished Hazel Creek three times and Deep Creek once. I knew of Kephart and had read his books. A friend from Bryson City, where Kephart lived when he felt the need to come to town, sent me a quote from the *Asheville Citizen* dated April 3, 1931, the day of Kephart's death. The headline read AUTHORS DIE INSTANTLY IN WRECK NEAR BRYSON CITY, and carried these words from Kephart: "I owe my life to these mountains and I want them preserved that others may profit by them as I have."

"I have," I said aloud, sitting on the massive stone marking Kephart's grave, "I have, indeed." It was twilight and the scattered lights of Bryson City looked like cheap strings of Christmas lights, every other bulb burnt out. The wind was up and the night was cool. I had set up camp down along the bottom end of Deep Creek, but I decided to sit a while longer on the hilltop and watch night settle in the valley and the lights of the small city shine soft as moonglow.

*

Why?

Of so many mountains, why these?

Why the Smoky Mountains? They seem such an unlikely destination for a man like Kephart, for anyone looking for true wilderness. There is, scientists and earth watchers tell us, no true wilderness left, at least not here. Recently, two scientists set out to determine just how much of the earth's wilderness is left. The study lasted eighteen months. No region could be accepted as wilderness that showed roads, buildings, airports, railroads, settlements, pipelines, dams, even power lines. What, then, is left?—almost nineteen million square miles, or roughly one-third of the earth's surface, is still wild, at least by this study's definition. Where is this wilderness, where are these last of the earth's pristine wild lands?—Antarctica, remote parts of the Soviet Union and North America, large parts of Africa and South America, smaller parts of Asia and Europe.

In North America the prime remnant wilderness lands are located mostly in Alaska and parts of northern Canada and the Arctic. Of all these patches of wilderness barely 20 percent are now protected. Each year a little more of the earth's great diversity and richness slip away and with them go not only beauty and solace, solitude and renewal, but much of the planet's possibility and potential. With them our desperate hope for the future grows fainter, fainter.

If there is less and less wilderness, there are still those places, even among the roads and dams and towns and power lines, where wildness hangs on. There are such places in these mountains, remnants of a land that is as tenacious as it is bucolic, as hard as it is beautiful. Tucked deep in these narrow valleys and shadowy coves, life goes on, luxuriant and unyielding, a broth of water and wind, stone and root, seed and bloom.

On summer afternoons on my grandfather's farm in the Ozarks when the heat sat on the land like hot iron, we gathered on the porch at noon and traveled through the well-thumbed pages of the old man's big black world atlas. There were few rules or limits: we journeyed to every land that seemed to offer cool rivers full of fat trout. Innocent fantasy, harmless dreams of old men and a young boy. Thoughts of such places cooled us, helped ease the heat, helped get us through afternoons that sizzled like the heavy walls of a blast furnace. No matter how pleasant and exciting our back-porch travels were, though, no other mountains, no matter how exotic, moved us as deeply as the hard-luck hills we lived in, for they were our lives—what was real, immediate, honest, the source of our joy and pain, our small gains and endless failures. If they were not the limits of our dreams, they were the boundaries of what we knew, the world out the back door, the wildness beyond the trees.

There is something in me that needs mountains and fast mountain streams. The rough-edged Smoky Mountains remind me of the Ozarks. Like the Ozarks, they are enough, all I need, time moving in the rush of a fast mountain stream, caught in the glint of light off rippled water or in a trout's cold black eyes, iridescent flanks, a single red leaf spiraling in the press of an autumn wind. There is no true wilderness here, but there is wildness, honest and deep and as much as a man could hope for. These mountains are sincere. They are a place of margins rather than pristine grandeur. There is as much ruin along these ridges, deep in these valleys, as there is natural glory. In these thick forests man and the land have collided again and again, battled for hundreds of years, and still there is no clear victor. Like the trout in these rocky streams, the mountains know no compromise. Consequently, the Smokies are a land marked more by loss and bankruptcy than prosperity.

Mountains are the scribblings of time on the surface of the land, a good place for a man to rub life's immediacy and its Jobaic persistence. Mountains absorb life yet do not hide it, either its fecundity, beauty, or its cruelty. In the high country every ridge seems a lodestone. Touch a great, smooth chunk of granite, wade a river, sink into a heavy sleep beneath hemlock trees—everywhere the feel of undiluted process, motion, raw possibility. And you are just another part of it all. Here man does not matter, does not count. Here he is just another expression of life, neither feared, envied, acknowledged, or especially needed. The stream, the trout, the mountains, go on with or without me, dancing, as they have for so long, to time's madder music, rhythms older than interstellar dust.

Life in the Smoky Mountains is hard, often luckless, impoverished, yet there is to these mountains richness of another kind, hard to measure, a legacy of holding out, holding on to a wildness deep in root and seed, blood and bone.

Sitting on the big stone over Kephart's grave up on School House Hill, I remembered a line of his, words full of celebration and wonder at these mountains. "There is not," he said, "a cranny in the rocks of the Great Smokies, not a foot of the wild glen, but harbors something lovable and rare." More high country irony—that mountains so thoroughly used, even abused, can still lay claim to some of the most sublime mountain country east of the Mississippi River.

No matter where I might be, these mountains stay with me, always. In any city, at any time, during any season, I can shut my eyes and see these summits dark and brooding against an indigo-blue sky and hear the low rumble and roar of swift trout water down rocky gorges and feel the weight of a good trout on my line, the tug that hauls me into the world of stream and water, mountains and trout. These mountains persevere, hang on. And every time I wake and find that I too am suffering from Kephart's disease, the unsettling feeling that I have everything that I want and so little of what I need, I go to the mountains, wade a fine stream, fly-fish until there is only the pure feeling of honest exhaustion and a light in the sky like that of a bed of embers, a perfection of reds, reds without names or definition or description. Coming to these mountains has nothing to do with pilgrimages, with looking for some piscatorial Holy Grail. Such adventures are luxuries and require large sums of what I don't have: money. I am only interested in the company of trout and the beauty they demand, a wildness that is as essential to their way of life as fast, clean water, life of a different kind for a time, a life as true and spare as smooth stone, as uncompromising as trout or wild orchids blooming in the cool shade along a mountain stream. The reassurance of no assurance is the medicine I need, the convenience of no convenience, the soothing order buried at the heart of chaos.

These mountains are enough. Here, on the Carolina side of the mountains, along Hazel Creek and Deep Creek, Snowbird Creek and Slickrock Creek, the years pass and the trout rise and the country is good. There is quiet and beauty in abundance. A brown trout on Slickrock Creek, a fish sometimes marked by a telling bloodred back, hits my fly with raw ferocity and Slickrock is all the holy water I require; it is the Afjord in Norway, the Te Anau in New Zealand, the Sustut, the Lower Talarik, the Big Horn, the Madison, the Bow. Wildness is rare and beautiful, moving, valuable, and profound whether it is experienced in the outback of British Columbia or Iceland or thigh-deep in a cold Smoky Mountain trout stream running unseen through the fingers of ten million visitors a year.

Along a few of the trout streams of the Smokies I have mingled with fish and water and light and I have felt the press of time, the great power of the present, the energy that fashions both the past and the future. It is not how many experiences we pile up in our lifetime, but what we make of them, how they mix with blood and memory, how they enrich our lives. Mountains and trout streams sustain me, are the handles through which I have glimpsed the slight and the immeasurable, the vast and the small. Being among them is never disappointing, even when there are no fish. For there is always the sensation, so deeply satisfying, of belonging, of being genuinely connected.

Estimates vary on just how many visitors a year pass through the Great Smoky Mountains National Park. Some say six million, others put the crowds at closer to eight or ten million. However many there are, most of them keep to the roads, the paved highways. They are eager to see whatever a road passes near. We have come to the point where we like our wilderness the way we like our food—fast and easily digestible, served up on the go, through the car window. The Great Smoky Mountains National Park's great appeal is that it is a drive-through park, that great good place where you can have a wilderness experience without ever having to leave your car. And the road does twist and turn through some magnificent countryside. There are frequent pull-offs and overlooks of great mountain vistas suitable for snapshots and a quick picnic. If the trash cans are full, it's all right. Wilderness, it seems, is for a great many of us just another handy place to dump beer cans, dead cars, plastic garbage bags full of chicken bones, and used plastic diapers. Along its main roads, even along the pastoral, often inspirational Blue Ridge Parkway climbing out of the Smokies and into the Blue Ridge Mountains, these mountains are like any other major national park, more trash than treasure.

Off the roads, off the main trails, back up in the thick woods, down steep slopes, along rock-strewn streams, these mountains have an admirable mean streak to them. Despite the hard-pressed towns, the creaky old dams, the telephone poles and electric lines and pipelines that climb and fall with nearly every ridge, despite every attempt to tame them, domesticate them, these mountains refuse to be easy, charitable, friendly. No compromise, none at all. Way off the roadways, deep in the hollows and stream valleys and in the thick forests that are not virgin but second, third, even fourth growth in some places, wildness persists, thrives. I am in wonder of these mountains for many reasons, but none more than their capacity for absorbing abuse and their capacity not just to hang on, but to endure.

I come for the beauty and the good fishing rather than grand truths, though these too are here scattered about the creek bottoms like weathered stones. The soft light of dusk, a trout's rise, the sound of nothing but water over stones are glamour and excitement enough. Mountain solitude is deep and wide and abiding and yet coiled tight as a snake, something alive, ready to give way at any instant to something as ordinary as birdsong or as confounding and bewitching as a trout's sudden inexplicable leap out of a stream's cold waters and into the sun's bright, warm light.

On a fresh, cool Sunday morning in March I met Allie Carlyle down the hill from one of Bryson City's many churches. The service was ending and the choir was on its feet, full of robust, uplifting song. We sat on big stones near large oak trees. Allie Carlyle looked to be in her forties, maybe more. Whatever her age, she was beautiful. The years and the mountains had been uncharacteristically kind. Long, soft, braided red hair, deep green eyes, skin the color of new butter, still cool, soft, fresh. As striking as her looks were, though, it was the old cane fly rod in her hand that caught my attention. Her voice was no louder than a whisper that blended with the church organ's inspirational chords. She, too, told me of nearby mountain streams full of trout.

"I don't know why I'm trusting in you, but I am," she said. "Keep all this to yourself. There's knee-deep silence up on those creeks, quiet that hasn't been broken just yet. Leave some when you go. It's a policy I try to keep." She turned then and looked up at the redbrick church up the hill and hummed along with the choir as it sang. In song her voice was loud and bold and there were uneven streams of sunlight moving wildly through her hair. After the hymn closed, after a weak chorus of amens, Allie Carlyle leaned close to the stone on which I sat, told me she had moved to town to teach after her father died some years back.

"There was the old farm," she said, and I noticed a definite roll to her whisper, like the rise and fall of emotion, "but I sold it. Unfair odds did it. Too many rocks, a soil way past hope, even luck, and just me. I have a son. Can't feed a boy on beauty, can't pay the bills with scenery. So I moved to town and called it a compromise. I earn a living for me and the boy and we get to stay in the mountains. Mountains can get to you, you know. I mean only that for me there's just no finer place to wait out Judgment Day."

You could hear the shuffle of robes and feet and chairs as the choir rose to sing again, put fire to sin with a powerful gospel song. Organ music wrinkled out of every chink and crevice in the old church, gave the wind a rich new tone and texture. Allie Carlyle picked up the melody, hummed along, smiling, absent-mindedly twirling the old cane fly rod in the fingers of her left hand. I said good-bye and walked down toward the river and then out toward Deep Creek, thinking that time spent in the mountains is indeed well invested and how lucky I have been to have invested so heavily: when I am old and bent and my mind is dim, the dividends of mountain time will nourish me still.

Franklin Burroughs

Lake Waccamaw
to Freelands

(SOUTH CAROLINA/NORTH CAROLINA)

On a bleak Sunday morning with a northeast wind driving a fine, misty rain into the windshield, Daddy and I headed up from Conway toward Lake Waccamaw. The first twenty miles
were through familiar territory, but when we got
beyond Highway 9, which runs from west to east
and crosses the Waccamaw at Bellamy's Landing, we entered what was for me almost a new
country, although it ought not to have been. My
mother's father had been born here, in the small
community of Buck's Creek, on the west side of
the Waccamaw, and had found his wife in Little
River, a few miles to the east. But he was up-
wardly mobile, moved to Conway, and left Buck's
Creek and Little River emphatically behind him.
My mother and her sisters and brothers do not
seem to have consorted much with their country cousins, and I became aware of this group of
relations only as they died, at which time my
sister and I would be put into our least inhabit-
able clothes and, on some unendurable summer
day, be driven over roads that shimmered in the
heat until they seemed to float above themselves
in an asphalt mirage. We would eventually arrive
at Buck's Creek or Nixon's Crossroads or Little
River, and there be introduced to any number of

Bryans and Stones and Vereens and Vaughts, all of whom made a collective, blurred impression of awkward diffidence, a lack of the fluency and self-possession I expected of grownups. The service would be Baptist, and entirely without the sanctioned impersonality of the Episcopalian disposal of the dead. To me at that time, accustomed as I was to the archaic remoteness of *The Book of Common Prayer*, it all seemed a poor show, insufficiently distinguished from the earnest and fumbling sincerity of ordinary life.

So now we drove on through Buck's Creek and toward North Carolina. This part of the county seemed untouched by all the changes that had taken place; it was still a region of small farms, with an occasional church or crossroads store. I had no topographical maps, and had to make do with two road maps, one of Horry and one of Columbus County, North Carolina. As we passed into North Carolina, subtle differences became apparent. We were leaving behind the pattern of gentle undulation typical of most of Horry County, with sandy ridges falling off gradually to bays, branches, and swamps, and entering a flatter, more sparsely populated country. The farms were smaller and fewer, the fields as flat as runways, and the black soil here looked heavy and impermeable, like clotted mud. The roadside ditches had a fine growth of cattails, indicating that water stood in them year round. It felt as though we were going into a lower and lower country as we went further and further upriver, but that of course was not possible. In an alluvial terrain, distance above sea-level is not what counts; what counts is distance above swamp level. The swamps around Lake Waccamaw, which we were now entering, are on average about forty feet above sea-level; those around Conway are about half that. But the high land around Conway may be twenty or thirty feet above the level of the swamps, while here such high land as there was would be only three or four feet above the swamp. We were at the southern edge of Green Swamp; the stretches of ground high enough for farming and human habitation are labelled on old maps as islands, and some of them still go by that name: Sweetgum Island, Pine Island, Clifton Island. These were originally savannahs, forested with longleaf and loblolly pine, and now they sustained a few meagre farms.

Because I had no adequate maps, we decided to turn east at Pireway, North Carolina, and cross the river, continue up it for a few miles on that side, and then re-cross at Freeland. That would give me at least two points of reference, some way of measuring my progress down from Lake Waccamaw.

The river at Pireway was unexpectedly broad—perhaps seventy yards across—and there was a landing on the east bank, just downstream of the bridge. My first impression was of a row of cars and pick-ups there, neatly parked and glistening incongruously between the dark, rain-dimpled surface of the river and the gray trunks of cypress and gum rising from the swamp behind them. We were already in the middle of the bridge before we realized that there was a baptism in progress at the river's edge. Forty or fifty people stood in a semicircle in front of the cars and trucks, facing the river. Their attention was focussed on the minister, who stood in shallow water, flanked by a young man and a young woman. These three, facing the congregation, had their backs to us, but we could see that the minister was reading from a big Bible that he held up in both hands, his head and shoulders tilted back to balance the weight of the book.

I slowed down and stopped, trying to take it in—the lowering skies, the skeins of Spanish moss moving softly in the wind, this solemn gathering by the river. Our normally acute sense of sabbath-day propriety deserted us entirely, and I think we would have sat parked on the bridge, gawking as rudely as any tourists, had not several somber faces in the congregation lifted to look at us, and the minister, by a slight twisting of his neck, indicated that he was aware of our presence. It was enough to show me what we were—two men in a truck, with Yankee license plates and a canoe on top, stopping to stare. I put the truck into gear and slunk on across the bridge, still watching out of the corner of my eye. My last view was of the faces turned back to the minister, and of the black current as it eddied around his knees, pulling at the severe crease of his pant legs, and at the waterlogged hem of the young woman's dress.

We drove on and talked about this and that. The rain would pick up for a moment, then relent; the windshield wipers kept up their steady rhythm of polish and smear, polish and smear. Although the hardwoods were at the point of unfurling into leaf, the flat land did not look hopeful. The clouds hung low and unbroken, it was chilly, and one had the sense of seed rotting in the drowned furrows. Daddy spoke practically of what a cold christening the two young people by the river were in for, when time came to wade out deeper—waist deep, maybe—and be dunked down below the surface. Often, he said, when a young woman was being baptized, her mother would sew lead battens into the hem of her skirt, so that it would not imperil anybody's modesty by floating up around her hips as she stepped into deeper water.

I asked if he had ever seen a Waccamaw baptism before, and he said he had once, just after the war. On a Sunday morning he and his brother Jack, a merchant in town, had put in at Red Bluff and run upriver to fish the Little Savannah territory. The war, like every war, had had the effect of undermining local pieties: before it, fishing was permissible in salt water on Sunday, but not in fresh water, unless it was your own private pond. Sunday hunting was unthinkable. This was not a matter of law—game laws in Horry County were generally regarded as a challenge, not an inhibition—but a matter of decency. After the war, people began to fish in the river on Sunday—at least townspeople did—although they did so somewhat self-consciously, as Jack and Daddy had that morning. Unsanctified or otherwise, they caught enough fish, cranked up the fine new Martin outboard motor, and headed back to the landing. Jack was at the tiller, and Daddy said that when they rounded the corner above Red Bluff he had two simultaneous perceptions—one of a crowd of people looking a good deal like a herd of cattle at a watering hole, and the other of the little Lumberton boat heeling over so sharply that he had to grab the gunwales, and heading back upstream and out of sight. Jack had a lot of regular customers in the Red Bluff vicinity. He and Daddy tied the boat to a piling upriver, sat on the bank, and waited out the service, until at last the congregation dispersed, and they could slip back to the landing unobserved, load the boat, and get home to a cold Sunday dinner.

We re-crossed the river at Freelands. It was small here, not twenty yards wide, and I was happy to see a good sandbar downstream, which meant that the water was low enough to furnish me plenty of campsites. Then we continued north to the lumbering town of Hallsboro, turned back east, and reached Lake Waccamaw not long before noon.

A kind of expectation, based on obvious metaphors, attaches to sources and headwaters. I knew almost nothing about Lake Waccamaw. A natural lake of any sort was a rarity in the Carolinas, and this one was further distinguished by the huge swamp that surrounded it. It has long attracted speculative interest, of one sort or another, although nobody seems to have taken much interest in the river that flowed out of it. Both of the botanical Bartrams went there. In July of 1765, John Bartram found slaves building tar-kilns to the east of the lake, and was characteristically delighted by "the great variety of lovely plants & flowers & in generally the finest lofty pines I ever saw" that grew on the savannahs, or "islands," that lay to the north. But "the so.west is very swampy. The outlet is at the so. end into the Wocoma river which runs a course of 50 mile & most of the way very stil water." He found fossilized shells, but had little conception of the extent of geological time: "it must be long ago when the sea flowed here: for the lake is now very fresh & produceth now the fresh water mussel as all our rivers do." His son William came there eight years later, describing it as "the beautiful Lake Wakamaw, which is the source of the fine river of that name [that] runs a south course of seventy or eighty miles, delivering its waters into Winyaw Bay at Georgetown." He deemed the "vast rich swamps" to the northwest of the lake, "fit for the production of rice" and his sense that, if only the swamps could be cleared and drained, they would provide the basis for a prosperous and sustainable agriculture, remained alive throughout the nineteenth century. But nothing substantial was done until the twentieth century, and then it was the logging industry, and not agricultural interests, that began digging canals, building causeways, and slowly diminishing the Waccamaw watershed.

But on this Sunday morning, Lake Waccamaw, seen from the county road that runs along its western shore, was a disappointment. The shore was low, scarcely a foot above water, and as perfectly flat as the lake itself. It was lined with summer houses, each house basically a box on stilts at the water's edge, and each with a dock extending a hundred feet or so out into the lake. Each dock had a boatshed at the end, and a big outboard runabout suspended from the rafters of the shed, so that the effect was of coming upon a lake where all the boats had gone to roost. There were no people about—it would be a few weekends yet before smoke from the charcoal grills would waft along the waterfront and the boats and water skiers would buzz round and round, like waterbugs in a birdbath. The lake itself, approximately round and about six miles across, looked immense in the light mizzle of rain. The wind had raised a chop on it; nothing about it suggested depth or lucidity.

The county map showed something called Waccamaw State Park, located at the end of the road and just beside the outlet. It turned out to be an exercise in minimalism, consisting of a fifty-five-gallon oil drum placed at the end of the sandy little road, and an unimproved landing. There was a certain amount of sodden garbage in the drum, and considerably more—wrappers, styrofoam cartons, bottles, cans, and other familiar excrescences of a vigorous and diversified economy—scattered around the landing. We stopped and got out and looked at the Waccamaw River, separated from Lake Waccamaw by a low concrete dam, over which there flowed an inch or two of water. The river spread out into the swamp, but a main channel was distinct. It looked like any little branch or creek near Conway—Crabtree Creek or Sterrit Swamp or Smith Lake: somewhat sluggish, quickly losing itself among the second-growth gum and cypress, in the lower branches of which was caught more undegradable junk—aluminum cans and plastic bottles and vaguely obscene streamers of cellophane.

After we had put the canoe in and before we loaded it, Daddy suggested that it might be well to paddle a little way downstream, to be sure that the river was passable. This was in part a sensible precaution, but I thought it also likely that he wanted to see at least a small stretch of the headwaters of a river upon which he had, over the course of seven decades, spent so many hours. And so we launched out, experiencing again the initial, and mostly illusory, sense of precariousness and hazard that you get when you step into a canoe after being landlocked for the winter. The stream took a couple of sharp turns; we ducked under a big water oak that had blown over, and made a bridge of itself, and under sagging, black-barked grapevines, some of them as thick as a man's thigh, and then came to a second oak, this one lying too low across the stream to duck under. We could see where a boat had been dragged around its upper end, and so got out, walked over a short, miry portage, and looked downstream. The river was clear as far as we could see, which was about two canoe-lengths. "Well, do you want to go ahead with it?" I thought so, although it looked like there would be a lot of portaging, of packing and unpacking the canoe. I had half expected that, and had my gear pretty well consolidated into a single pack and two waterproof plywood boxes. So we returned to the landing, loaded the canoe, and said goodbye. Daddy said he would wait at the landing for half an hour, in case things got bad enough downstream for me to change my mind, and go back down to Freeland and put in there. "Just yell," he said. "From the looks of what we saw, it'll take you all afternoon to get out of earshot."

I reached the portage and carried over the gear and the canoe, nervously timing myself as I did so. Seven minutes—at that rate, I could be spending more time afoot than afloat this afternoon. Within two turns, there was another tree, its crown fallen squarely into the center of the stream. But when I got to it, I found that half a dozen limbs on the underside of the trunk had been sawed off, making just enough room for me to squeeze through. The cuts were made with a chainsaw, and it seemed strange to me that a passage had been made here but not on the upstream tree. Both trees were uprooted, and both lay in the same direction, as though victims of the same storm. But I was glad to profit from this ameliorated windfall, and gladder when it became apparent, within the next hundred yards, that the sawyer had continued on downstream. He was obviously a thrifty man in a small boat. The openings he cut were narrow, and it usually took a certain amount of tugging and prying to get the canoe through, but I never had to portage again.

Except for the saw cuts and, for the first mile or so, an occasional soda bottle or hamburger carton, there was impressively scant evidence of man. The forest—red maple, water and laurel oak, tupelo and black gum—had, like all the Southern woods, been logged more than once, but not recently. Big, dark grapevines were everywhere, crisscrossing the understory of the swamp and hanging low across the stream. I went what I estimated to be three miles without seeing anything that distinguished itself in any way; I might have been going in a circle. I wished that my botany were better—as was the case everywhere in the low country, there were a good many trees, and a great many shrubs, that I did not know, and so had no way of recognizing what might be distinctive about this swamp. There is a real consolation, an antidote to isolation, in being able to name by their right names all the things that surround you, and I could not do that here. There were many young red maples, their pale gray bark splotched and stippled with white, and their winged seeds, brilliantly red, hanging in thick clusters; but apart from them, the swamps of the Waccamaw were, as Bishop had reported them, indeed desolate.

The rain had suspended, but the raw east wind was steady. There were few signs of life. From time to time a pair of wood duck would flush ahead of me; their squealing made a large commotion in this still and silent place. The one telling observation I was capable of making was that the high-water mark, indicated by bands of pollen and the upward limit of a shaggy, brownish-green moss on the trunks of trees, was less than six inches above the stream, although the stream itself, after a dry spring, was not high. This was an indication of the vast size of the swamp I was in—in time of freshet, the water could spread out horizontally for miles, and so rose very little. At present, the floor of the swamp was out of the water, although you would stop short of calling it dry land. It was dank and oozing, and when I had made my one portage, each footprint had filled immediately with water. I had about four more hours of day-light, and began to get a little uneasy about finding a place to camp. In the swamps around Conway, you could count on the occasional hummock, and these would normally be indicated by one or two big loblolly pines, which do not like wet feet, but which seem to colonize any little elevation in a swamp, no mat-ter how remote. So I looked sharp through the treetops, hop-ing to see pines, but there was nothing.

I went around one tight bend after another, pulled under fallen trees, and then went around one more corner and there, silent and sudden, was more sky than I had seen since Lake Waccamaw, and, on creosoted pilings, a one-lane bridge, so low that I would have to duck going under it. The road that crossed it was sand, with a very thin layer of tar on top, and last year's dead weeds sticking up through every crack and break in the tar. After the closeness of the swamp, it had a slightly un-real quality, like a low-budget hallucination, and this quality did not vanish when I pulled in against the bridge and stood up, and looked both ways, up the road and down the road. Judging from the weeds, no traffic had passed this way since at least last summer. The bridge looked new—the creosote was still black and glistening, and the trusses had not begun to sag and settle. It was undoubtedly a logging road of recent con-struction, but it seemed peculiar that there should be no sign of traffic—log roads are built for immediate use, and are used until they are used up. This one was a riddle, and it added to the afternoon's feeling of emptiness and abandonment.

But it would at least be a dry place to camp, if not a very in-viting one. I checked my watch and decided to paddle for an-other hour. If I had found nothing better by then, I could return and sleep on the low causeway, or the bridge itself, without much risk of getting run over. Below the bridge, the river re-entered the obscurity of the swamp, and so did I, but with a certain expectancy now.

Two bends downstream, I saw something gleaming ahead of

me in the swamp, by the edge of the stream. Seen first through a screen of vines and branches, it had an unnatural radiance, like fox-fire or phosphorescence, yet it resolved itself, as I drew around the corner and saw it clearly, into nothing more than a stack of lumber—to be more precise, a stack of ten-foot cypress rails. They looked like the sort of split rails that are used for suburban fencing when a rustic effect is desired, or by the coupon-clipping gentlemen farmers of the Shenandoah Valley. But these rails had been sawed with a chain saw. The sawyer had taken some trouble to make them wedge-shaped and irregular in cross-section, so that, from even a short distance, they looked like they had been split with a maul and wedges. Looking into the swamp behind the railpile, I could see a scattering of sawdust on the dark leaf-mold, and the stump of the cypress, and the trodden ground where the man had worked. The pile of rails would have amounted to something less than half a cord of wood—a good day's work. The neatness of the pile, stacked tightly between two young maples, was impressive, and so was the degree of trust or isolation it implied—in Horry County, anything left unlocked beside the river in the morning would be circulating in the local economy by mid-afternoon. Or at least that would have been the case in my boyhood but—who knows?—perhaps the denizens of the Waccamaw had at last become the self-respecting, godfearing, and trustworthy yeomen of American legend.

But what impressed me most was simply the odd lambency of the new-cut wood, which contrasted strongly with the muted grays of the living trees that surrounded it. The cypress was tawny in color toward the center, shading out to the pallor of sapwood beneath the bark. Its brightness was mirrored and doubled by its reflection in the black water, where, wavering in the slow whorls and eddies of the current, it seemed to issue continuously out of itself, and continuously to disappear, like flame. It was strange to see all this and yet know that it was only a pile of wood, and that, whether left here or taken to fence in somebody's yard or hog-lot, it would soon weather to the neutral tone of ordinary lumber.

Soon after this, the river opened up into a long straight

stretch, twenty-five or thirty yards wide. For the first time, I could see whole trees reflected in the water, and not just over-hanging branches. The swamp was slightly lower here, and the trees stood in shallow water. But off to the east, obscured by the intervening treetops but still unmistakable, I could see the crowns of pines. Closer at hand, almost every cypress that stood out into the river had a trotline suspended from one of its low branches. There were also, at wide intervals and in no discernible pattern, plastic bottles anchored in the stream, serving as buoys of some sort, but I could not guess their purpose, and when I tried to pull one up, it didn't budge.

As I reached the end of the straight stretch, there was a sudden commotion in the swamp to my right, a great thrashing and splashing, and I stood up in the canoe just in time to catch the quickest glimpse of the white tails of two deer. If the canoe had startled them, their own noisy flight seemed to give them the illusion of a pursuer, and their frantic plunging continued for as long as they were in earshot. When I sat back down and looked ahead, there was a big water oak across the stream, and a sluggish flow of water passing into the swamp around the upper end of the oak. My sawyer had not touched this one, which seemed to indicate that I should work my way around the upper end, through the swamp, and back into the river on the other side. But within a few yards, the flow of water played out, and lost itself, and me, in the swamp.

I had gotten out and dragged the canoe some distance, in water not much deeper than the rubber bottoms of my boots, looking back to the right all the while, in every expectation of seeing open water in that direction, when I heard the buzz of an outboard motor ahead of me and to the left. It drew toward me and passed, invisible through the trees, but causing a fractional surging and then a faint subsidence in the water at my feet. Even allowing for an overcast day, an unreliable sense of direction, and the featureless confusion of a swamp, it made no sense at all, and there was nothing to do but drag the canoe back out the way I had come, and reconsider the river.

By the time I got back to open water, the outboard had faded on out of hearing upstream. It might have been the trotliner,

I thought. I paddled upstream a short distance and there, to the east, was what was unmistakably the outlet, exiting from the side, rather than the end, of the long straightaway. It must have been at about this point that I had flushed the deer on the opposite bank, and, attending to them, had missed the outlet. As I turned into it, I heard the whine of the outboard, coming back downstream, and in a few minutes an aluminum johnboat came skimming toward me. It contained a man, at the tiller, and two girls. Because I was close in against the bank, they were nearly on me before they saw me and the man turned quickly to shut the motor down, and the boat settled abruptly into the water, wallowing for a moment in its own wake.

"Well where'd *you* come from?" he asked, and I set about explaining, with considerable embarrassment, how I'd happened to be out of sight when he had come by before. He looked doubtful, but then said for me just to follow him, and I couldn't go wrong. He asked if I'd had any trouble getting down this far, and I told him no, that everything had been smooth sailing, because somebody had cleared out the channel enough. "I done that," he said, "and you might notice I left one right there below the lake. Don't want all them big boys on Lake Waccamaw coming down here. Anybody can paddle, I'm glad to see 'em. I live right round the corner here, not quarter-mile away. You stop by, and stretch your legs a little." I thanked him and told him I would, and he cranked up and, putting ahead of me at barely more than paddling speed, led me down the stream, then up a short dredged-out channel to his house.

"This here is my daughter and her friend," he said with a nod in their direction as I got out. "They been after me to take 'em ridin' in the boat, so we was just out ridin'." The two girls, shy and friendly both, gave me quick, ducking nods and a bright laugh, and skipped up to the house. I tried to take in my host, and his house, and a strange little boat, half full of water, that was tied to a cypress-knee beside us. We shook hands, and he told me his name was Thomas Spivey, and that they all lived here, himself and his Daddy and Mama and his wife and daughter, and that he didn't ask anything more.

He looked to be in his middle thirties, of about average

height, but of much more than average trimness and tautness. Everything about him was cleanly and pleasingly weathered. His face was brown, square, and well creased around the eyes, and his hair evoked Hollywood's idea of what a backwoods-man ought to look like—black as a horse's mane, long, and combed straight back. His hat, the style of a hunter's hat with a narrow brim that turns up in back, was made of cotton, and it had originally been brightly patterned with the trademarks of the most popular American beers—the kind of cheap hat sold mostly to high school boys who hope to be mistaken for hard-drinking college boys at Myrtle Beach or Surfside. But the hat had faded out almost to whiteness, with only the faintest traces of the colorful designs left in it, and hooked in its narrow band were a dozen or so small bass bugs, that were definitely not ornaments—the enamelled paint on them was cracked, and you would say that their tail feathers and rubber legs were much the worse for wear, except that any kind of fishing lure is always much the better for wear, which is the proof of its efficacy. His shirt at the shoulders was as bleached out as the hat; you had to look down a way to see that it was a gray work-shirt, worn to the softness of flannel. He wore blue jeans, all the stiffness and most of the dye gone out of them too, and his boots, despite the muddy landing where we stood, were newly oiled and clean.

He saw me looking at the boat at our feet. It was, with very slight modification, the aboriginal design of the whole region, and indeed of all naval architecture in any part of the globe where good-sized trees grew in convenient proximity to the water. Compared to it, my canoe, and the bark canoes that inspired it, were newfangled high-tech gimcrackery. "That's a old-timey log boat," he said. "I dug it for my Daddy." I had seen specimens of such boats in museums, and they had been fairly common on the river in my father's youth, but this was the first one I had ever seen in a state of nature. It was unmis-takably primitive, with the slighty lumpy, imperfectly symmet-rical quality of something made from modelling clay. I asked Thomas about it, and he told me to come on up to his shop, he was working on one there.

The shop, standing between his house and the river, turned out to be a shed, and a rough shed at that—a pieced together tin roof that looked like it had been salvaged from an old tobacco barn, supported on cypress poles that stood, erratically braced and trussed, directly on the ground. There were no walls and no floor, just the slick, trodden earth and a few planks nailed between the poles to provide a work table and a place for tools. In a pile of tawny chips on the ground lay the new log boat, almost complete. It was ten feet long and not quite thirty inches wide—slightly smaller than the one at the landing. The boat was bluntly double-ended and flat-bottomed, with the bottom rising noticeably as it narrowed toward the bow and stem. Its sides had only a slight flare—most of the rotundity of the log had been cut away. Inside, it was gouged out to a depth of about ten inches. There was no seat, but this boat, like the one at the landing, had a fish box—two partitions, or bulk-heads, of log had been left, about a foot apart, in the middle of the boat, and the space between them had been dug out and two half-inch holes drilled through the bottom. A cypress lid was fitted over the fish box; the hinges which held it, and the nails which held the little cypress decks at each end of the boat, were the only hardware involved.

It began raining again while we were under the shed—"I'm going to put me some hot-top up there this summer, fix her up nice," Thomas said, by way of comment on a good many leaks—and so we stood and talked for a while. He showed me his tools, which were basically a foot-adze and a hand-adze, which he called a howel. Both were wickedly sharp, but otherwise they looked more closely related to agricultural implements—a hoe and trowel, say—than to anything you would expect to find in a craftsman's shop. He took a piece of scrap plank and demonstrated the foot-adze. The handle was long enough for him to stand almost erect, with the board under his forward foot. The blade came into the wood a few inches ahead of his big toe. With a few neat strokes, he dug a groove in the plank, one that would compare favorably with what a weekend carpenter could do with a mallet and chisel—the depth of the cut was uniform, the edges clean and straight, and the bottom nearly smooth. The howel had a short, curved blade, and he worked it with a quick flipping motion of the wrist to shape and smooth the wood until its surface looked almost as though it had been planed.

I asked him about the various things I had seen coming down. The rails were his: "Fence-railing. Sell all of it I can make. But it's hard to find cypress anywhere. Sometime I find a old log about half buried out in the swamp. Might have been there a hundred year, and still sound as a dollar. I hook up a come-along to a tree and snake it out that way. Them bottles up there in the straightaway? They mark a couple old logs sunk in the river. This summer when she gets down real low I'll get 'em out. I make all kind of things out of cypress—benches, swings, fenceposts."

What he most liked to make were the boats, but it took an unusually fine piece of cypress to make one, and that drastically limited his production. The one in the shed was already bespoken by a doctor in Tennessee, who would pay him two thousand dollars for it. "That seems like a lot of money, but what people don't realize is, there ain't much cypress left." He did other things too: trapped some in the winter—raccoons, bobcats, otters, and mink—and caught snakes in the summer. He had sometimes worked as a dragline operator and swamper for Georgia Pacific—"That bridge you come under? I done that, working right by myself. It was so you could drive clear acrost to Hallsboro, but there was that bridge an another one, and some of them boys over on the Hallsboro side got mad at G. P. about something, and burnt the tother one down. So the road don't go nowhere now"—but he preferred making a living on his own, here at the edge of the swamp. "If you do good work, and garntee it, your name'll travel. I been on television three time, showin' how I build my boats and catch snakes. Now I can't keep up with what folks want to buy. I had a man to write me from Fairbank, Alaska, asking about log boats. But I tell you this—I don't care how many folks want it or how fast they want it, when I build a thing I build it right, and if it ain't right I fix it or buy it back. I ain't got nothin' but my name in this world, and folks will tell you about Thomas Spivey, when he does a thing, he does it right."

The rain had stopped again, and he showed me around. He

kept his snakes in a low, reassuringly well-built cage of hardware cloth. At present there was only one—"They ain't out good yet, and this early one that is out is like to be so poor he'll die on you, but this is a right good one for this time of the year"—a moccasin of about thirty inches, tightly coiled under a small watering trough inside the crate. He sold the snakes to universities for research and the production of antivenom. Almost any snake has some value, but moccasins were the silk of the trade, and he pursued them from the Virginia line all the way down to Georgia, living out of his pick-up truck, hunting them at night with a spotlight in the hot weather.

Beyond the cage was a greenhouse, built very much like the workshed, with juniper posts and dirt floors, but enclosed in builder's plastic. Here I met his father, who was transplanting seedling tomatoes from various styrofoam containers—cups, boxes, hamburger cartons—that looked as though they might have drifted down from Waccamaw State Park. Mr. Spivey's hair was nearly white, and he was a good deal stockier than his son. Like his son, he treated me as though I were doing him a favor by interrupting his afternoon—"Ain't a thing I'm doing here can't wait"—and he told me about his greenhouse. He had always liked to farm some, but had reached the point where he couldn't do it any more, and a few years ago Thomas had built him the greenhouse. "Daddy done good out of it," said Thomas. "Made us right proud." He raised mostly vegetables, with a few flowers and houseplants, and sold them locally, to neighbors who were too busy to bother with a vegetable plot, but still liked the taste of fresh tomatoes in the spring, or a good bunch of collards. "It took some money to build," said Mr. Spivey; "they don't give that plastic away. But I told Thomas when we built it: 'We ain't got nothing so we ain't got nothing to lose.' You can't lose nothing if you ain't got nothing, and you can't get nothing without you lose something. We didn't inherit nothing but our name, and a man's name ought to be enough. It's been enough for us."

Much of what he said had this somewhat oracular quality, and he spoke with a deep placidity. Thomas listened respectfully, saying little, but plainly agreeing with his father. "It was me taught Thomas how to dig a log boat, and I never see any-body to do a better job of it. He built that one down there at the landing, and give it to his Mama and me as a gift. I want you to paddle that boat before you leave. His Mama and me go fishing ever day, if the water ain't froze over. It froze right over this winter: temperature of zero degree, plus the wind chill. But otherwise, if it ain't froze or Sunday, we go right out ever day. Cold weather, we take and put a lard stand right on the fishbox, build us a little fire in it." I asked him what they caught, and he called the fish by names I had not heard for a long time—morgans and goggleyes and bonnet brim; jackfish and stumpknockers and redfin pike.

I did not go into the house. Like the other buildings, it was low, did not appear very sturdy, and seemed to incorporate a good deal of recycled material. It looked like something casu-ally improvised out of whatever was handy. It occurred to me that the average middle-class American, seeing such an estab-lishment in passing, would probably express a degree of in-dignation, either against the people who were willing to live there, or the society which reduced them to it. But talking with the Spiveys was a great antidote to this sort of reaction; I felt no tendency to wish other circumstances upon them. They had been here, on this bit of highland in the swamp (which is named, rather *too* appropriately, but there it was, right on the Columbus County roadmap: Crusoe Island) since way back, Mr. Spivey told me. From all appearances, his remark about nobody inheriting anything was strictly accurate: there was nothing in this ancestral homestead that would have been as old as Thomas Spivey himself, and nothing that seemed likely to outlast him. In the cluttered, grassless yard, and the make-shift style of the architecture, there was more than a sugges-tion of life on a frontier, or an extended bivouac. It contrasted strongly with the neatness, enterprise, and skill of the two men themselves.

Northern travellers in the South, throughout the nineteenth century, commented upon the squalor and primitiveness in which most rural whites of the non-slave-owning sort lived; the contrast to the thrifty and tidy farmsteads of New England or Pennsylvania was irresistible. Houses of unchinked logs, mud and stick chimneys, unglazed windows, and dirt floors seem to have been common, and even more prosperous dwellings struck outsiders as lacking rudimentary amenities. Buildings, and indeed the material culture in general, made no statements, affirmed no traditions. The Spivey house belonged to a regional idiom of architecture that was neither traditional nor contemporary in aspiration. It was purely extemporary, improvised to provide shelter, and not a great deal more, against a generally mild climate. It was not pleasant to imagine an August night in one of its small rooms, with the air thick with mosquitoes from the swamp and dank with mold and mildew. But it seemed clear that Thomas Spivey preferred this way of life—a man who could operate a dragline and build bridges as solid and neat as the one upstream could command a respectable salary, and live in an FHA-approved house: for that matter, he could build it himself.

I was torn between wanting to stay and talk and needing to get on downriver before the rain resumed or darkness fell. We said goodbye to Mr. Spivey and walked back toward the shed. As we passed Thomas's truck, there was a strange grunting and growling from beneath it, and then a dog emerged: a fyce bitch, obviously old and fat as a woodtick. She ambled gravely up to Thomas to get patted. He scratched her ear, and pointed to her back, which was rumpled and greasy: "She 'bout lives under that truck; likes to hump her back against the pan and get oil all over it. Helps keep off the fleas. She's a smart dog. Fourteen year old and still the best squirrel dog you'd ever want. She'll eat anything, though—only dog I ever see that'll eat tomatoes, right off the vine." She rolled over on her back, and Thomas gave her an affectionate pat on the stomach. "You ain't exactly perishing to death, is you?" he said to her, and we walked on. The little dog lay on her back, her forepaws limply aloft, peering after us, and seemed to give some thought to getting up and following us, but decided against it, sighed, and settled down to a nap.

When we stepped back into the shed to get a paddle, Thomas

showed me more of his handiwork, stashed under a tarp and waiting to be sold. It was all strongly and simply made—a crib that, with the addition of a lid, could have doubled as a rabbit hutch; some shallow wooden bowls, of the sort that are used for kneading bread; a milking stool. These things were truly rustic, and belonged here, but they were not destined to stay here. They would be sold in shops along the highway between Wilmington and Myrtle Beach, along with suntan lotion, beach towels, firecrackers, darkglasses, and T-shirts that announced their wearers' willingness to cross state lines for immoral purposes. Some of the work was done on commission. There was a section from the bole of a hollow cypress, three feet long and standing on one end, with a little raised roof, below which was a crude crank, on the other end. "That's a wishing well. Lady in Charlotte asked me to make one for her last year. Now her sister's got to have one." There was no trace of irony or amusement in his voice. Next to the well were two benches, which looked like the next thing the lady in Charlotte might buy, to get back ahead of her sister. They were not the kind of product you would associate with any self-respecting craftsman, and could be forgiven only if you saw them as a gleeful exploitation of our enormous, uninformed nostalgia. But Thomas Spivey did not see them so.

Mr. Spivey's log boat was too heavy—about four hundred pounds, Thomas reckoned—to pull up and tip over, so we bailed it with a scoop. I expected it to be tippy—I had had some experience with little one-man fishing boats, made from planks, plywood, or cypress strips, that were of its size and general design. But this one hardly seemed to notice when I stepped in and sat cross-legged on the floor. The bows were raised enough so that the boat did not plough through the water; once under way, it moved along easily, and held a steady course. I paddled up the dragline cut to the river, turned, and came back. Thomas then took the boat, to show me some things about it. One was its stability; he could stand comfortably on the back deck of the little boat, or paddle it from the fishbox—its weight kept the center of gravity low. He had an easy, loose-jointed way of being in a boat, his legs folded under him, the paddle, no longer than a pizza spatula and with a considerably narrower blade, managed with one hand.

It was time to go sure enough, although I felt reluctant. I asked him if he would sell me one of the wooden kneading bowls, and he consented. We dickered for a while over the price—I wanted to pay him the retail price, which was low enough, but he insisted on wholesale. The bowl was a pretty thing, the howel marks still visible in the pale, almost grainless wood. "That's tupelo," he said. "Only thing to make a bowl out of. My uncle, he's took to makin' 'em now, and he'll just make 'em out of anything; juniper or sweetgum or maple. Me and him's had some discussions about that; we don't get on so good. Your tupelo won't never warp or check on you; them others will." I thanked him for everything and shook his hand and got back into the canoe. As I stashed my new possession into the pack, he said for me just to keep it dry till I got home, and then to rub some cooking oil into it. "Do that, and every couple years rub a little more oil in, and she won't never give you no trouble. I garntee it to last. You bring it back if it don't."

As I resumed my trip downriver, I thought about the log boat, and its merits in a place like this. Thomas Spivey had had nothing good to say about canoes. He considered them noisy, hard to manage in a wind, and, as he put it, *slippery*—"You stand up in one and it's gone right out from under you." For his purposes, the log boat *was* better. Deep in the water, it moved as quietly as an alligator. When you are fishing along the river bank, moving with the current and casting in toward the bank, stealth is everything and speed is nothing. A wood canvas canoe, paddled slowly, is one of the quietest things I know, but there is a slight slapping noise associated with its progress and, when moving under minimum power, it is susceptible to any gust of wind, which forces you to do a certain amount of bracing and prying with the paddle. The log boat kept you low; you nudged it along with only the slightest twist and flex of the wrist. Paddling it, Thomas had seemed to merge with the slow deliberations of the river, and the muted backdrop of the swamp. It belonged here, where its design was as indigenous and functional as that of the cypress tree itself. I wondered about the doctor in Tennessee, soon to be the owner of the boat back in Thomas's shed, and I hoped that he lived over in the western part of the state, and had some bayou or swamp for it, and would know how to use it. But I suspected that the odds were against it; there were not many people of means who still did the kind of unsophisticated, yet highly skilled, fishing and hunting for which this boat was intended.

I passed several hummocks high and dry enough for camping, and each was prominently posted by Georgia Pacific. Despite Thomas's assurance, I felt a little skittish about pitching my tent directly under a sign that forbade my doing so, and so kept paddling and hoping for less forbidden earth. I was soon regretting it: the hummocks came further and further apart, and the darkness settled rapidly—once the sun has gone below the horizon, light fails quickly in a swamp. There was still light in the sky, but almost none at ground level, when I heard a car door slam, an engine start, and had a glimpse of headlights as the car pulled away. From the Columbus County map, I knew that this had to be Old Dock, where a county road crossed the Waccamaw. I found a narrow strip of dry woodland between the road and the river, and pulled ashore there, pitched my tent, and cooked and ate my supper in the last gloom.

Susan Cerulean

Searching for Swallow-Tails

(FLORIDA)

It's an emphatic ninety-eight degrees on this first day of June, when I meet up with Dr. Ken Meyer and his field crew in southwest Florida's Big Cypress National Preserve. That's not counting what the crew's tree climber, Megan Parker, terms the "phenomenal humidity" spun our way by the year's first hurricane shaping up over Cuba. This is my fifth trip to the preserve to observe Meyer's groundbreaking field studies of the rare swallow-tailed kite, a spectacular, fork-tailed black and white raptor. Florida is the breeding season stronghold of the northern subspecies of this bird, now thought to merit formal designation as an endangered species. Although it once nested in as many as twenty-one states, at present it occurs only in Florida and small portions of five other southeastern states. At the moment, the kites have hatched what young they can this season, and the chicks are close to leaving the nests. Meyer and his crew are working every hour of long summer daylight to study and mark the young birds.

The crew, consisting of Meyer, Parker, and two technicians, Deb Duvall and John Arnett, began work before sunrise this morning, and have already outfitted two kite chicks with radio transmitters when I meet them at noon. The crew is schlepping climbing gear, toolbox, water, and a heavy plastic duffel fifteen minutes down a winding trail to a slash pine topped by the third kite nest on the day's agenda. Two, six, ten, then sixteen agitated adult swallow-tailed kites circle the tree, calling urgently, confirming that we are in the right place. The nest is about sixty-five feet high, wedged among the topmost branches of a loblolly pine tree.

"This is a damn nice tree—something that can actually support my weight," jokes Parker, just arrived from Idaho to assist Meyer with the tree climbing. "It's a big tree, compared to the garbage Ken's been showing me!"

Safety for the kite chicks, the nest trees (no injurious climbing spurs are used), and the climber is Meyer's top priority. The logistics are daunting. Parker doesn't pull on her climbing harness just yet. Despite the presence of the anxious adult kites, Meyer must confirm that the young bird is still in the nest before he sends the lanky climber up to retrieve it. We can't spot the chick with our binoculars. Meyer comments that the nest looks a little rough around the edges. Parker and Duvall scout the underbrush, turning up feathers, fragments of a wasp nest (a major food item brought to the young birds by their parents from the surrounding forest), a plundered wild turkey nest and hen's feathers, and fresh whitewash on the ground.

Within sixty to ninety seconds of our arrival, they have also located the dead chick, tangled in the underbrush at the base of the nest tree. Ants crowd the bird's eyeballs and swarm the length of its frail wing bones.

"This bird is only four weeks old," Meyer tells me, gently fingering the small corpse. Its white, almost translucent feet and beak hang limp and bleached with death. "It would not have left the nest on its own for at least another week."

Meyer kicks up downed nest material around the base of the tree. It's not much to see: pencil-thin pine branchlets, pale lichens and a greenish curly relative of Spanish moss. High wind is the number one killer of nestling kites, Meyer tells me, and from the location of the twigs and the condition of the bird, Meyer is almost positive that last night's violent storm knocked this chick from its nest. He can even deduce the direction of the deadly wind.

"I'm going to sit over here and get depressed," sighs Meyer. "I really thought we'd get this nest." I join him in the scanty shade of a slash pine. We watch wood storks going in and out of a nearby cypress dome. Adult kites plane and cry overhead. I can almost believe that they are trying to call the young one back into life.

After a quick water break, we resume the struggle through the grapevine and palmetto, and scour the surrounding trees, hoping to spot a surviving sibling.

"Just tell us, birds, just tell us," I chant to the sky. "Have you got another baby out there somewhere? Don't make us work so hard."

"They are telling us," points out Meyer. "We just don't know how to listen well enough."

Field technician John Arnett isn't waiting for the birds to talk. When he found this nest three weeks ago, he suspected there was another nearby. Now he emerges through the pines with a rare grin on his face: "There's another nest over here! And nobody dead under it!"

But a quick visual survey indicates that, unfortunately, neither is anyone remaining in the nest. We pack up gear and water bottles and head for the trucks. It's really, really hot. When I unlock my car, the metal handle raises a blister on my skin. Visible waves of superheated air pour from the dark blue interior. Everyone agrees to drive north to Sunniland to stock up on ice and drinks and snacks.

Inside the mini-market, Parker eyes the meat sweating inside a glass-covered grill.

"That hot dog's probably been circling for weeks, but it looks good to me," says Megan. "Just shows you how low I'll go after a day in the field."

We make our purchases and stand under the shade of the gas station drinking icy tea and cokes. Nobody talks much. We dig our fists into a communal bag of spicy, lime-flavored tostitos.

"I love this job," muses Deb Duvall. She pauses dreamy-eyed, takes another pull on her soda. "Or maybe it's the caffeine and chips."

A thunderstorm is circling in from the south and east. The temperature has eased into the low nineties. For most people, the work day is ending. But for the swallow-tailed kite crew, there remains a 5 P.M. appointment with a nest tree across Highway 29 and south a bit, at the twenty-six-thousand-acre Florida Panther Refuge. The crew unloads the climbing gear, rope, five ten-foot sections of aluminum ladder, cameras, and banding equipment, and lashes it snug against the roll bar of the refuge's high-tired swamp buggy. At first the buggy seems like overkill; we think the truck would have done fine. But the bumpy trail, strewn with sharp lime rock, gives way to long, deep, serious puddles. The giant tires spew mud ten feet to the right and the left of the vehicle, and we're glad to ride high.

"The fact that things are so quiet makes me doubt the young are still in the nest," opines Ken when the refuge personnel show us their nest. "There should be begging, there should be feeding. I'm inclined to think it failed rather than fledged—no adults close by. If it had fledged it'd most likely still be in the nest or perching somewhere close by."

"One minute more," Debbie asks. "I think I see something light up there."

Parker adds: "If I saw something light, it was fuzzy." That, of course, would mean the head of a chick. The two women crouch on their haunches, discussing sunscreen and binoculars, waiting for telltale movement in the nest.

But there's nothing up there, at least not showing.

We see a fledged bird with a short tail on the way out, flapping over the trees. Its flight is labored. Probably seven weeks old, Ken estimates. First one he's seen out of the nest this year.

"The birds are growing as we speak, at the other nests we've got marked," frets Meyer quietly, thinking about the next day's agenda. Almost everything we know about swallow-tailed kites is based on the slender period of time, during breeding season, that they spend in North America. To learn more, Meyer has designed a long-term study based on radio-tagging and monitoring sixty-five young birds. The best age for radio-tagging young swallow-tails is around thirty-five days. At this age, about four to six days before they can fly, the birds are large enough to be properly fitted with transmitters but too young to jump from the nest. It's a hard-edged window of opportunity that has this crew scrambling all over the southern peninsula of Florida.

"Synchronized breeding didn't evolve for this purpose," Meyer muses, with a wry laugh. "But it provides the animals with effective predator protection—from us! It's working well for them."

We drive out through a grassy prairie, framed in drifts of soft dwarf cypress, as pretty as any meadow I've ever seen. Anywhere. Clear pink meadow beauties, jewel-like sundews, and white bog buttons punctuate the marsh grasses. Rosy gold light pours from the flat-bottomed thunderhead rising Himalaya high over Naples, thirty miles to the west. The sky sprawls round as a bowl. Six or eight different cloudscapes dominate as many points of the compass. We stop the car so we can turn full circle in one place, standing on the ground. The energy of the warm eighty-seven degree gulf water is building these thunderheads, these Florida mountains, as high as the moon. The wind is steady, and for the first time today, holds a hint of cool.

The next morning, the crew converges in Ochopee at 6 A.M. and prepares to drive two-and-a-half hours north to the KICCO Wildlife Management Area near Avon Park.

In the truck, Meyer explains the urgencies and the logistical nightmare of working with his chosen bird.

"We know so little about swallow-tailed kites. We can't even tell male from female without drawing blood or performing surgery. I don't know where the birds go after they fledge, or anything about what happens to them on their wintering grounds in South America. But at the rate natural communities are being destroyed here and in the rain forests, I feel some anxiety about what it will take to keep the birds around.

"To get the information, the data I need, I've got to find sixty nests and radio-tag thirty young birds during this season and the next two. Probably because of the high water all over south Florida, we've had a heck of time finding nests this year. Over the past six years, the average amount of time just to find a single nest was fifteen hours, with a standard deviation of three — that's pretty consistent from year to year. But this year, the average time to simply find one nest was over thirty hours.

"Kites are great birds, but you have to work so hard for the tiniest bits of data. I just have to resign myself to small sample sizes and obscure statistical tests."

At the wildlife management area, we unlock the wire gate and drive a mile beneath enormous live oaks to a stand of tall pines where John Arnett has located an active nest. We attempt to chigger-proof our clothing with spray-on repellent, then beat down a rough path toward the pine through chest-high underbrush.

This time, the chick is on the nest. Parker is pleased with the tree's ample sturdiness ("God forbid something should have that diameter!" she crows).

So far, so good. The task now is to get a climbing rope for Parker over a major limb in roughly the middle third of the crown of the tree. Meyer knots a lead egg sinker to heavy monofilament line loaded on a Mitchell spinning reel. He slips the dull gray sinker into the leather basket of a wrist rocket slingshot, which he supports on his left forearm.

Over and over, Meyer zings the sinker skyward. Again and again, it falls short or tangles in a thick bit of foliage. The technicians take a turn when Meyer's wrist gets sore.

"This isn't going to work," Meyer says, fifty minutes and innumerable shots later. "We're wasting a lot of energy going horizontally. Maybe we should bag it." This is what he says, but what he does is figure out another way to get a rope up the towering pine. He switches to the next weapon in his arsenal, the dummy launcher, a sort of dull gun made by marine supply companies to shoot line between boats. The launcher, powered by a twenty-two shell, is also used to train retriever dogs, some-one tells me. The launcher has plenty of power, but it is extremely noisy and its aim is crude.

Boom! I cover my ears too late.

Boom! Over and over, the big red dummy hangs up tight as a pine cone on improbable branches, never where it seems to be aimed, and sometimes alarmingly close to the nest.

Boom!

"Somebody else want to do this?" offers technician Arnett. "I'm almost permanently deaf."

Deb returns to the truck for earplugs and more line, and Meyer takes over the firing.

"Let's see how long we can make this take," says Meyer, only half-joking, taking stock of the lowering sky. Three hours have passed since we began tackling this tree. Meyer polls his crew, and they deliberate, weighing the time they can spend on this nest against the likelihood of the approaching storm. They allot themselves three more shots with the crude launcher.

"Actually, I feel like I'm getting a little more consistent," says Meyer, considering the placement of his twelfth shot. "What do you think about that one?" He addresses his question to Parker. It is her weight, after all, that the branch must bear.

Parker trains her Bausch and Lomb binoculars on the tree, trying to pick out the trajectory of the thin glistening line.

"Oh, I see it, I see it!" she exclaims. "My feeling is . . ."

Meyer laughs: "Whenever she starts with 'my feeling,' it's not going to be any good."

Parker reassures him: "The limb that it's over is fine if we can just get it close to the trunk."

Meyer does, and the crew shifts into action. With heavy silver duct tape, they fasten the end of the monofilament to white clothesline, then tie on the blue climbing rope. The adult birds have resumed their vigil, calling, circling, full of concern. Parker guesses that for them, there's something very predatorlike about the colorful ropes snaking up the tree.

Thunder grumbles closer.

Meyer wraps the climbing rope three times around the thick-based pine and secures it tight with a bowline and two clove hitches. It's a beautiful rope, azure crisscrossed with green fibers and a dash of hot pink.

"Are we worried about the thunder?" someone murmurs. Again, the crew defers to the climber.

"I'm happy to go but I don't know what we're expecting here in terms of weather. I'm not afraid of it, but I want to use some judgement," considers Parker, studying the movement of the wind in the tops of the pine trees. "I kind of want to go 'cause we've rigged it."

The storm decides otherwise. Gusting wind shakes free a torrent of rain and nails it down with a convincing bolt of lightning. The crew sprints back to the oaks and hunkers under a plastic blue tarp spread over the bed of the truck. We eat, make weather predictions, tell stories, wait. I turn to Megan Parker, holding a corner of the tarp over her lightly built, six-foot frame. How did she come to be a climber of raptor nests?

"Some years back I got hired by the Peregrine Fund to study laughing falcons and bat falcons in Guatemala. I knew I was going to be climbing trees, so I had a friend rig a twenty-foot climbing rope in a tree in my yard. It seemed so high and so complicated. All those knots. Once I got there, I had to climb these huge trees, maybe ninety feet tall, every day. There was no one around to spot or coach. Just me and a Guatemalan, before light, pantomiming. When you are so naive, one thing isn't worse than another. But it was a real macho thing, I was the only woman. I wasn't about to complain. There was a lot of up and down, making all the mistakes you can think of, without an audience. They would nail sticks together to make a ladder 100 feet up. I would never do that again without protection.

"After a while it became the most comforting thing in the world to be up there five or six hours a day. The trees twist through every dimension, with these big comfortable branches. Once I got up there, it seemed sort of womblike. And every tree had its own definite personality. You wouldn't believe what I saw from up there: troops of monkeys, incredible hummingbirds, neat insects."

Parker completed her thesis on laughing falcons in Guatemala, and now lives in Idaho, studying the vocalizations of a wolf pack for the nonprofit Wolf Education and Research Center near Stanley, Idaho. She lives in a nylon canvas yurt ("the size of a closet") near the spectacular Sawtooth Wilderness. Two dogs and Polarfleece sheets keep her warm through the minus-forty-degree winter nights. It's the stuff of woods-woman fantasies. I'm intrigued by this lovely, unpretentious woman wearing faded blue work pants, a worn t-shirt inscribed *Cinco de Lobos,* thick sunbleached braid. Why does she come back to Florida at all?

"This is the only chance I get to climb anymore," she explains. "And I love the birds. I sure don't come back for the Wal-Marts. The closest Wal-Mart to Stanley is two and a half hours away, in Boise!"

Finally, the rain lets up. Parker pulls her purple climbing harness over her hips, adjusts the brightly colored mechanical ascenders fitted and tied to her height and stride. Suddenly she is hanging free, five feet off the ground and about that same distance from the trunk of the eighty-foot tree. She pauses to adjust a knot. Smoothly she kicks up the rope, so fluid and effortless that we are hardly aware of the technical competence, the daring, the balance, the physical strength all bound up in this single upward movement. For the next five minutes, the only sound I am aware of is her breathing, heavy and audible. Bits of bark dislodge from the tree and drift over us. The attending adult kites are highly agitated by Parker's approach. She slings a piece of red webbing over the branch supporting the climbing rope, pulls her body up, ties on to the main trunk with a safety rope.

"This makes me so nervous," breathes Meyer, almost a prayer. Parker ties and reties protection anchors above her body, moving steadily toward the dinner plate–sized nest. None of us take our eyes off the climber, as if we might will her safe through our attention.

I remember what she told me at lunch: "Climbing has got more to do with rhythm than strength. It's just basically climbing a ladder. That's all there is, but you can fight it, and then it takes a tremendous amount of strength. What I do is just get totally focused and quiet and just blast up there. The hardest thing is balancing up there while you're waiting for the bird to come back up."

"Here comes the wind," say Duvall and Meyer simultaneously. We feel the prefacing breeze of storm on our skin.

And then we see big wings, kite wings, held unnaturally stiff against the gray sky. Parker's got the half-grown chick by the feet. Carefully she slides it into an orange cloth sack.

Meyer lets out a long breath and all the pent-up praise and encouragement he's been holding inside: "You did a great job, Megan. I thought you had many feet to climb yet. You're the best, that was just great."

Parker sends the bag quickly down the rope. "I'd sure appreciate as much speed as possible," she calls. "I'm about to get a haircut from one of these parents." We can see and hear the fluttering commotion of the adults, about eight feet above her head.

Meanwhile, the technicians have arranged a simple work space on a green waterproof ground cloth under the tree. Meyer is teaching his technicians as he works.

"Okay, the way I get him out of the bag is I feel for the head. I'm going to try to reach in and get one of his shoulders. You peel the bag back, contain the feet. Don't want to pull the toes too hard, you can damage them."

The ungainly chick, with its brown speckled head and chest, has none of the sleek elegance of the adult swallow-tailed kite. It clutches pine branchlets from its nest in its talons. I think about the twiggy nests in these tallest of trees, how tightly these birds must cling to such sparse support from the moment they hatch.

Duvall slips a soft, green, handstitched hood over the bird's head to calm it. Then the bird is weighed: 505 grams, the second heaviest so far, says Meyer. He measures the feet and bill, then bends a silver identification band around the bird's leg.

Now the bird is cradled on its back in Duvall's hands.

"Fast heartbeat, Deb?" asks Meyer. He knows she loves this intimacy with the kites.

She nods yes. "Mine, too."

The chick barely moves in her hands. But its thin, piteous cries through the hood seem to stimulate an intensified response from the attending adults far above.

Meyer and Arnett fit the bird with a backpack harness holding a radio transmitter. The bird struggles as the soft Teflon ribbon harness slips over each wing. Nothing in its young life has prepared it for this experience. Meyer centers a square of soft material on the bird's sternum. This is the deliberately weak link in the harness. Here, cotton attachment threads will rot and weaken through wear and exposure during the twenty-seven-month life span of the tiny transmitter on the bird's back, eventually allowing it to fall free.

"I haven't checked the right cable wrap, but the left is great," Ken reports. He's using pliers to snug the harness, then super-glues the transmitter in place. "I want to leave a certain amount of play because the bird is still growing; even if it were full grown, you'd leave a little bit of slack."

"I'm not having much fun up here," Parker reminds us from the tossing treetop.

"We're almost done, Meg," Meyer reassures. He checks his watch, frowns.

"Twenty minutes. I promised her fifteen." For the moment, the adults have swung far away into the stormy sky. The absence of their cries is a relief.

Now, the last step, the most intrusive. A kite's sex organs are internal, so it's impossible to tell a male from a female until it mates. This year, a colleague of Meyer's in Miami has offered to sex the birds based on blood samples obtained in the field.

"Put its head at my two o'clock," Meyer instructs Duvall. She extends the wing, and holds it in place so Meyer can withdraw a tiny sample of its blood. I am asked to hold the wing tip. Three tiny bird mites scurry up my arm. There is no sound from the chick, although its chest heaves as the needle enters a prominent vein. Drops of sweat roll off Ken's forehead and mingle with bits of white feather shaft on the green plastic dropcloth. Then it is over. Arnett labels the tiny tube: "STK 10."

Meyer looks up at the sky. Lightning traces closer. "We're done, Megan, we're just waiting for the puncture to heal, and we'll have him back up."

"Okay, I'm putting him in the bag. If you'll just check its wing to make sure its not bleeding when you get it . . ."

"Sure," says Parker. She hauls the bright cotton bag against the gray sky, and then out of our sight. A cool rain begins as Parker rappels down the brilliant rope. I can see that she's got the rope wrapped around her leg as a break, controlling the speed of her swift descent with leather glove on her right hand. Faces upturned, we watch her. Rain falls into our eyes, rain from far higher than the nest and the young bird, from higher even than the adult kites hanging noiseless, now, in the sky.

E. O. Wilson

Paradise Beach

(FLORIDA)

What happened, what we *think* happened in distant memory, is built around a small collection of dominating images. In one of my own from the age of seven, I stand in the shallows off Paradise Beach, staring down at a huge jellyfish in water so still and clear that its every detail is revealed as though it were trapped in glass. The creature is astonishing. It existed outside my previous imagination. I study it from every angle I can manage from above the water's surface. Its opalescent pink bell is divided by thin red lines that radiate from center to circular edge. A wall of tentacles falls from the rim to surround and partially veil a feeding tube and other organs, which fold in and out like the fabric of a drawn curtain. I can see only a little way into this lower tissue mass. I want to know more but am afraid to wade in deeper and look more closely into the heart of the creature.

The jellyfish, I know now, was a sea nettle, formal scientific name *Chrysaora quinquecirrha*, a scyphozoan, a medusa, a member of the pelagic fauna that drifted in from the Gulf of Mexico and paused in the place I found it. I had no idea then of these names from the lexicon of zoology. The only word I had heard was *jellyfish*. But what a spectacle my animal was, and how inadequate, how demeaning, the bastard word used to label it. I should have been able to whisper its true name: *scyph-o-zo-an!* Think of it! I have found a scyphozoan. The name would have been a more fitting monument to this discovery.

The creature hung there motionless for hours. As evening approached and the time came for me to leave, its tangled undermass appeared to stretch deeper into the darkening water. Was this, I wondered, an animal or a collection of animals? Today I can say that it was a single animal. And that another outwardly similar animal found in the same waters, the Portuguese man-of-war, is a colony of animals so tightly joined as to form one smoothly functioning superorganism. Such are the general facts I recite easily now, but this sea nettle was special. It came into my world abruptly, from I knew not where, radiating what I cannot put into words except—*alien purpose and dark happenings in the kingdom of deep water.* The scyphozoan still embodies, when I summon its image, all the mystery and tensed malignity of the sea.

The next morning the sea nettle was gone. I never saw another during that summer of 1936. The place, Paradise Beach, which I have revisited in recent years, is a small settlement on the east shore of Florida's Perdido bay, not far from Pensacola and in sight of Alabama across the river.

There was trouble at home in this season of fantasy. My parents were ending their marriage that year. Existence was difficult for them, but not for me, their only child, at least not yet. I had been placed in the care of a family that boarded one or two boys during the months of the summer vacation. Paradise Beach was paradise truly named for a little boy. Each morning after breakfast I left the small shorefront house to wander alone in search of treasures along the strand. I waded in and out of the dependably warm surf and scrounged for anything I could find in the drift. Sometimes I just sat on a rise to scan the open water. Back in time for lunch, out again, back for dinner, out once again, and, finally, off to bed to relive my continuing adventure briefly before falling asleep.

I have no remembrance of the names of the family I stayed

with, what they looked like, their ages, or even how many there were. Most likely they were a married couple and, I am willing to suppose, caring and warmhearted people. They have passed out of my memory, and I have no need to learn their identity. It was the animals of that place that cast a lasting spell. I was seven years old, and every species, large and small, was a wonder to be examined, thought about, and, if possible, captured and examined again.

There were needlefish, foot-long green torpedoes with slender beaks, cruising the water just beneath the surface. Nervous in temperament, they kept you in sight and never let you come close enough to reach out a hand and catch them. I wondered where they went at night, but never found out. Blue crabs with skin-piercing claws scuttled close to shore at dusk. Easily caught in long-handled nets, they were boiled and cracked open and eaten straight or added to gumbo, the spicy seafood stew of the Gulf coast. Sea trout and other fish worked deeper water out to the nearby eelgrass flats and perhaps beyond; if you had a boat you could cast for them with bait and spinners. Stingrays, carrying threatening lances of bone flat along their muscular tails, buried themselves in the bottom sand of hip-deep water in the daytime and moved close to the surf as darkness fell.

One late afternoon a young man walked past me along the beach dangling a revolver in his hand, and I fell in behind him for a while. He said he was hunting stingrays. Many young men, my father among them, often took guns on such haphazard excursions into the countryside, mostly .22 pistols and rifles but also heavier handguns and shotguns, recreationally shooting any living thing they fancied except domestic animals and people. I thought of the stingray hunter as a kind of colleague as I trailed along, a fellow adventurer, and hoped he would find some exciting kind of animal I had not seen, maybe something big. When he had gone around a bend of the littoral and out of sight I heard the gun pop twice in quick succession. Could a bullet from a light handgun penetrate water deep enough to hit a stingray? I think so but never tried it. And I never saw the young marksman again to ask him.

How I longed to discover animals each larger than the last, until finally I caught a glimpse of some true giant! I knew there were large animals out there in deep water. Occasionally a school of bottlenose porpoises passed offshore less than a stone's throw from where I stood. In pairs, trios, and quartets they cut the surface with their backs and dorsal fins, arced down and out of sight, and broke the water again ten or twenty yards farther on. Their repetitions were so rhythmic that I could pick the spot where they would appear next. On calm days I sometimes scanned the glassy surface of Perdido Bay for hours at a time in the hope of spotting something huge and monstrous as it rose to the surface. I wanted at least to see a shark, to watch the fabled dorsal fin thrust proud out of the water, knowing it would look a lot like a porpoise at a distance but would surface and sound at irregular intervals. I also hoped for more than sharks, what exactly I could not say: something to enchant the rest of my life.

Almost all that came in sight were clearly porpoises, but I was not completely disappointed. Before I tell you about the one exception, let me say something about the psychology of monster hunting. Giants exist as a state of the mind. They are defined not as an absolute measurement but as a proportionality. I estimate that when I was seven years old I saw animals at about twice the size I see them now. The bell of a sea nettle averages ten inches across, I know that now; but the one I found seemed two feet across—a grown man's two feet. So giants can be real, even if adults don't choose to classify them as such. I was destined to meet such a creature at last. But it would not appear as a swirl on the surface of the open water.

It came close in at dusk, suddenly, as I sat on the dock leading away from shore to the family boathouse raised on pilings in shallow water. In the failing light I could barely see to the bottom, but I stayed perched on the dock anyway, looking for any creature large or small that might be moving. Without warning a gigantic ray, many times larger than the stingrays of common experience, glided silently out of the darkness, beneath my dangling feet, and away into the depths on the other side. It was gone in seconds, a circular shadow, seeming to blanket the whole bottom. I was thunderstruck. And immediately seized with a need to see this behemoth again, to capture it if I could, and to examine it close up. Perhaps, I thought, it lived nearby and cruised around the dock every night.

Late the next afternoon I anchored a line on the dock, skewered a live pinfish on the biggest hook I could find in the house, and let the bait sit in six feet of water overnight. The following morning I rushed out and pulled in the line. The bait was gone; the hook was bare. I repeated the procedure for a week without result, always losing the pinfish. I might have had better luck in snagging a ray if I had used shrimp or crab for bait, but no one gave me this beginner's advice. One morning I pulled in a Gulf toadfish, an omnivorous bottom-dweller with a huge mouth, bulging eyes, and slimy skin. Locals consider the species a trash fish and one of the ugliest of all sea creatures. I thought it was wonderful. I kept my toadfish in a bottle for a day, then let it go. After a while I stopped putting the line out for the great ray. I never again saw it pass beneath the dock.

Why do I tell you this little boy's story of medusas, rays, and sea monsters, nearly sixty years after the fact? Because it illustrates, I think, how a naturalist is created. A child comes to the edge of deep water with a mind prepared for wonder. He is like a primitive adult of long ago, an acquisitive early *Homo* arriving at the shore of Lake Malawi, say, or the Mozambique Channel. The experience must have been repeated countless times over thousands of generations, and it was richly rewarded. The sea, the lakes, and the broad rivers served as sources of food and barriers against enemies. No petty boundaries could split their flat expanse. They could not be burned or eroded into sterile gullies. They were impervious, it seemed, to change of any kind. The waterland was always there, timeless, invulnerable, mostly beyond reach, and inexhaustible. The child is ready to grasp this archetype, to explore and learn, but he has few words to describe his guiding emotions. Instead he is given a compelling image that will serve in later life as a talisman, transmitting a powerful energy that directs the growth of experience and knowledge. He will add complicated details and context from his culture as he grows older. But the core image stays intact. When an adult he will find it curious, if he is at all reflective, that he has the urge to travel all day to fish or to watch sunsets on the ocean horizon.

Hands-on experience at the critical time, not systematic knowledge, is what counts in the making of a naturalist. Better to be an untutored savage for a while, not to know the names or anatomical detail. Better to spend long stretches of time just searching and dreaming. Rachel Carson, who understood this principle well, used different words to the same effect in *The Sense of Wonder* in 1965: "If facts are the seeds that later produce knowledge and wisdom, then the emotions and the impressions of the senses are the fertile soil in which the seeds must grow. The years of childhood are the time to prepare the soil." She wisely took children to the edge of the sea.

The summer at Paradise Beach was for me not an educational exercise planned by adults, but an accident in a haphazard life. I was parked there in what my parents trusted would be a safe and carefree environment. During that brief time, however, a second accident occurred that determined what kind of naturalist I would eventually become. I was fishing on the dock with minnow hooks and rod, jerking pinfish out of the water as soon as they struck the bait. The species, *Lagodon rhomboides*, is small, perchlike, and voracious. It carries ten needlelike spines that stick straight up in the membrane of the dorsal fin when it is threatened. I carelessly yanked too hard when one of the fish pulled on my line. It flew out of the water and into my face. One of its spines pierced the pupil of my right eye.

The pain was excruciating, and I suffered for hours. But being anxious to stay outdoors, I didn't complain very much. I continued fishing. Later, the host family, if they understood the problem at all (I can't remember), did not take me in for medical treatment. The next day the pain had subsided into mild discomfort, and then it disappeared. Several months later, after I had returned home to Pensacola, the pupil of the eye began to cloud over with a traumatic cataract. As soon as my parents noticed the change, they took me to a doctor, who shortly afterward admitted me to the old Pensacola Hospital to have the lens removed. The surgery was a terrifying nineteenth-century ordeal. Someone held me down while the anesthesiologist, a woman named Pearl Murphy, placed a gauze nose cone over my nose and mouth and dripped ether into it. Her fee for this standard service, I learned many years later, was five dollars. As I lost consciousness I dreamed I was all alone in a large auditorium. I was tied to a chair, unable to move, and screaming. Possibly I was screaming in reality before I went under. In any case the experience was almost as bad as the cataract. For years afterward I became nauseous at the smell of ether. Today I suffer from just one phobia: being trapped in a closed space with my arms immobilized and my face covered with an obstruction. The aversion is not an ordinary claustrophobia. I can enter closets and elevators and crawl beneath houses and automobiles with aplomb. In my teens and twenties I explored caves and underwater recesses around wharves without fear, just so long as my arms and face were free.

I was left with full sight in the left eye only. Fortunately, that vision proved to be more acute at close range than average— 20/10 on the ophthalmologist's chart—and has remained so all my life. I lost stereoscopy but can make out fine print and the hairs on the bodies of small insects. In adolescence I also lost, possibly as the result of a hereditary defect, most of my hearing in the uppermost registers. Without a hearing aid, I cannot make out the calls of many bird and frog species. So when I set out later as a teenager with Roger Tory Peterson's *Field Guide to the Birds* and binoculars in hand, as all true naturalists in America must at one time or other, I proved to be a wretched bird watcher. I couldn't hear birds; I couldn't locate them unless they obligingly fluttered past in clear view; even one bird singing in a tree close by was invisible unless someone pointed a finger straight at it. The same was true of frogs. On rainy spring nights my college companions could walk to the mating grounds of frogs guided only by the high-pitched calls of the males. I managed a few, such as the deep-voiced barking tree frog, which sounds like someone thumping a tub, and the eastern spadefoot toad, which wails like a soul on its way to perdition; but from most species all I detected was a vague buzz-ing in the ears.

In one important respect the turning wheel of my life came to a halt at this very early age. I was destined to become an en-tomologist, committed to minute crawling and flying insects, not by any touch of idiosyncratic genius, not by foresight, but by a fortuitous constriction of physiological ability. I had to have one kind of animal if not another, because the fire had been lit and I took what I could get. The attention of my surviv-ing eye turned to the ground. I would thereafter celebrate the little things of the world, the animals that can be picked up be-tween thumb and forefinger and brought close for inspection.

Marilou Awiakta

Daydreaming Primal Space

(NORTH CAROLINA/TENNESSEE)

I

A Cherokee elder told me, "Look at everything three times: Once with the right eye. Once with the left eye. And once from the corners of the eyes to see the spirit [essence] of what you're looking at."

Viewed from the "corners of the eyes," the mountain forest is the round, deep space—immediately immense, intimate, resonant—that the French philosopher Gaston Bachelard calls "the friend of being." It is also the first space in Appalachia that humans inhabited and called home. For centuries, these American Indians sang and danced and lived poetry as a habit of being. They considered themselves co-creators with the All-Mystery, the Creator, whose wisdom spoke through Mother Earth and the universe. In harmony with this voice, men and women spun a web of life so deftly that no limb bent, no flower crumpled beneath its weight. They made each strand strong and elastic, like the spider's, which has almost the tensile strength of fused quartz, drawn out silken fine. The web was an extension of the forest—a sturdy, secure dwelling open to the flow of wind and light and vision. Round living in round space. It gave the people a twinkle in the eye.

When Europeans arrived, they found many such webs among the mountains. The Cherokee had spun the largest, stretching almost the length and breadth of southern Appalachia. Some of the newcomers liked living in the round. Either they brought this holistic ability with them, or they learned it from the Indians or from Mother Earth herself. They looked at everything three times, with a twinkle. For a while everyone lived in harmony.

Other European settlers believed in the perception of the right and left eyes only. Philosophically, their point of view contained the seed of a dichtomy that would bear deadly fruit: God is God; nature is "the other." They feared the wilderness, the "savages" who lived there, and the amorphous power of the intuitive both represented. Out of fear and acquisitiveness they responded. "This new land needs to be squared up," they said. "Squared, boxed, labeled—*brought under control.* These 'primitive' webs are in the way. We'll tear them down and stamp out the spinners." And they did. Or so it seemed.

But the forest knows better.

That's why we're going there by way of a daydream.

II

Even in a daydream, no wise person enters the primal forest without looking at it three times. Having taken its measure from the corners of the eyes, we must use the right and the left eye to take clear bearings: our point of departure, the lay of the trail from beginning to end, the experiences we should anticipate.

We are going from contemporary space to primal space, from life on the square to life in the round, and from the line to the curve of time. There are corresponding differences in language and in the movement of thought, which this essay reflects. The language is intimate, for in the primal mind there is no *psychic distance* between the singer and the song; listeners share the web of context and experience. Also, instead of following the conventional Western linear progression (A, B, C, etc.) and reasoning from the outside in, the essay begins with the center, Part I, and moves in a widening spiral to the conclusion, developing the thought from the inside out. This is the traditional American Indian mode that originated in primal space, where everything is connected.

Experientially, it is probably a familiar mode. Imagine you and I are hiking the Appalachian Trail, beginning at Newfound Gap in the Great Smoky Mountains National Park. The deeper into the forest we go, the less we look at our watches. A vast, varied maze of evergreens and hardwoods leads our gaze from mountain to mountain, each more deeply steeped in blue haze, until the last faint curve becomes a wave between sight and feeling. We relax into the flow of wind in branches, of streams rushing over smooth boulders. Our thoughts web out. Peace webs in. Time is seamless—a slant of sunlight on treetops.

The longer we stay in primal space, the more jarring it is to return to what many American Indians call "the other world" — a world not of poetry but of lists:

SQUARED. . . . . THE OTHER WORLD TIME SQUARED TO THE CLOCK. LIFE SQUARED to television/credit card/truck/car/train/jet—to cubicles piled in high rude rectangles. FILL IN THE SQUARE: name/address/telephone/sex/age/ race/occupation. STAY IN THE LINES. KEEP TO TIME SLOTS: work/ play/eat/sleep/love. Box 'em, label 'em, stack 'em up. COMPETE! Claw to the top of the pyramid. COMPUTE! COMPUTE! COMPUTE! ("No, you can't have your veteran's benefits. The computer shows you 'dead.'") GET HERESY UNDER CONTROL. The Creation is clear-cut: God is God; nature is "the other." Choose your side. WOMEN, SQUARE your shoulders, starve your bodies straight. Curves are out. MEN, SQUARE your hearts. Produce! Produce! Feelings don't raise the GNP. The shuttle's SEALS are at RISK . . . ? LAUNCH it! Seven people smeared across the sky translate to the TV monitor, "OBVIOUSLY WE HAVE A MAJOR MALFUNCTION." . . . Obviously.

Via television millions saw *Challenger* and its astronauts explode and scrawl a fiery hieroglyph on the curved wall of space.

A warning. *"Humans have lost connection—with ourselves and with each other, with nature and the Creator."* We do have a major malfunction. We've felt something seriously amiss for a long time. Now, in the blood of seven—a number sacred to the Cherokee and mystic to many of the world's peoples—we have clear warning. To survive, we must set ourselves right and reconnect.

One way to heal the deep slashes that sever us from relationship and hope is to go back to our home ground—our primal space—and find within it the deepest human root. In Appalachia, as elsewhere in America, that root is American Indians. They were the first to call the mountains home, as most Appalachians of every ethnic background continue to do. Perhaps if we study how indigenous people spun their original web, we can adapt their skill to our own time.

But how can we reach our primal space and the people who "sang and danced and lived poetry as a habit of being"?

We cannot see them with the right and left eyes, which only perceive facts and knowledge. We have to *experience* poetic habits of being from the corners of our eyes. To do that we use the phenomenology of the French philosopher, Gaston Bachelard, which reveals the imaginative movement of inner space. In *The Poetics of Space* he says, "All really inhabited space bears the essence of the notion of home." Through thoughts and daydreams, we bring all our past dwellings with us to our present abode—especially the "original shell" (home) where we were born. This original shell is also "the topography of our intimate being," our soul. Remembering the shell, "we learn to abide within ourselves."

A cross-country trucker from Knoxville put this same idea more plainly: "Wherever I go, I got my mountains inside of me. They keep me steady. Headin' back to East Tennessee, I keep pushin' 'til I get 'em in sight again. When I see that first blue line rise up, I know I'm home."

We're on our way to primal space in Appalachia, to the "spinners" and their web. But we can't get there through Bachelard's paradigm of the house as "the original shell." Although he looks at it from the corners of his eyes, the cast of his gaze—

the perception governed by culture—is of the West. It is irreconcilable with the traditional worldview of American Indians and therefore with the model of the web.

For Bachelard, a given is the dichotomy between humanity and nature, between culture and the powerful forces of the universe. Their relationship is adversarial. In the dynamic between human and universe, "the house helps us to say: I will be an inhabitant of the world in spite of the world." This dichotomy is the antithesis of the American Indian belief in the sacred tie to Mother Earth and to the universe as revelations of the wisdom of the Creator, who stands behind. Severance of the tie is basic to Western thought. It ranges God and man together; nature and all identified with it—including indigenous peoples and women—are "the other."

With this cardinal separation as a base, it is logical that Bachelard derives his idea of the house as a "tool for the analysis of the human soul" from the psychological paradigm of Carl Jung, in which the house is detached from nature and compartmentalized. The attic is the intellect—the rational mind—which polarizes with the cellar, the realm of the irrational and intuitive, where "the walls have the entire earth behind them" and we are afraid. The cellar is the unconscious. It cannot be civilized. To be used, it must be rationalized, dominated, "*brought under control.*" In a word, "squared." The other rooms of the house stack up, and we inhabit them one at a time. The mode of the house cannot be applied to the web—an extension of the forest, where the dweller feels the vibration of any one strand as a vibration of the whole.

Furthermore, in the web, the balance of gender replicates the balance of Nature's dynamics and is crucial to communal harmony. "Men and women spun. . . ." The power of change and transitoriness (male) must stay in balance with the power of continuance (female). Otherwise, there is discord and death for the people. From this point of view, Bachelard's "oneiric" house is a bird with one wing, which claims to be two-winged. Although Bachelard says he is studying the "houses of man"— that is, of "humanity"—and the experience of inhabiting, all of the dwellers are male. The wing of their experience is powerful and true. But where is the balancing wing of continuance? No woman speaks of her experience—not even in the cellar, much less in the attic. There is no bedroom and no kitchen in Bachelard's house (extraordinary omissions for a Frenchman) and no nursery—no comfortable space for the fecund and regenerative.

Only in a later chapter, quoting Michelet's meditation on birds making a nest, does Bachelard come close to female experience and gender balance:

> Michelet suggests a house built by and for the body, taking form from the inside, like a shell, in an intimacy that works physically. . . . "On the inside," he continues, "the instrument that prescribes a circular form for the nest is nothing else but the body of the bird. It is by constantly turning round and round and pressing back the walls on every side that it succeeds in forming this circle. The female . . . hollows out the house, while the male brings back from the outside all kinds of materials, sturdy twigs and other bits. . . . The house is the bird's very person."

Even with so pregnant an opportunity as this, Bachelard does not apply nature's principle of gender balance to humans. Indeed, he cannot. The psychic distance is too great, for the sacred tie that would transfer it has been severed for centuries.

It would seem then that although the process of phenomenology—the daydreaming of images—is wonderfully applicable to primal space and the web, its paradigm is not. However, Bachelard finally dreams his way out of the squared house and into an immense cosmic dwelling, which "is a potential of every dream of houses. Winds radiate from its center and gulls fly from its windows. A house that is as dynamic as this allows the poet to inhabit the universe. Or, to put it differently, the universe comes to inhabit his house." This house expands or contracts as Bachelard desires. It is "infinitely extensible"—a "sort of airy structure that moves about on the breath of time." Unwilling to be enclosed, the space we love "deploys and appears to move elsewhere without difficulty; into other times and on different planes of dream and memory."

Gaston Bachelard is dreaming the web!

Gradually he makes his way toward it, gathering images from nature that have the quality of roundness, like Michelet's bird nest. "When we examine a nest," he says, "we place ourselves at the origin of confidence in the world. . . . Our [man-made] house, apprehended in its dream potentiality, becomes a nest in the world, and we shall live there in complete confidence if, in our dreams, we really participate in the sense of security of our first home." The shell, with its "protective spiral," engenders similar confidence and evokes the intimate connection of body and soul. Bachelard dreams on through "the curve that warms"—the curve that is also "habitable space harmoniously constituted"—until he comes at last to the primal forest of his ancestors. Here he meditates on "intimate immensity" and "roundness," implicitly yearning for wholeness, for cosmic connection.

Sharing his feeling and transposing his forest to our own in Appalachia, we ponder the mountains and imagine "an airy structure that moves about on the breath of time," a dwelling that is "open to wind and light and vision." Alas, the webs are torn down, the spinners stamped out.

But the forest smiles. Deep in her nooks and crevices she feels the spinners and the harmony of their web. We will dream our way to them.

III

Daydream at midnight: We're back on the Appalachian Trail, somewhere in North Carolina—looking for a Cherokee web and "poetry as a habit of being." By the pressure of our toes against our shoes, we feel the trail descending. Flashlights give us narrow glimpses of a rut here, a rock there. It's like a Cades Cove woman said, "You don't know what dark is 'til you seen night come down on the mountain."

As the trail swings into the open along a ridge, we stop. From the corners of our eyes we see the essence of the mountains. By day, clothed in trees and blue veils, they are so beautiful it's tempting to relax in their embrace and forget they are also what we see jetting against the moonlit sky—mass and mystery, immovable. Only a fool thinks of "conquering the mountains." Mountains nurture the reverent. For the irreverent, the consequences are inevitable—and often fatal. If you're born and raised in Appalachia, this wisdom comes with your mother's milk. Mountains teach you to face the realities of life, to "abide in your own soul"—and survive.

Carefully, we feel our way through the folds of darkness. Since our right and left eyes are virtually useless, other senses become our eyes. The roll of a pebble, the breath of dew-cooled pines, a startled flutter in a nearby bush magnify the vast silence of the forest. Wind and stream are the murmuring current of time, taking us back to where poetry is sung and danced and lived. . . . In the distance a fire flickers—not running wild, but contained, like a candle. The spinners.

Coming closer, we encounter the first strands that define their web: a whiff of wood smoke, the brisk "*SSH . . . ssh, SSH . . . ssh*" of shell-shakers and a chant/song that *dips . . . lifts . . . dips . . . lifts*. It's as if, in the still of the night, Mother Earth is making music from her heart. The music draws us on, even shapes our courtesy. Extinguishing flashlights, we approach the large clearing slowly, for it is ceremonial ground, consecrated ground. Around the perimeter of the web, people are moving among the trees. We stop, wait for someone to acknowledge us.

Waiting is part of the poetics of primal space—a silence that allows the gathering of thought, the savoring of meaning. Alternating activity with rest is nature's way. It engenders endurance and reduces possibility of conflict, giving time for stasis to evolve. Even so, the night is chill and to stand in the dark, outside of community looking in, is lonely. The people, the trees, even round Brother Moon seems to be quietly looking us over. Only the steady heartbeat of the web reassures us:

"*SSH . . . ssh . . . SSH . . . ssh. Dip . . . lift . . . dip . . . lift*. . . .

A woman comes to greet us. Her bearing is confident, kind— immovable. We are respectful. She is the Ghigau, the Beloved Woman, chief of the Women's Council and a principal leader of the nation. Unhurried, she works the conversation around to the key question, addressed to me because of my black hair and high cheek bones. "Who is your mother?" (Meaning of what clan. She would have asked a man the same question.) I answer as my ancestor would have, "My mother is of the Deer Clan from the Overhill (Cherokee) at Tenasi."

With this filament of information in hand, the Beloved Woman begins connecting us to the web. In the forest, as in every town in the nation, the community revolves around seven mother clans. Like protective shells, they ensure the continuance of kin and care in the midst of change. They also keep the peace among the town, for it is forbidden to fight with relatives. Seven arbors, one for each clan, ring the ceremonial ground. In the woods behind them, families have cleared the underbrush and made camp; their small, embered fires are like red stars scattered in the dark.

As the Beloved Woman weaves a path among them, people in the shadows speak or wave to her but courteously avoid looking at us directly. We sense they're taking our measure from the corners of their eyes, intuiting cues for responses. And we do the same. Even by glance, aggression and dominance have no place here.

"*SSH . . . ssh . . . ssh. Dip . . . lift . . . dip . . . lift. . . .*"

The harmony vibrates every strand of the web, as natural and pervasive as air. Breathing the rhythm, we know we should slowly follow the poetic habits of being to their source. Otherwise, we will be disrespectful, unfit—and unwelcome—in the dance. The primary habit is connecting.

As the Beloved Woman settles us into the Deer Clan, people good-naturedly move over a little—give us greetings, a place by the fire and food from a communal spread nearby—roasted beef, corn, boiled squash and peas, bean bread and spring water, which we dip from a bucket. We take up threads of conversation as they're offered—"Where do you come from? How was your journey?"

Looking at these amenities twice only, we might mistake them for mere courtesies. But the spinners live *poetically*, always moving in harmony with the spirit beyond the tangible. We see the courtesies as they do: the greetings are the first silken strands attaching us to the web. The place by the fire signifies acceptance into the circle. The food and words are tokens of care for us to spin into response. We are entering the ceremony of connecting that originates in the dance. Following its measured pace, we accept what it offered with appreciation—eat slowly, talk with intervals of silence to allow thought to gather and be expressed.

Like an artist's brush, the firelight strokes the spinners only enough to suggest the full life beyond what we see:

the planes of cheek in the faces close to us and zestful twinkles in the eyes;

the ebony swing of a woman's hair as she bends over her baby, the smile between two elders who glimpse a young couple edging toward deeper shadows;

a warrior's arm guiding a toddler away from the fire;

and slightly apart from the group, the silhouettes of the Beloved Woman and a man walking together, intent in conversation.

"Is that her husband?" I ask the woman beside me.

"No. A chief. The council meets tomorrow."

Societal balances are different here than where we come from, but they generate a peaceful, easy feeling. Gradually we meet other friends and relatives of the clan (and by extension of ours)—a leisurely flow of men, women and children who mingle freely with the adults, not boisterous but *busy*. Conversation and laughter are abundant yet muted. Everyone understands the parameter of behavior at the ceremonial grounds. People gather here to celebrate the oneness of life, to recenter their spirits in the All-Mystery. Although the grounds are inclusive of human needs, there can be no alcohol, no rowdiness, nothing to disturb the harmonies of regeneration and renewal. Do these harmonies translate to twinkles in the eyes? We think so.

They also translate into energy. The dance has been going on for two nights already. When some of the women move a faint "*ssh . . . ssh*" comes from shells covered by their long skirts. Every clan has its team of shell-shakers and male singers, its poetic expression of continuance and change. The leading of the dance alternates among the seven clans, leaving other people free to participate or rest as they have energy and inclination.

"When do you sleep?" we ask.

"When we are tired."

"And when do you get up?"

"When we are rested."

They are amused by our questions as people in the square world would be by someone asking, "What is a clock?" In the web, as in the universe, everything cycles, circles, assumes a round shape, connects to everything else. Our dwelling is an "airy structure," a cosmic house "open to wind and light and vision." The owl glides freely here. The cricket chirps in counterpoint with the dance. The raccoon ambles impudently at will. The spinners address them with familial respect as Grandmother, Grandfather, Sister, or Brother. We are among all our relations, which include the standing people—the vast, staunch company of trees who have seen generations of walking people come and go. Resting confidently against the bosom of Mother Earth, we gaze along the mountains' curve into the dome of the sky, where even the tiniest star has a worthy place—as we do at home in the web.

We inhabit all its parts simultaneously. There is no attic here, no cellar, nothing to keep us from orienting to our whole space and whole being. Instead of cubic rooms, the web has spheres, which—like the auras of a circular rainbow—are distinct and diffuse at the same time. In the outer aura are the campsites, where embering dots signify the presence of perhaps three hundred people. If two hundred more should arrive, the web is "infinitely extensible." Or if that many should depart, it simply contracts. Wind extends the psychic space of our dwelling, bringing scents of deep forest, of distant streams and pollens. From the communal cooking area come aromas of whole beefs roasting on the spit. We know that someone prepares for the morrow—just as looking up at Brother Moon keeping watch over us, we know his sister, the sun, is moving toward the east. Our relatives are dependable—they give us a purring feeling.

In the next aura, people flow continually—visiting, doing errands, or just enjoying themselves while they wait to dance. As comfortable in the night as in the day, the spinners look at everything three times and move easily from the intellect to the intuitive and back again—a habit that many from the "other world" find "primitive and irrational." But in the round world it seems the natural way—in fact, the only sensible way—to move.

The circle of arbors marks the beginning of the web's spiritual center, the aura where meditative energy concentrates. At sundown on the first day of the dance, the spinners had begun the ceremony of connection with special prayers, songs and dances to evoke harmony with Mother Earth, the universe and the All-Mystery. Then they made a great cone-shaped fire of seven sacred woods—to burn continuously until the final day. The ceremonial dance began, a dance so ancient that no one knows its time of origin, a living poem passed from generation to generation. The dancing lasts until dawn.

During the day, although the people move freely in the outer part of the aura, they hold its flaming center in constant reverence. Its sacred meaning is visible at all times from every strand of the web. Because there is no psychic distance between the source, its image and those who express it, the fire is not symbolic in the Western sense. It is analogous to the atom's photon, which is made of the same material as the star. The fire, like the sun, shares the essence of the All-Mystery, Creator, just as the individual shares the spirit of the people. The fire embodies the light of all. To understand its meaning, however, we must experience it in the dance.

We sit among the Deer Clan but withdraw into our inner space . . . into a silence that allows the fire's image to deepen . . .

"*SSH . . . ssh . . . SSH . . . ssh. Dip* . . . lift . . . dip . . . *lift.* . . ."

There is ancient magic in the sound. Tuning our ears to the song, we hear predominantly the tonalities of *a*. They seem to resonate from the core of time to a place inside us we feel but cannot name.

Bachelard's voice, soft and discreet, enlarges our thought:

> It is impossible to think the vowel sound *ah* without a tautening of the vocal chords . . . . The letter *a*, which is the main body of the word *vast*, stands aloof in its delicacy . . . . This delicate little Aeolian harp that nature has set at the entrance to our breathing is really a sixth sense, which followed and surpassed the others. It quiv-

ers at the mere movement of metaphor; it permits human thought to sing . . . . I begin to think that the vowel *a* is the vowel of immensity. It is a sound area that starts with a sigh and extends beyond all limits.

Through their powerful intuitive skills, the ancient spinners understood the vowel *a* and its effect on the sixth sense. They also knew that dance touches the sixth sense in a similar way, making an "Aeolian harp" of the whole body. In combination, the song dips and lifts the people into immensity while the dance holds them secure. This balance repeats in the dance pattern itself, which alternates man/woman/man/woman.

Looking through the web to the great cone-shaped fire and the figures circling round it, we juxtapose on them the image of Michelet's bird, turning round and round, shaping her nest from the inside out. And we understand the cardinal poetic of primal space: The All-Mystery—the source of all light and energy—animates the breast of Mother Earth and turns her round and round, shaping the spinners, their web and their ways to "curve and hold the curve." Man/woman/man/woman. The power of change and transitoriness balanced with the power of continuance—strong shining wings that keep all life aloft. This is the Great Law, the Poem ensouled in the universe. The people sing it, dance it, live it.

Now when we look at the Deer Clan sketched in firelight, we realize the fuller implications of their habits of being:

The Beloved Woman talks with the chief, reflecting the wisdom of both genders active in government.

The warrior *and* the woman nurture the children, who are spread among us like seeds in the forest. Sometimes the woman is a warrior also.

The old couple rejoices in the life cycle of the young, in the assurance that the people will continue.

We ourselves are included in the web through a social interpretation of the Poem. Regeneration and renewal is the theme of primal space. The plane of our cheeks feels stronger. Twinkles well in our eyes.

We are hopeful that the square world we come from can regain its round shape. As we speak to the Deer Clan of problems there, an old man across the fire listens, eyes half-closed. With his forefinger he touches his head and heart, then makes a slashing gesture between them. Nods of agreement around the circle. "Head-severed-from-heart"—disconnection—has long been a source of conflict with European settlers of the two-eyes-only type. Many spinners believe that this unbalanced condition will cause the whites to destroy the Indian webs and, in the end, to foul their own nest.

Although these thoughts are not articulated, the Beloved Woman feels their movement. "There are also whites who *do* keep head and heart connected," she says. "We can learn from their good ways and they can learn from ours. Maybe we can find the balance between . . ." Her years of work in this endeavor give weight to her words and a tone of irony as she adds, ". . . if not in seven years, then in seven hundred."

Her illusion to the medicine man's prognosis—that a cure will work "in seven days, and if not in seven days, in seven years"—is well understood. There is wisdom in it. And stoic humor.

It is time to dance.

People begin to stand up, stretch their legs. It is the Deer Clan's turn to lead. One of the shell-shakers shows me the cuffs that cover her legs from below the knee to the ankle—row after row of turtle shells, with a scattering of pebbles in each.

"How much do the cuffs weigh?" I ask.

"About forty pounds. It takes years of practice to be a shell-shaker."

And, I think, years to build up the stamina. Holding the rhythm of continuance is not a task for the frail.

Neither is singing. The dance is brisk, the songs vigorous and long. It takes the breath of male athletes to sustain them simultaneously. Some of the singers pass near us. They are strong-legged and supple. It is said that they can run for days with only a modicum of rest, and their skill as warriors is well known. Yet tonight they turn their energies to ceremonies celebrating life, which (apparently unknown to the Hollywood of our time) is what most tribal dances are about.

Along with many other members of the clan, we follow the shakers and singers as they cross the web toward their arbor. The closer we come to the center, the more people gather quietly together. In the aura of the arbors, they move very little, and in the circle ringing the dancers they are almost immobile, absorbed in the rhythm. Around the tall fire almost a hundred people jog counter-clockwise in unison—woman/man/woman/man . . . round and round . . . adults on the inside, children on the perimeter . . . round and round . . . quick, trotting steps . . . arms bent at the elbow . . . faces contemplative . . . round and round. . . .

Vibrations from stomping feet pass through Mother Earth to our own, making us feel part of the dance already; and though we are silent, our throats contract with the *a* sounds of the song:

"*SSHH* . . . *sshh* . . . *SSH* . . . *ssh* . . . *Dip* . . . *lift* . . . *dip* . . . *lift*. . . ."

The music spirals up, soaring and gliding on perfectly balanced wings. When the shell-shakers cease, the dance ends and the song trails off on a haunting note, like a cry of the loon.

Slowly everyone leaves the dance ground. We wait at the edge . . . watching flames . . . following smoke as it drifts toward low-hanging stars.

Deer Clan singers file in silently and circle close to the fire. Leaving a space between each pair of them for another person, they begin a slow, rhythmic pace, calling out on every fourth beat, "ahYO . . . ahYO . . . ahYO . . . ahYO. . . ." Smoothly, the shell-shakers join them, "*SSH* . . . *ssh* . . . *SSH* . . . *ssh*." As we spiral in with other people, the tempo slowly increases, then holds steady. We settle into a rhythm that has endured for hundreds of years . . . round and round . . . . The chant lifts and dips in myriad tones of *a* and *o*, synchronizing perfectly with the shells. So intricate is the balance that we cease to analyze and give ourselves up to music . . . to warm energy rising within, melting away fatigue and cares . . . round and round . . . . Shell curves to song and song curves to shell . . . the whole moving, moving . . . memories come and dreams far beyond our knowing . . . membranes dissolve between flesh and leaf and sky, releasing all the atoms' tiny stars. . . . They stream round and round . . . into the All-Mystery, a radiant cup that holds our spirits in perfect stillness and perfect peace. . . .

IV

Round, deep space
immense
intimate
resonant
the friend of being,
our first home
in Appalachia.

If we really experience its sense of security in our dreams, we can live in our present home with confidence. Whatever our ethnic origins, we have in common our primal space and ancestors who knew how to live in harmony with it. This heritage is the ground of our hope. It holds us steady as we face the realities of our time, a time "squared" almost beyond endurance.

In Appalachia, as elsewhere in the world, the effects of humanity's "major malfunction" are evident. Through lack of reverence for the web of life, humans have upset the balance of nature on a global scale. Poison is invading the ozone layer, the forests, the waters, the food chain—perhaps even the very heart of Mother Earth. *Challenger's* fiery hieroglyph merges with warnings from scientists, theologians, artists and others who "feel it in their bones": we are reaching the point of no return. We must stop the rending of our web and begin to reweave it.

The pattern of survival is in the poetics of primal space. Balance, harmony, inclusiveness, cooperation—life regenerating within a parameter of order. The pattern repeats the deepest heart of Mother Nature, where the atom—with its predictable perimeter—freely makes its rounds to create new life. Continuance in the midst of change, cardinal dynamics that sustain the universe.

The Cherokee have used these poetics for survival. In 1838, after the Trail of Tears, the Nation's web was in shreds. Surveying the damage, the elders said, "In the seventh generation, the Cherokee will rise again." With the wisdom of the spider, the people ingested what was left of their web and began to spin. It was seven generations later, in 1984, that the Cherokee Eastern and Western Councils reunited at the Red Clay Historic Park near Cleveland, Tennessee—on the very ground where the last council before the Removal was held. For three days I lived in the web that the Cherokee wove on the knolled mountain meadow in the same pattern they had used in 1837.

Recently I discussed the reunion of the Cherokee with Wilma Mankiller, principal chief of the Cherokee Nation of Oklahoma. She is a poet-chief, in the classic American Indian tradition. Traditionally reared, she is also a shell-shaker for her clan at the ceremonial grounds, where many Cherokee come regularly to sing and dance and live poetry as you, the reader, and I experienced it in our midnight dream. I asked Chief Mankiller, "In essence, do you think the Cherokee survived because they kept dancing?" "Unquestionably," she answered. "We've held the center. We've maintained connection."

Survival. It *is* possible. A hopeful twinkle glimmers in our eyes as we Appalachians contemplate primal space—our first home, our friend of being. The question is: Do we have the courage to *be* a friend in return? For the sake of renewed relationships, will we unstack the boxes, take off the labels, and open ourselves to the flow of light and air and vision? It will mean giving up the idea of dominance for the concept of harmony with "all our relations." It will mean balancing the power of change and transitoriness with the power of continuance, in every dimension of our society. Most of all, it will mean that we heal the sacred and severed tie between humanity and nature as the expression of the All-Mystery—the Poem, the Great Law ensouled in the universe, which teaches us to live in the round. Looking three times at what lies before us, I chant: *Out of ashes/peace will rise/if the people are resolute/our courage is our memory.*

Bland Simpson

The Great Dismal

(VIRGINIA/NORTH CAROLINA)

> I can fancy that it would be luxury to stand up
> to one's chin in some retired swamp a whole
> summer day, scenting the wild honeysuckle and
> bilberry blows, and lulled by the minstrelsy of
> gnats and mosquitoes!
>
> HENRY DAVID THOREAU,
> *A Week on the Concord and Merrimack Rivers,* 1849

"Everything changes," Reggie Gregory said.

We were sitting in hobbled chairs out in his
tractor shed at Tadmore, the fog-enshrouded wilderness wall just beyond us, the wet air of the November afternoon full of mist one minute, roaring with winter rain the next. Hurricane Kate had
just blown up through Apalachicola and Georgia,
flooding full the creeks and swamps and pocosins
of eastern North Carolina. Seagulls were stark
chalk-white against green winter cover in the
fields, cotton remnants where stubble stood were
drooping gray and dripping wet, and more than
a few men were afield with shotguns in all this
wet weather.

Reggie was speculating about whether or not
the Dismal Swamp Canal along U.S. 17 would
stay open, shrugging over its prospects. But what
he was really concerned about, and feeling very

deeply, was how much the Swamp he had known and ranged all his life was now changed forever, not just cut over, but preserved. The Swamp was saved, but because this meant his progeny could never hunt and trap it as he had, in a way Reggie felt the Great Dismal was almost lost to him.

Though he was the park ranger for the Dismal Swamp State Park—fourteen thousand acres bounded by Bull Boulevard on the south, Forest Line Ditch on the west, the state line to the north, and the Canal on the east—his dealings with people in government, whether state or federal, mystified him. He was playing a role that no one had really written, only titled.

"I bout have no contact with the State," he told me. "They give me that old four-wheel-drive, but it rides so rough I'd rather use my own truck, even if I have to put my own gas in it. I don't write them, don't call em, nothing. Never hear from them.

"Oh, the new man from Raleigh came to see me. I asked him what had happened to the other fellow. He said, 'Oh, he's gone now. I've taken his place.' I said, 'Well, good—I didn't like him worth a damn.' Course I didn't mean it, I was just sayin that. And that was the only time I saw this new guy. I don't have nothing to do with them folks up in Raleigh, cept I get a paycheck from em, and I go back in the Swamp, and check on it, see that it's still there."

The old man leaned back and his chair creaked and the woodstove he had built breathed with a slow and steady insuck of air as it burned away on wood he had cut and split. On the refrigerator in the corner was a brunette in a revealing macrame bathing suit—"Navy boy put that up, fellow who was rebuilding his truck in my shop here," Reggie said. On the shedwalls were hoses, cords, funnels, headgaskets, on the floor a small ballpeen hammer. Beyond a bandsaw and a drillpress was a new bulldozer trailer he was welding together, not yet finished but not far from it. He said he had gotten new orders not to maintain the roads and ditchbanks in the state park with his bulldozer and brushhog, but from now on only with a chainsaw and an axe the state would stake him. Won't be no road, if that is the way they expect me to keep it up," he said, ever mystified.

North Carolina had a treasure in its park here, he thought, a set of jewels no one knew what to do with. Reggie thought the state should cut out a juniper thicket, take the money and put a campground over on the Canal by U.S. 17, and make it possible for people to come into the Carolina Swamp and stay awhile and get to know it. He was made head to toe of peat and juniper and Swampwater, and he had an ingrained contempt for those in power who assessed his home grounds from afar or who came in sporadically and at best gave the territory a few minutes of cursory windshield appraisal.

"The state's got a juniper thicket right there on the Forest Line Road, right side, worth a million dollars today, that one thicket. Damn fools want to give it to the Interior crowd. Would of done it hadn't been for me—I went to see this guy over there in Bertie, Monk Harrington, told him what they was getting ready to do, and he and Melvin Daniels blocked it. I think that's the reason they got pissed off at me, they knew I'd done it. It didn't make any sense to me. Just gon give it to them."

So it came to light that Reggie had run afoul of some bureaucrat or politician, and someone was trying to clip the old Swamper's wings: telling him to clear the jungle's roads with the meanest of tools; upbraiding him about his taking an occasional deer from the Swamp, hunting for which he said he had had express permission; and ordering him to clear his any and every action in the Swamp with another warden in a nearby park. It all made him mad, and sad, at once. No title, no redrafted job description would have made him one whit more or less proprietary about his place in the world, his Swamp, than his very birthright had made him. He said:

"One of the head men out of the Raleigh office a year or two ago was down here riding with me and we was riding with the head man of the Interior up here, going right down Corapeake Road, and of course all that road belongs to us, the park, and he said, "'Reggie, we just as well give them this road, hadn't we?' And I said,

"'Sir?' And he said,

"'Don't you think we just as well give them this road, cause, hell, we own both sides of the road?' I said,

"'If you gon give em this road, why not give em the whole damn park, just as well, cause we ain't gon have a thing left if you do!' And the Interior man he just laughed.

"We got some of the dumbest bastards in the world running this state."

The mistshroud and the storm were so socked in that it was nearly dark by half past three. For a spell then it rained steadily and more heavily, and had it not been November and I not known better I might have taken the loud battering on the tin roof above us for hail. It was hard to hear, but Reggie did not raise his voice except for occasional emphasis. We had been sitting there without rising by now for nearly three hours, and we had entered a new moment. There was something sterling in the emotional air, some melding of Reggie Gregory's fierce integrity and the overscoring storm outside.

It was a high and affecting sadness, and I struggled to follow the muffled voice that articulated it as Reggie drew more deeply into his own soul for the things he said next, as he drew upon the wells of that sadness and grew tearful.

"Excuse me if I get a little sentimental sometimes. That old Swamp is my home, my living, my life. Now they gon take it away from me. And all I ever worked for and enjoyed, my grandson won't ever be able to go in there and enjoy it, what I did, and that's what tees me off. Just on account of some screwball, that don't know no more about this Dismal Swamp than I know about Washington, D.C., and ain't never been here."

From his rear pocket he pulled a handkerchief, wiped his eyes and his nose and shook his head, and then recalled for me and for himself too another man, another loss, and music that came to us in the shed across the distance of a half a century.

"There was a colored fellow named Holly, drove the Cedar Works train in the Swamp way back. And he had a son that worked with him, was the brakeman. And there was two logs, just like that out over the ends of the flatcars, and one day the son, coupling up the cars, he backed up and them logs came together on him, mashed him, killed him. And it like to ruined Holly. And when he'd go out, years after that when they come on south through the Swamp, on through here, see, our field,

Papa's field, joined that railroad. He'd come right by with that trainload of cars, and that old fellow could blow the whistle in there, and late evenings when he'd come out, every day, he would blow that steamwhistle in the engine and play 'Nearer, My God, to Thee.' Pretty as anything I ever heard in my life.

"Couldn't help from crying sometimes."

One fall fifteen years before Reggie Gregory was born, a young poet stood on a boardinghouse porch in Canton, Massachusetts, knocked on the door, and waited to see the love of his life. He knew she was not expecting him, but he was dressed up in a new suit the girl's own mother had bought for him, and he bore with him two slender books of poetry he had written for his love. He was twenty years old, there in all earnestness — surely she would see him.

Surely she would not. He had surprised her by riding the train all night from Lawrence to Canton and presenting himself so. The girl refused to entertain him there at the boardinghouse, or anywhere else in town. What of the gift of his heart? He showed her the identical small volumes of verse, the entire edition of his five-poem collection, and offered one to her. Each of them was to keep and cherish a copy, like halves of a heart locket or, better still, like wedding rings.

She looked at the little brown book he held out to her, its name "Twilight" stamped in gold foil onto the dark pebbly leather, took it from him as if she had been delivered no more than a newspaper or a prescription, and shut the door where he stood as she disappeared into the house.

Robert Frost was crushed.

He wandered down the railroad tracks, tore his half of the covenant of love into shreds, and scattered these remains along the roadbed of the train. All that was left to do was to destroy himself.

On Election Day, 1894, young Frost set out, traveling by train from Lawrence to North Station, Boston, from South Station there to New York City, then by steamer south to Norfolk, Virginia, where he disembarked the next morning. After he had had breakfast — all he would eat that day — he asked the way to the Dismal Swamp.

Now he was on foot, dressed only in light clothing and a thin topcoat, and it was the end of the day before he reached Deep Creek, sundown before he saw the Canal. The moon was nearly full, and Frost, fearful since childhood of the dark, trudged along towards the wilderness, stopping to lighten his grip by pitching out some clothes and a couple of books.

Brambles and forest enclosed the road, tunneling it after a while. The mudhole quagmire he walked down soon sank beneath a shallow sheet of water, and now the poet strode upon a plank walk perhaps a foot above the water. What would he do? Dive in and drown in the cold waters of the Canal? Make his way by swimming, by boat, to the western side and walk off into the Big Swamp, there to lie weak and starving up against some gumtree none save he had ever seen? Or would the enormous black man with a shouldered axe that Frost fancied he sensed hard on his heels finally lop off his head?

If Robert Frost had in mind a poem of his own death, some epitaph short or long that might form and play in his head as he sank into the mire, he did not write it here in the Great Dismal. Somewhere between Deep Creek and the old Northwest Lock ten miles to the south, it must have dawned on him that his romantic suicide would have no effect on its intended audience, Miss Elinor White, if his body were never found and neither she nor anyone else ever heard about it.

At Northwest Lock about midnight that night, he boarded a small steamer bound for Elizabeth City, where it lay docked for most of the next day awaiting a party of duck hunters. They were boisterous, well-provisioned, liquor-swilling, and they swept him along with them for a night and a day of it down at the old Nags Head Hotel.

"I was trying to throw my life away," he repeatedly told Lawrance Thompson, his biographer, but instead he walked and boated right through the Great Dismal, and, now, Robert Frost's Swamp adventure was over.

In time he would win the two things the want of which had driven him towards the Dismal and death: Miss White and the world's respect for him as a writer. And in our time his few lines about the bird that is now so populous in the drier

Great Dismal stand as an elegy to the great cypress and juniper Swamp, the wet Desert, that once was.

THE OVEN BIRD

There is a singer everyone has heard,
Loud, a mid-summer and a mid-wood bird,
Who makes the solid tree trunks sound again.
He says that leaves are old and that for flowers
Mid-summer is to spring as one to ten.
He says the early petal-fall is past
When pear and cherry bloom went down in showers
On sunny days a moment overcast;
And comes that other fall we name the fall.
He says the highway dust is over all.
The bird would cease and be as other birds
But that he knows in singing not to sing.
The question that he frames in all but words
Is what to make of a diminished thing.

The hunt camps on stilts, the cabins on the shore, are all gone from Lake Drummond now, all except a weathered hut on the southwest shore stove in by a huge gumtree, the tan-and-brown shanty at the mouth of Jericho that the Refuge may soon remove, and the gray house a few hundred yards to Jericho's east that lies sunk to its ceiling, so only attic and roof and eaves protrude from the Lake. Wasps buzz around the tin roof of the sunken ruin, and gableboards creak and sway loose to the rhythms of the winds and waters.

Jake Mills and his boy Mark and I had gone into the Lake for a spell of fishing in early May of 1987, and though we caught nothing in the Lake larger than a potato chip, it was a fine, cool weekend, a grand time to tour the old Lake and see the remains of hunt habitation along its marge. As we had headed up the Feeder on a Friday afternoon in our seven-and-a-half-horse johnboat, a couple of bikers espied our boatload of goods—blue-and-white-striped canvas tent, beat-up Coleman stove, red coolers and green—and one of them said:

"Y'all going camping?"

"Yeah," Jake said.

"Takes a lot of stuff to go camping, don't it?"

"Yeah," Jake said again, now sensing that we were being cased and adding, "but it's just a bunch of junk, though, really."

At midnight that night we went out upon the Lake, and it was cool and clear. I studied the treeline pattern where the Feeder came out, so that we might find our way back into the little notch through the woods and not spend all that cold night cruising the shore. Back at the spillway when we returned, there were many low mists playing rapidly across the water.

Saturday morning we were back out on the Lake just past ten. There had been pollen in sheets all over the Feeder Ditch going out, and we had slowed to study the hunter's camp on the north shore of the Feeder just west of the spillway—a log cabin with a hundred A-1 sauces propped in the kitchen window, deer antlers all along the outside wall, big longhorn steerhorns at an upstairs window, a dogpen big enough for a dozen hounds.

Songbirds were everywhere singing out to beat the band. Blackbirds swarmed in a hollow gum along the southeast shore, its top blown totally out. We saw mallards, kept flushing a great blue heron that would fly ahead of us, settle, then take off again at our approach.

These ruins lay about the Lake: a privy on the north shore, tilting over at a sixty degree angle, an ornate wrought iron rail pitched off into the woods, a corrugated tin building that looked like a pair of pony stalls, an upended kitchen sink and a hotwater heater in the water, matrices of charred pilings here and there in the shorewaters where hunt clubs had obeyed the federal order to remove their camps by burning them where they stood, a bike reflector on a gumtree, and a chipped chamberpot tied to a tree with a red bandana.

Our fishing was far better back at the spillway Saturday afternoon, where ten gates were open and spilling. Jake and Mark pulled in ten catfish and a couple of perch, and were happily frying them up for our big Swamp souse-down when one of a group of fey, urban campers happened by and said, "What're you fixing there?"

"Catfish," Jake said.

"*Catfish?!*" the man said, horrified. "You mean you're going to eat *catfish?*"

"That's right," said Jake, defiantly flipping one and splattering grease, "catfish."

The spillway spit was filthy with caterpillar worms and toads that night, but these had secreted themselves away by the time I awoke next morning to the cries of a kingfisher strafing the Feeder Ditch. I wandered off into the big trees and tangles past an old sluice near the boat railroad, tracking for fifteen minutes or so a rufous-sided towhee. Then we fried bacon and scrambled eggs and ate up and cleared out, listening as we loaded and moved slowly down the ditch to the urban men, who having polished off a couple of boxes of Suzanne's Danishes now suspected fellow campers of stealing their cache of deli roastbeef and were sounding off about it, shrill and petulant in their designer-labeled camp outfits.

When we were out of earshot, Jake said of them and their complaint: "You were talking about diminishment here in the Swamp? Well, there it is! There it is."

A little ways more down the Feeder, we cut the engine and flipped a huge dead belly-up snapping turtle with one of our aluminum tent stakes, admired its claws that could easily strip the flesh from a deer, or a man. Through the cooter there was some purchase on the primeval Swamp whence it came, and we were still speaking of it granting it the honor due a lion of the ancien régime, like Sir Walter Ralegh, the Last Elizabethan, at his beheading—as we passed the Bongo Club and Blind Man Road outside South Mills and entered the Swamp again beyond Tadmore, where buttercups by the billion were putting forth.

The Lake is pink-rimmed in spring, when all the maple in the marge of the morass puts forth like cherry, and the cypress that still stand in the shallows are the lightest and most feathery green. Fetter-bush hangs abloom at the mouth of Jericho Ditch, bullfrogs ga-lunk there where the Lake just slides off into the Swamp, and thrushes sing their looping, liquid songs. Standing up on the ditchbanks to be counted are fronds and fiddleheads, for ferns are in near riot here—cinnamons, royals, sensitives, Virginia, and narrow chains, thirty species in all, with even the rare log fern presenting itself nowhere more than in the Dismal. The whole jungle swarms over itself in remarkable convolutions of fecundity, yellow and black butterflies and dragonflies and lavender moths alighting everywhere, slow-croaking frogs in the musky sloughs of North Jericho Ditch, grapevines leafing out where they twine upon holly, Swamp magnolia blossoms coming on, pollen swirled thickly in the still dark waters of the ditches, and everywhere hanging over and falling into these little canals the heady yellow jasmine sweet-scenting the air.

I was staring at an eight-foot wild azalea way up Jericho one bright late April day, its white flowers tinged with pink, when a female wood duck with six ducklings came paddling down the ditch. When she saw me she squealed and went off to the north, dragging her left wing and playing sick-bird, while the six little ones kept on downstream, stepped up their paddle-pace, and ducked under the lowest hanging branches till I moved along. Warblers were singing, mourning doves too, and a pileated woodpecker crying out from somewhere east of Jericho Ditch finally went lope-flying across the road and dropped down into a thicket from which three great, thick-barked pines loomed up and towered over all.

A big beautiful maple at the confluence of Jericho and Williamson Ditches was a huge pink ball, its flight-seeds still hanging all a-cluster. I had picked up a shotgun shell from the road, a Charles Daly 12, and was idly turning it in my hand when I heard the deep varinoted horn of a diesel engine. The long train went rumbling through the Swamp over the ancient roadbed, setting up a strong drumming rhythm of the rails that went on and on till I thought what an awfully long train this was, and how much its rocking rhythm now reminded me of the high-spirited, highstepping black marching band from P. W. Moore High School in Elizabeth City when I was a boy, the beat going:

BUM bu DUM bum
BUM bu DUM bum
BUM bu DUM bum
Bu-bu-bu-BUMP!

After a few minutes I realized that the freight train was miles west of the Swamp, and what I had been listening to for some time now was another marching band, this one working out on the playing field of John F. Kennedy High School in Suffolk, snug up against the northwest corner of the Swamp. The drumming of train and band had been so well conjoined that, but for the syncopation of the musicians, I might well have imagined the train to be ten or twenty miles long.

A hundred thirty-five years before, early in the Civil War, Virginia's William Mahone played shrewdly and well upon the imagination of the Federal commander of Gosport Navy Yard. Mahone, who had built one of the rail-lines through the northern Swamp, ordered his engineer to move slowly, easterly, towards Gosport, blowing his whistle long and often. Aware that the Gosport commandant had intelligence Lee might be advancing on Norfolk, Mahone counted on this theatrical military play—echoing train-rumbles and steam-shrieks—to convince the Federals that Southern soldiers were railing in on them. The Federals fled the mock attack, and Gosport fell bloodlessly, if briefly, to the South.

I stood at that pink-maple corner in the Great Dismal and thought of the freight train I had just heard, how it had rumbled slowly over Mahone's old roadbed, the causeway of Swamp earth packed upon a never-rotting cypress corduroy, a roadbed so fine that the president of Norfolk and Western could say in 1949 that it "requires astonishingly little maintenance." And at that moment too, I had not only the strongest sense of the history of this place, but also the stern feeling that history here was finished.

Nothing more will happen here, I thought. Just the endless leaf going down to leaf, the cold gray winter when waters from the west recharge the peat muck and mire, the hyperfecundity of the jungle in spring, the yellow flies of July and August, high summer's curse of the Swamp. Scientists will descend on Great Dismal till in time perhaps the Swamp will have been studied to the death of its mystery. Perhaps. But as I mused on Mahone that late April morning, his track-clattering trains, his successful gambit against Gosport for the Confederacy, I thought too:

gone are the Nansemonds, and whatever other Indians named or no who used God's own smokehouse, this Swamp, as their own; gone are the shinglegetters, and all the armies phantom or real of runaway slaves; gone too the legions of lumbermen who ran the narrow-gauge rails into the most remote reaches of the Swamp and in our time, or our fathers', tore down the rest of the cypress and juniper in the thousand-year-old woods and sent it out into the world as lifeboats for the Coast Guard and cedar shakes for cottages all over the East and South and as barrels to bring back coffee from Colombia far away.

Now there were only a few fishermen, fewer hunters, and no trappers; some birdwatchers come in for the glories of this songbird swamp, spectators like myself. The historical adventure of this place, I thought, ended when the *Emma K* made her last run down the Canal, or when Holly made his steamwhistle sing "Nearer, My God, to Thee" that last time in the fields of Tadmore, or when Union Camp gave George Washington's Entry back to the American people, whence it came, and pulled out of these logwoods for good. Or maybe it really ended the last time Shelton Rountree spent a night camped on the Lake, the hair shivering and standing on the back of his neck at the bobcat's piercing nightcry, or the day the inveterate moonshiner Alvin Sawyer got busted for what must be good at his gargantuan still in the southern Dismal, or the morning Reggie Gregory walked from his kitchen out to his tractor shed staring as he trod the familiar fifty yards at the curtain of green to his left with deep and regretful certitude in his heart, knowing that even if he were offered the million dollars that Mose White made off the lost stand of juniper Reggie had carried him to, he could no longer find his own way back to the hollow cypress where yearly he had cached the traps whose steady catch pulled him through the Great Depression, and would never again oblige the rusting steel that lay awaiting his hand. Bear and deer will mark the spot, or some hiker lost and anxious will stumble inadvertently over the caved-in log and just as unpurposefully kick to flinders the rusty dust, logsplinters and all. Which moment, which event, marked the passing of the Swamp's adventure, who knew? Only the gods who made it, and they say little to the living of such things. I turned from the pink maple that shimmered in the breeze, and from the bethumping drums that had so well succeeded the rhythms of the rolling stock, walked south to my car at Five Points, and went down to the Lake for lunch.

Three weeks later, a few minutes past two on the hot Sunday afternoon of May 18, 1986, a westbound Norfolk and Western steam engine pulling a company-picnic excursion train approached a switch called Juniper in the northern Swamp. One of the tracks in the heat of the day and under the pressure of the train became unsettled and shifted. The engineer—Robert Claytor, chairman and chief executive officer of Norfolk Southern and one of the most experienced steam engineers in America—felt a lateral motion as the locomotive passed over the turnout; a passenger in the first car behind the auxiliary water tender said the tender rocked violently," and a passenger in the fourth car back reported a jerk, side motion jerk, and to me it sounded like a loud explosion under the wheel . . . the sound of steel hitting steel." The trailing truck of the eighth car rode for some seven or eight yards up atop the steel ribbon, fell outside it, and then this and the next thirteen cars derailed, flipped, and jackknifed off to the rails' side and settled in the absolute Swamp as if they belonged there.

So much for the end of adventure in the Great Dismal, I thought when I heard of the trainwreck. Nothing is ever settled.

"The whole food counter started coming towards us," Navy Captain Robert Brewer told *The New York Times*. He and his two sons were in the dining car. "We realized we were going into the woods."

There were a thousand men, women, and children aboard this rolling entertainment gone awry, and nearly two hundred of them were injured, mostly cuts and broken bones. The trainwreck was hard to get to, all the more so after two mobile cranes sent by the Navy in Norfolk to the site of the disaster got stuck in the stone driveway and blocked access from the east. Helicopters from the Coast Guard, the Navy, the State Police, all roared in, but only a small medevac copter—the "Nightingale"—could land at the scene of the derailment. Still, in three hours thirty emergency medical units evacuated these thousand people from the wreck in the Swamp. No one was killed, and no one later died of injuries, but, as Captain Kenneth Murphy of the Chesapeake Fire Department said, "There was some hollering."

And now the cries of the wounded that May day are ghost-cries on the winds that sough through the last juniper and cypress and whistle over the wilderness. And they join the desperate callings-out of Byrd's lost men on the 1728 survey line, and the mournful shanties and songs of Washington's rice-farmers and shingle-men, the shrieks and lamentations of French navymen with a payload of gold who by legend fled from a British man-of-war up the Southern Branch of Elizabeth River and into the Swamp where they hid their treasure and died at the hands of their pursuers, and the last rasping death-rattle breath of some outlaw slave with hellhounds on his trail, and with the name of Thomas Moore's death-cold maid that issuing from the lips of her lover wild and possessed rang on the Lake shore so long ago. This vast wild region is a place well fit for a grand gathering of ghosts, a place simultaneously aswarm with the spirits of all ages here, of fin, feather, fur, and man-flesh; nor am I exempt.

I see myself on the Lake's north shore, at the mouth of Jericho and Washington, sitting one bright balmy October day with my little twins Hunter and Susannah, they just half a year old and already picking up the brown cypress needles from the ground and trying to devour them, and I at half my three score years and ten staring out at the rust-gold rim of Drummond in the fall. And I see two lovers one stormy April eve along the old Canal, my own sweet Ann Cary Kindell and I watching the quiet mists rise off the water and hang in the darkening pines. And at last I see in our Great Dismal Swamp not so much the indomitable sorrow it suggests as the incalculable and evolving beauty that it is.

Stephan Harrigan

The Soul of Treaty Oak

(TEXAS)

According to Stephen Redding, a mystical arborist who lived on a farm in Pennsylvania called Happy Tree, the Treaty Oak expired at 5:30 in the afternoon on Tuesday, July 25, 1989. Redding felt the tree's soul leave its body. He heard its last words—"Where are my beloved children?"

Redding had read about the bizarre plight of the Treaty Oak in the *Philadelphia Inquirer,* and he had come to Austin to help ease the tree's suffering, to be with it in its terrible hour. The Treaty Oak by that time was an international celebrity. People in London, Tokyo, and Sydney had heard the story of how Austin's massive, centuries-old live oak—once showcased in the American Forestry Association's Tree Hall of Fame—had been *poisoned;* how a feed-store employee named Paul Cullen allegedly had poured a deadly herbicide called Velpar around the base of the tree in patterns that suggested some sort of occult mischief. It was an act of vandalism that the world immediately perceived as a sinister and profound crime. As the Treaty Oak stood there, helplessly drawing Velpar through its trunk and limbs, it became an unforgettable emblem of our ruined and innocent earth.

Stephen Redding—a big man with dark swept-back hair and a fleshy, solemn face—was only one of many people who felt the tree calling out to them in anguish. Over the years Redding had been in and out of jail for various acts of civil disobedience on behalf of threatened trees, and he hinted darkly that the car wreck that had left him dependent on a walker may not have been an accident ("It was very mysterious—a dark night, a lonely intersection"). In preparation for his visit to the Treaty Oak, Redding fasted for six days, allowing himself only a teaspoon of maple syrup a day ("My means of partaking a little bit of the lifeblood of the tree kingdom"). On his second night in Austin, he put his hand on the tree's root flare and felt its slow pulse. He tied a yellow ribbon around its trunk and planted impatiens at its base. For almost a week he camped out under the tree, criticizing the rescue procedures that had been prescribed by a task force of foresters, plant pathologists, chemists, and arborists from all over the country. Finally Redding grew so pesty that the city decided to escort him away from the tree. That was when he felt it die.

"It was so intense," he told me in his hotel room a few days later. "I just kind of fell back on my cot without the energy even to sit. I felt like someone had dropped a sledge on my chest."

"I heard that you saw a blue flickering flame leave the tree," I said.

"I'd prefer not to speak about that. If you want to enter the rumor, that's okay. I don't want to confirm it. You could suggest that rumor has it that it looked like a coffee cup steaming. And if the rumor also said there was a hand on the loop of the coffee cup you could say that too."

I was surprised to realize, after an hour or so of hearing Redding expound upon the feelings of trees and the secret harmony of all living things, that I was listening not just with my usual journalist's detachment but with a kind of hunger. Anyone who went by to pay respects to the Treaty Oak in the last few months would recognize that hunger: a need to understand how the fate of this stricken tree could move and outrage us so deeply, how it could seem to call to each of us so personally.

When I read about the poisoning, I took my children by to see Treaty Oak, something I had never thought to do when it was in good health. The tree stands in its own little park just west of downtown Austin. Although in its present condition it is droopy and anemic, with its once-full leaf canopy now pale and sparse, it is still immense. It has the classic haunted shape of a live oak—the contorted trunk, the heavy limbs bending balefully down to the earth, the spreading crown overhead projecting a pointillistic design of light and leaf shadow.

The historical marker in front of the tree perpetuates the myth that Stephen F. Austin signed a treaty with a tribe of Indians—Tonkawas or Comanches—beneath its branches. The marker also states that the tree is six hundred years old, an educated guess that may exaggerate the truth by two hundred years or so. But the tree is certainly older than almost any other living thing in Texas, and far older than the idea of Texas itself. Stephen F. Austin may not have signed his treaty beneath the Treaty Oak, but even in his time it was already a commanding landmark. According to another legend, the tree served as a border marking the edge of early Austin. Children were told by their mothers they could wander only as far as Treaty Oak. Beyond the tree was Indian country.

It was a cool evening in early June when we went by Treaty Oak that first time. I looked down at the kids as they looked up at the tree and thought that this moment had the potential to become for them one of those childhood epiphanies that leave behind, in place of hard memory, a mood or a shadowy image that would pester them all their lives. The several dozen people who had gathered around the tree that evening were subdued, if not downright heartsick. This thing had hit Austin hard. In its soul Austin is a druid capital, a city filled with sacred trees and pools and stones, all of them crying out for protection. When my neighborhood supermarket was built, for instance, it had to be redesigned to accommodate a venerable old pecan tree, which now resides next to the cereal section in a foggy glass box. Never mind that Austin had been rapaciously destroying its environment for years. The *idea* of trees was still enshrined in the civic bosom. In Austin an assault on a tree was not just a peculiar crime; it was an unspeakable crime, a blasphemy.

"Oh, poor thing," a woman said as she stood in front of the

ailing oak. Like everyone else there, she seemed to regard the tree as if it were a sick puppy rather than an implacable monument of nature. But you could not help personifying it that way. The tree's inanimate being—its very *lack* of feeling—only made it seem more helpless. Someone had left flowers at its base, and there were a few cards and brave efforts at poems lying about, but there was nowhere near the volume of weird get-well tokens that would come later. On the message board that had been set up, my children added their sentiments. "Get well Treaty Oak," my seven-year-old daughter wrote. "From a big fan of you."

Would it live? The answer depended on the experts you asked, and on their mood at the time. "The Treaty Oak was an old tree before this happened," John Giedraitis, Austin's urban forester, told me as we stood at the base of the tree a few days after Stephen Redding had declared it dead. "It's like an old lady in a nursing home who falls down and breaks her hip. She may survive, but she'll never be the same afterward."

Giedraitis was sipping from a Styrofoam cup half filled with coffee. "If this were a cup of Velpar," he said, holding it up, "about half of the liquid that's in here would have been enough to kill the tree. We think this guy used a whole gallon."

The Treaty Oak poisoning had thrust Giedraitis from his workaday position in an unsung city bureaucracy into a circus of crisis management. His passionate way of speaking had served him well in countless television interviews, and now when he walked down the street in Austin, people turned to him familiarly to inquire about the welfare of the tree. He replied usually in guarded language, in a tone of voice that betrayed his own emotional attachment to the patient. Two years earlier, Giedraitis had proposed to his wife beneath Treaty Oak's branches.

"There was never any question in my mind that Treaty Oak was where I would propose," he said. "That's the power spot. That's the peace spot."

"This is a magnificent creature," he said, standing back to survey the ravaged tree with its startling network of life-support equipment. A series of screens fifty-five feet high guarded the tree from the sun and made the site look from a distance like a baseball stadium. A system of plastic pipe, carrying Utopia Spring Water donated by the company, snaked up its trunk, and every half hour the spring water would rain down upon the leaves.

"You know," Giedraitis went on, "it's hard to sit here over the last six weeks like I have and think it doesn't have some sort of spirit. You saw those roots. This thing is pressed to the earth. This thing is *alive!*"

Giedraitis said he thought the tree might have been poisoned as long as five months before the crime was discovered. He first noticed something wrong on March 2, when he took a group of visiting urban foresters to see Treaty Oak and happened to spot a few strips of dead grass near the tree. The dead grass was surprising but not particularly alarming—it was probably the result of a city employee's careless spraying of a relatively mild chemical edger at the base of the tree.

Treaty Oak seemed fine until the end of May, when a period of heavy rains caused the water-activated Velpar that was already soaking the roots of the tree to rise from its chemical slumber. On the Friday before Memorial Day weekend, Connie Todd, who worked across the street from the tree, noted with concern that its leaves were turning brown. She thought at first it must be oak wilt, which had been decimating the trees in her South Austin neighborhood. But when she looked closer at the leaves, she saw they were dying not from the vein out—the classic symptom of oak wilt—but from the edge inward. Todd called Giedraitis, who looked at the leaves and knew that the tree had been poisoned.

But by what, and by whom, and why? Whoever had applied the poison had poured it not only around the base of the tree but also in a peculiar half-moon pattern to the east. Giedraitis called in tree experts from Texas A & M University and the Texas Forest Service. Samples were taken from the soil to see what kind of poison had been used. Eight inches of topsoil were removed. Amazonian microbes and activated charcoal were injected into the ground.

When the lab reports came back on the poison, Giedraitis was stunned. Velpar! Velpar is the sort of scorched-earth herbicide that is used to eliminate plants and competing trees from pine plantations and Christmas-tree farms. Velpar does not harm most conifers, but it kills just about everything else. The chemical is taken up into a tree by its roots and travels eventually to the leaves, where it enters the chloroplasts and short-circuits the chemical processes by which photosynthesis is conducted. The tree's reaction to these nonfunctioning leaves is to cast them off and bring on a new set. But in a Velpar-infested tree, the new leaves will be poisoned too. The tree dies by starvation. It uses its precious reserves of energy to keep producing new leaves that are unable to fulfill their function of turning sunlight into food.

When Giedraitis and his colleagues discovered that Velpar was the poison, they immediately realized that Treaty Oak was in a desperate condition. As its tainted leaves fell to the ground and a deadly new crop emerged to replace them, outraged citizens called for the lynching of the unknown perpetrator from the very branches of the tree. They suggested that he be forced to drink Velpar. Du Pont, the maker of Velpar, offered a $10,000 reward for information leading to the conviction of the person who had so callously misused its product. The Texas Forestry Association chipped in another $1,000. Meanwhile a twenty-six-person task force bankrolled by H. Ross Perot convened in Austin and considered courses of treatment. The sun screens were erected, and the tree's upper branches were wrapped in burlap to prevent them from becoming overheated because of the loss of the leaf canopy overhead. Samples showed that the soil was contaminated to a depth of at least thirty-four inches, and so the dirt around the base of the tree was dug out, exposing the ancient roots that had bound the earth beneath the oak for hundreds of years. When the root system became too dense to dig through, the poisoned soil was broken with high-pressure hoses and sluiced away.

A Dallas psychic named Sharon Capehart, in Austin at the invitation of a local radio station, told Giedraitis that the workers had not dug far enough. The tree had spoken to her and told her what their samples confirmed—that there were still six inches of poisoned soil.

Capehart took off her shoes and crawled down into the hole and did a transfer of energy to the tree.

"It was a tremendous transfer," she told me. "But she needed it so much. It was like she was drawing it out of me."

Capehart had determined that Treaty Oak was a female. In another lifetime—when the tree was in human form—it had been Capehart's mother in ancient Egypt. The tree had a name, which it passed on to Capehart, stipulating that she could release it only to the person her spirit guides had revealed to her.

Meanwhile the vigil in front of the Treaty Oak continued. Sharon Capehart wasn't the only one beaming positive energy to the tree. To the protective chain that now cordoned off the Treaty Oak, visitors attached all sorts of get-well exotica: holy cards, photographs, feathers, poems ("Hundreds of you/Fall everyday/The lungs of the World,/by our hands taken down./ Forgive us ancient one"), even a movie pass to the Varsity Theatre, made out in the name of Treaty Oak. People had set coins into the brass letters of the historical marker, and on the ground before it were flowers, cans of chicken soup, crystals, keys, toys, crosses, everything from a plastic unicorn to a bottle of diarrhea medicine.

All of this was so typical of Austin. Looking at this array of talismans, I was convinced anew that Austin would always be the never-never land of Texas. What other city would take the plight of an assaulted tree so grievously to heart or come to its rescue with such whimsical resolve?

There was a suspect. Sharon Capehart had an intimation of a "sandy-haired gentleman with glasses, around the age of thirty-eight," and that was about what the police turned up, though the man was forty-five. His name, Paul Stedman Cullen, had been put forward to the police by several different informants. Paul Cullen worked in a feed store in the nearby suburb of Elroy and lived alone in a truck trailer, where he read science fiction and books on occult magic with solitary fervor. According to the police, his arrest record—for drunken driving, for drug possession, for burglary—dated back more than twenty years. He had lived in California in the sixties, during the salad days of the drug culture, and now he drove a truck with a sign in the rear window that read "Apollyon at the Wheel" and was a self-confessed member of the Aryan Brotherhood.

Paul Cullen had poisoned the tree, the informants told the

police, because he wanted to entrap its spiritual energy to win the love of a woman or to ward off a rival. They described the poisonous circle he had drawn at the base of Treaty Oak and mentioned the books—including one called *The Black Arts*—that he might have used as ritualistic manuals.

"Any pagan knows better than to kill a tree," an outraged Austin pagan known as Bel told me. "And *The Black Arts* is nothing but metaphysical masturbation. The reaction of the pagan community to this act is one of disgust."

Before Cullen could be charged with a crime, the tree had to be coolly appraised, using a complicated formula devised by the Council of Tree and Landscape Appraisers. The formula takes into account a tree's species, location, condition, historical value, and trunk size. (According to the guidelines, the current value of a "perfect specimen shade tree" is $27 per square inch of trunk cross section: "The cross section area is determined by the formula 0.7854D, where D equals the diameter measured.") When all the figures were applied, the mighty entity of Treaty Oak was judged to be worth $29,392.69. Because the tree's value was more than $20,000, Cullen was charged with second-degree felony mischief.

"It's tree worship!" Cullen's attorney, Richard C. Jenkins, shouted at me over the phone as he proclaimed his client's innocence. "In my opinion, Paul is a political prisoner. He's being sacrificed in a new kind of witchcraft rite. He could go to jail for *life!* People have really jumped off the deep end on this one. Usually this kind of treatment is reserved for murder victims. Rape victims! Child-molestation victims! But a tree? Come on! I mean, it's a *tree!*"

Though the poisoned soil had been removed from the base of Treaty Oak, the tree was still full of Velpar, and the chemical crept slowly up its trunk and branches, killing off the leaves flush by flush. As a last desperate measure, the tree scientists drilled holes in the trunk of the tree and injected thirty-five gallons of a weak potassium-chloride solution, hoping that this salty flood would help the tree purge itself of the poison.

Sharon Capehart, in Abilene for a radio talk show, felt the

tree weeping and calling out to her for another energy transfer. As soon as she was able, she got in her car and headed toward Austin. "Around Georgetown I could really feel her weeping and wanting me to hurry hurry. I told her, 'Just wait. I'm putting the pedal to the metal. I'm getting there.'"

Capehart arrived at Treaty Oak wearing high heels, a tight black skirt, and a red jacket. Her blond hair was teased in a manner that made it look as if it were flaring in the wind. There were four or five other women with her, students and assistants, and they made a circle around the tree, holding out their hands and drawing the negative energy—the Velpar itself—into their bodies and then releasing it into the atmosphere. I was told I would be able to smell the poison leaving the tree, and I did detect an ugly gassy smell that may have been Velpar or may have been fumes from the Chevrolet body shop next door.

Capehart and her team did one transfer and then took a break, smoking cigarettes and waiting for their bodies to recharge their stores of positive energy.

During the second transfer the women each held a limb of the tree, and then they all converged on the trunk, laying their hands flat against the bark. Capehart's head jerked back and forth, and she swayed woozily as a couple of squirrels skittered around the trunk of the tree just above her head.

"Are we doing it, or what?" she called from the tree in triumph. "Two squirrels!"

Capehart's spirit guides had told her that I was the person to whom she should reveal the name of the tree. "Your name was given to me before you ever called," she told me in her hotel room after the transfer. "They let me know you'd try to understand."

She dabbed at her lipstick with a paper napkin and tapped the ash off her cigarette.

"Her name is Alexandria," she said. "Apparently Alexander the Great had started the city of Alexandria in the Egyptian days, and she was named after that. She was of royalty. She had jet-black hair, coal-black, very shiny. She was feminine but powerful. She had slate-blue eyes and a complexion like ivory."

Alexandria had been through many lifetimes, Capehart said, and had ended up as a tree, an unusual development.

"None of the guides or spirits I've communicated with have ever come up in a plant form before," Capehart said. "This is my first as far as plant life goes."

The energy transfer, she said, had gone well. Alexandria had told Capehart that when she began to feel better, she would drop her leaves upon the psychic's crown chakra. Sure enough, as Capehart stood at the base of the tree, she felt two leaves fall onto her head.

"There ain't no way that tree is dead. That spirit has not left that tree. She is a high-level being. They never leave without letting everybody notice."

Entrusted with the name of the tree, I felt compelled to visit it once again. She—I could not help but think of it as a female now—did not look to me as if she could ever recover. There was a fifth flush of poisoned leaves now, and the tree's branches seemed saggy and desiccated. There was not much cause for optimism. At the very best, if Treaty Oak survived, it would not be nearly the tree it had once been.

But even in its ravaged state it remained a forceful presence, a hurt and beckoning thing that left its visitors mute with reverence. And the visitors still came, leaving cards and crystals and messages. All of the attention paid to the tree had created, here and there, a discordant backlash. An anti-abortion crusader had left a prophecy, saying that, because of all the babies "slaughtered without mercy" by the city of Austin, "the tree that she loved will wither and die. Tho' she care for it night and day forever, that tree will not survive." Others complained, in letters to the editor, in press conferences, in editorials, that the money and resources that had been bestowed on the tree should have been used for the poor, the mentally ill, the Indians. They saw the circus surrounding the tree as a sign of cruel indifference, as if this spontaneous display of concern subtracted from, rather than added to, the world's store of human sympathy.

I talked for a while to a man named Ed Bustin, who had lived across the street from Treaty Oak for years and who used to climb it as a boy, working his way up its steady branches to its spreading summit. Another neighbor, Gordon Israel, had gathered up some of Treaty Oak's acorns with his children a year before and now had some eight seedlings that in another five or six hundred years might grow to rival the parent tree. A local foundry operator had put forth the idea to cast the tree in bronze, so that in years to come a full-size statue would mark the spot where Treaty Oak lived and died. And there were other memorial acts planned: The Men's Garden Club of Austin would take cuttings from the dying tree, and corporate sponsors were being sought out to pay for an expensive tissue culture that would ensure genetically identical Treaty Oak clones.

"I hope you live so I can bring my children to see you," read a note left at the tree by J. J. Albright, of La Grange, Texas, age nine. There were innumerable others like it—from other children, from grownups, from bankers, from pagans and Baptists, all of them talking to the tree, all of them wanting in some way to lay their hands upon its dying tissue and heal it. Perhaps this was all nonsense and I had just been living in Austin too long to realize it or admit it to myself. But I was enough of a pagan to believe that all the weirdness was warranted, that Treaty Oak had some message to deliver, and that no one could predict through which channel it would ultimately be received.

My own sad premonition was that the tree would die, though not in the way Sharon Capehart had predicted, in an ascending glory of light. I felt that at some point in the months to come its animate essence would quietly slip away. But for now it was still an unyielding entity, mysteriously alive and demanding, still rooted defiantly to the earth.

Standing there, feeling attuned to the tree's power and to the specter of its death, I recalled with a shudder a ghastly incident I had not thought of in years. When I was in college, a young woman I knew slightly had burned herself to death at the foot of Treaty Oak. I remembered her as bright and funny, carelessly good-looking. But one day she had walked to the tree, poured gasoline all over her body, and struck a match.

The newspaper report said that a neighbor had heard her moan and rushed to her rescue with a half-gallon wine bottle filled with water. By the time he got there she was no longer on fire, but her hair and clothes were burned away and she was in shock, stunned beyond pain. Waiting for the ambulance, they carried on a conversation. She asked the man to kill her. He of course refused, and when he asked her why she had done this to herself, she would not respond. But why here? he wanted to know. Why do it here at the Treaty Oak? For that she had an answer.

"Because," she said, "it's a nice place to be."

Barry Lopez

Theft: A Memoir

(GEORGIA)

In the cool Georgia morning under dog-woods my uncle's Mercury Marquis possessed animal-like qualities, like a workhorse taken from a shaded stall at dawn, sleek and quivering. Later, under the match strike of the summer sun, the car would be too hot to touch, and in the humid air my legs would stick to the leather seats. With the thud of the big doors just then, though, I only felt class coming to attention, the teacher taking his seat.

My uncle Gordon lit a Panatella cigar and headed us south out of Thomaston. We were driving to a farm in Macon County, a quarter-section of land on the east bank of the Flint River owned by a man named Arthur Drewpierce. The Drewpierces, my uncle told me, had been in that part of Macon County since before cotton, seven generations or more. He and Mr. Drewpierce had business to discuss that morning, he made clear as we drove along, gesturing occasionally with his cigar hand at a distant barn, offering a few lines of history or an anecdote. I knew when he asked me to accompany him, though,that he had a separate reason and thought it not likely that it was solely to meet Mr. Drewpierce. It was Gordon's way quietly to set a problem before me. He was then the Upson County superintendent of schools as well as the superintendent of schools in the county seat of Thomaston, but he had taught high school for many years and some at Auburn University, his alma mater. He was as devoted to the idea of a formal education as other men were to the pursuit of financial profit.

I lived hundreds of miles from his home, in an apartment in Manhattan with my younger brother and my parents. Whenever my brother and I came for a visit, Gordon would impress on us the need to understand the family's history, the incidents in our slow migration from the Delaware Water Gap in 1725 through Virginia to Georgia and Alabama. He would emphasize our obligations to the integrity and honor of that family, no matter what we may have heard from others of horse thievery or disinheritance.

He was neither obsessive about family history nor overbearing about integrity, only direct and serious. And because he undermined the gravity of these concerns with wit or humor he seemed neither pedantic nor sanctimonious. He appeared to suggest, however, that there was something debilitating that haunted human society. He implied that the knowledge he conveyed was crucial to survival, that Armageddons loomed for us, always. The threats he saw to civilization were vague. They had to do with the failure to remember, which explained some of his devotion to the study of history, and the failure to honor. The high polish of his shoes, the careful routine of his days, the deliberation with which he spoke, like his library and the perfectly maintained car, were his proofs against such menace.

We rolled south in the big Mercury. I sat with my elbow out the window in the car's slipstream. In the summer of my twelfth year I could almost manage this naturally.

Gordon was being promoted by businessmen and state educators for the House of Representatives. I understood that his driving out to see Mr. Drewpierce had something to do with this, that he wanted Mr. Drewpierce's views. I was staring at a feral wall of kudzu vine festooned in the roadside trees, wondering what he in mind for me, when he began to speak of Indians.

I'd heard some of these stories from him before, about the Kashita and Coweta, and about Andrew Jackson's fight with the Creeks at Horseshoe Bend on the Tallapoosa, His recountings seemed exotic; I knew no one else in Georgia who referred to local Indians. He lined out their histories with the same knowledge and authority he brought to discussions of what he called the War Between the States. I knew no other adult who took history as seriously. I listened attentively, knowing this was a prelude, that he was leading me someplace.

His language tended to be formal and dramatic and was sometimes biblical in its cadence; his views he decanted in slow measure. The sentences sounded rehearsed, but they weren't. The Creeks, he was saying, were a confederacy of tribes, the most powerful of which were the Muskogee. The ceremonies of a farming people held them to the earth, in particular *boskita*, an eight-day celebration built around the ripening of the last corn plants. (We drove a macadam network of backcountry roads with no signs as he spoke, passing isolated clapboard shacks elevated on stone pilings and weathered gray, passing the spindle-lattice of picked cotton fields and fields thick with sorghum and ripening corn, passing Herefords slow-grazing pastures in the awakening light.)

"But long before that . . ." He was pausing now, gathering the documents in his mind. " . . . long before the Muskogee, it might have been Aztecs who were here. Before that culture had either name or notoriety among the Spaniards, before they were a horror for the Mixtecs to behold, they might have been living right here on these creeks, tending their gardens, worshiping the sun."

He looked at me, to see how I was taking it in, gauging his next remark.

"A man named Whittier, from the university up at Athens, has been down to see Mr. Drewpierce. He wants to excavate along the river there at the edge of his fields. He believes Aztecs once camped there. Now Mr. Drewpierce, he has no strong feelings about this yet—either way. It's in a state of negotiation for him. Mr. Drewpierce reads his Bible closely on this and other matters though, so Mr. Whittier, you see, might not be able to dig there. We may or may not learn anything more of this campsite beyond what Mr. Drewpierce's man Otis found last fall, a few bits of pottery. He may decide to take a six-bottom plow to it, you understand."

I nodded yes. Yes I would not bring up the subject in Mr. Drewpierce's presence; and, yessir, if Mr. Drewpierce brought it up and suggested I go down to the site while you talked together I would go (and this, certainly, was why my uncle had brought me here). And, yessir, I wouldn't touch or take anything.

"Do they teach you these things in school?"

"Yessir."

"About the Aztecs?"

"Yes, I've heard of it, heard of them."

"I don't remember it well, just that the Aztecs came in from the north and conquered the Mixtecs and others, and then the Spaniards slaughtered them."

"And they had a great empire."

"Yes, they did. They were great builders and mathematicians. When you walk along the river, think about these people, how they started out on these creeks. Mr. Whittier is impassioned to prove his point, you understand, which could be a mistake—archeologically and with Mr. Drewpierce."

He looked at me with an amused smile. I basked in the level of his confidence in me.

Mr. Drewpierce was a tall man and I thought him disdainful at first. He wore a clean white shirt under a fresh-laundered pair of Union bib overalls and greeted us in a quiet voice. He steered us to a gather of green-and-white metal lawn chairs on his porch and called to his wife to bring us some lemonade.

I drank my lemonade in silence while the two men spoke, a light conversation of gossip, weather, and anecdote which I knew often preceded serious conversation in such a setting.

"Boy, I believe I know where you might interest yourself for an hour or two," said Mr. Drewpierce.

I glanced across at his long face, not meaning to stare at the way his dark eyebrows rolled down into the corners of his eye-sockets.

"Yessir?"

"You see that fence running yonder?"

"Yessir."

"Well, you go out there and follow that fence down to the river, and then you walk on up there about five hundred yards, to where the river comes on a bend, and right there in the crook of it is some mighty interesting things washing out of the sand."

I looked to Gordon, who nodded approval of a plan he was pleased to have helped fashion.

The morning heat and humidity had now become oppressive. Crossing the fields and walking the fence I began to sweat, a scent attractive to mosquitoes and, I suspected, chiggers. Canebrake rattlers lay in the field rows here and cottonmouth water moccasins were in the river. The country seethed with the threat of violence from small animals. I watched anxiously, too, for poison ivy. I was relieved when the banks of the river appeared at the end of the fence and I felt a faint, fitful breeze off the water.

I found the bend with no trouble, and saw the first pot-sherds before I'd walked a dozen feet. I squatted down on my haunches to study them: gray and reddish shards, some incised with stylized patterns resembling the impression of leaf fronds, some looking blackened by fire. I brought my fingers hesitantly into contact with their gritty edges protruding from the soil. *Aztecs.* I stood and walked farther along the curving bank. I discovered concentrations of potsherds in two more places, and nearby found glistening flakes of quartz, a sign of worked stone. I began a diligent search for arrowheads. That I would take nothing from this place had been my faith, but I felt now a need beyond all restraint and thought. I could not understand how taking a single arrowhead might matter at all.

I searched for nearly an hour, looking for any object that suggested weaponry or adversity. I found nothing. Disappointed, I instead pulled two potsherds from the soil to examine more closely. One looked as if it had been broken away from the smooth rim of a bowl or jar. The other was intricately hatched with fine lines. I washed the sandy red soil off both in the river. They glistened like fish in my hands, and now seemed very valuable. I pushed them deliberately into the pockets of my shorts. What Aztecs had once held, I now held. The thought worked on me that the confluence here was preordained, a cabalistic power was inherent in this simple act. In taking possession of these two pieces of pottery, I had transcended the intrusive nuisance of insects and heat, the threat of snakes and poisonous plants. I felt ownership.

I walked back along the fence to the Drewpierce place. My eyes cooled when I rested them in the pine-straw shadows of a loblolly copse, the Drewpierce woodlot. The light on the muddy surface of the river had been fierce, predatory.

They were still talking. I sat on the ground beneath a weeping willow, watching how the fabric of my shorts might disguise the shape of what was in my pockets. I hated having to wear shorts, that I was not old enough for pants.

The men talked on. I felt hungry. I began to imagine how I would explain what I'd found to my brother, tell him how I, myself, had located this obscure site, had discovered what once had belonged to Aztecs, and had carefully removed only these two pieces of pottery. If he reacted with jealousy I would offer him one. Or maybe just give him one on his birthday, anyway.

My uncle hailed me to the porch, and we said good-bye before Mr. Drewpierce would feel obliged to invite us for lunch, We drove east in the big car with the wind blowing through the open windows. We stopped at a family cafe in Marshalville for lunch. They all knew him. They called him Mr. Holstun when we walked in.

My uncle asked if I'd had a good time, but he did not ask what I had seen. Sitting there at the Formica table, I could not fit the desire to share my excitement to any story I might confidently tell. Riding in the car I felt a piece of pottery, its outline clearly visible, stabbing me in the leg. When I showed no inclination to discuss the site or Mr. Whittier's ideas, I felt sure Gordon knew I'd stolen something.

On the way home Gordon said the river site might not be Aztecan. He said he respected Mr, Whittier's views and hoped Mr. Drewpierce would allow Mr. Whittier to carefully examine what was there, but he believed the pieces of pottery now sitting on the Drewpierce mantlepiece would prove to be Mayan. The Mayans traded vigorously and extensively north of their homes in the Yucatan Peninsula, he said. Some of their pottery, he told me, had been found in sites as far north as New York State.

"These are all theories," he concluded. "Just speculation. Someday men will have the tools to confirm what they believe happened here"—he gestured out the window—"before we came along. And then in another time they will talk about us, about what we did, or what we might have believed. We make sense of ourselves as a people through history. That is why we should make no modifications in records of the past, you see, but only speculate."

On the long ride back to Thomaston I searched beyond his words for the power that had been undeniable and true on the river bank. An angry silence grew up between us for me, as if he had ruined something.

That night I lay wide awake, succumbing finally to shame and stupidity. The boyish fascination with notoriety that makes being any kind of outlaw attractive was gone now. I felt the false step, the bad faith, that ultimately makes the outlaw an outcast among his own people. I couldn't continue to deny it with bravado. If the house had not been asleep, I would have gone upstairs and asked Gordon not for absolution but to listen to my explanation, to the intelligence I had arrived at on my own through shame. I knew that night that I was on the verge of the territory of adults.

In the morning, my thoughts were jumbled and I said nothing to him. The act was ineradicable and I lived with it.

Gordon did not enter the race for a congressional seat, although he seemed assured of winning it. He didn't want it. I continued to see him once a year or so after that until he died in 1976. We enjoyed many fine and complicated discussions while I was in college, and in some ways I came to reflect his sense of values. The incident at the river, though we never referred to it, formed part of our understanding of each other.

Twenty-five years after that day on the Flint River, walking in a remote area on the west rim of Marble Canyon in northern Arizona with two archeologists, I came upon the ruins of an Anasazi dwelling, a structure about eight hundred years old. Scattered all around it in the dust were hundreds of potsherds, some beautifully decorated with red-on-black designs, others finely incised with a fingernail to accentuate a corrugated pattern in the clay. With the permission of the archeologists I moved several of these shards to photograph them against a background of sunlit canyon walls and white cumulus clouds floating in a bright blue sky. When I was finished I returned each piece to its cradle of dust.

It occurred to me, of course, to take a potsherd as a memento, but I had no such desire. I agreed with my companions that the shards formed part of a historical record, that they should be left for some other mind to come upon and to interpret after we are gone. I had no desire to take anything, either, because of the esteem I had for my companions, my regard for their profession and for our friendship. I couldn't shake a feeling, though, which had clung to me since I'd moved the potsherds, that something was wrong. Something was unfinished.

That evening I sat on my sleeping bag working up the day's notes by the light of a fire. Across from me one of my companions, Bob Euler, was cleaning our dinner dishes. He was older than me by about twenty years, a professor of archeology, a former university president.

"Bob?" I said. He looked up. "I want you to know that even though I picked up those potsherds back there to photograph, I didn't pocket them. I haven't picked up anything on these sites. I just want to tell you that plainly. I don't do that."

"Yes," he said, "I noticed."

Janisse Ray

Whither Thou Goest

(GEORGIA)

Only love can quiet the fear
of love, and only love can save
from diminishment the love
that we must lose to have.
WENDELL BERRY

The work of belonging to a place
is never finished.
SCOTT RUSSELL SANDERS

At night on the prairie of Wild Horse Island, in western Montana's Flathead Lake, the coyotes never stop howling. When they woke me, the half moon had risen finally, and Orion was directly overhead, like a sentinel. The coyotes had two camps, one to the east and one to the west, and their songs passed back and forth: bays, trills, howls, barks. Theirs was a night-tongue, calling interdependence and belonging, and I lay awake a long time listening and understanding none of it.

Every time I woke I could hear the coyotes, and I expected to sit up into the prairie and see one of the he-dogs poised, gray in the trickle of moonlight, watching. I think, although I did not wake to see it, that that happened.

Toward morning I dreamed of my grandmother. She had died, at the age of ninety-three, just weeks before I'd come to Montana. I'd spent the last fortnight of her life beside her bed, although most of the time she wasn't able even to speak. I dreamed I was haying a field on her land. I was on the old Massey Ferguson and the sun was close and brilliant, but not oppressive as it usually is in late summer in the South. My arms were bare and I was practically flying over this field. I knew that although my grandmother was dead, she was watching me from the line of water oaks at the edge of the pasture. Yet her body seemed to be the hayfield itself. I dreamed this so wholly that when I woke, I thought I was there, in my grandmother's grassy arms.

Before I even set foot on Wild Horse Island, I had steeled myself against it. Newly arrived in the West, I'd left the swamps and pine flatwoods of southern Georgia, where I was born and where I was encircled by kith and kin, and come to graduate school twenty-five hundred miles away. School was the only reason I'd come.

I'll admit up front that the West has things to teach me, but the last thing I did before leaving Georgia was buy a bumper sticker that said "Southern American: A Proud Heritage" and stick it on the truck, so there'd be no doubt where my loyalties lay.

"You won't be back," friends said. "You'll get out there and fall in love with the West, and one of those cowboys."

"I'll be back," I replied.

There I was, with a professor and fifteen colleagues, set to spend a weekend on an undeveloped island, a primitive state park—twenty-one hundred acres crawling with wildlife. Our assignment was to choose one animal species on Wild Horse and follow it for two days. We even got to spend the night, although camping's not publicly allowed, because Hank, my professor, is one of a handful of private landowners.

Hank led us up to the palouse prairie at the heart of the island, where two hulls of settlers' cabins still stand. "The island's shaped like a fish," he said. "You're standing in the narrowest spot. It fans out to the east and the west." To the east rose a short chain of low mountains. To the west, in the distance, lay the mainland, and the Salish Mountains beyond.

"If you get lost," he said, "just follow the lake shore back. If you get hurt, we'll find you."

Easing away, I headed up the nearest hill, overlooking Skeego Bay. As I shuffled through the grasses I wondered how "palouse" was spelled, and what it meant. The ecosystem resembled the savannas of the southeastern United Sates, except the grasses were different. Back home: wiregrass, bluestem, toothache grass. Here I was lost. Not knowing their names was like having poetry taken from me. The world was flat. When I flushed a meadowlark, I wondered if the bird species were similar as well.

The drainage of Skeego below was blue-green and blurry with Ponderosa pines, but what I saw was longleaf, the pine of my home with its similar natural history. Fire-loving longleafs historically dominated southern uplands, but they were rapidly disappearing. I'd been defending them for years. I missed them.

And the island itself. Just before I left Georgia, I made one last trip to Cumberland, a wilderness barrier island off the coast and a national seashore. There, sitting on a high bluff above tidal Christmas Creek, fasting, I'd seen so many wading birds, mostly white ibis and snowy egrets, that I'd thought water lotus bloomed across the mud flats. A mother raccoon with three young had passed through camp, and a flock of wild turkeys. The wild horses had let me get within twenty feet of them, and at night coyotes sang on Crooked River. The West was renowned for grandeur, but Cumberland Island coursed through my blood and who would want more than that?

My son felt the same. Just days before, he had asked, "Know what I miss?" and I expected him to remind me of some toy we'd packed away, or how he used to steer the truck for Grandpa.

"Cypress trees," he said.

I ran into pygmy nuthatches first thing. One Ponderosa pine was absolutely alive with them, so that the tree seemed to wear dozens of dangling earrings. They fed mostly from the cones, but also from beneath the bark, flaking and tossing it away with little rips of the head. Their tapping kept the tree chattering.

My grandmother had loved birds. For years she was the only person I knew who kept bird feeders, fashioned by Uncle Percy, just outside her kitchen door. "Won't you look at this purty little yellow bird," I'd hear her say. Or red bird. Or blue. I used to spend Saturdays with her, and those days at the farm would be long and slow. One noon, as we cleared up after dinner, she came back through the screen door from throwing scraps to the dog, smiling. "Listen at that," she said, in her sweet and royal way. "That big old woodpecker is just a'laughing." A pileated clung to the longleaf in the back yard. I'd never known anyone to notice, let alone take such pleasure in, a bird call.

Evenings, we'd sit and rock on Grandmama's front porch, trying to stay cool. She loved flowers too and the edge of her porch, outside the screen, would be lined with impatiens and geraniums. There would be a whir and a ruby-throated hummingbird no bigger than a fig newton would flash among the faces of blooms. "Bless gracious," she'd croon, "you're a fine little fellow." Then it would whir away.

On footpaths that turned to animal trails, I headed eastward along the north shore of the island: a shy belted kingfisher went shrieking away. Two dark-eyed juncos hid in a cedar loaded with light-blue nuts.

The trail, bordered with purple asters in places, started to climb, and after a couple of hours I came to a damp woodlands cliff. The cliff was threaded with ungulate trails, and harebells bloomed along one steep, cool face. I saw from the map that the terrain got steeper and rockier. I headed inland, toward the highest peaks. My breath said "flatlander, flatlander, flatlander."

I watched for sheep, bears, mule deer, mountain lion, but there was nothing except all the unidentified squirrels one desired. They left stump-faces littered with pine cone strippings like piles of artichoke leaves after dinner.

Late in the afternoon, I came out onto a high, grassy meadow. A substantial bird in a pine two hundred feet away spooked and circled out over the now-visible basin of Flathead Lake. Then I saw another, closer. Onyx lines of tears dripped from its eyes, and its tail flashed russet in the lowering sun. Kestrels!

Like a traveler who seizes one familiar word in a foreign language, I seized kestrels, as if they might unlock something for me. I wanted to jerk my body up and down, nodding vehemently and mutely; I wanted to flail my arms and say it over and over: kestrel, yes, kestrel. We have them. If I could erase the series of mountains that swept away from me and replace it with a field of broken cotton stalks, with the kestrel perched on the barbwire hunting, I'd be home.

My good friend Milton, a naturalist and a farmer, had written in a letter just days old that he'd seen the first kestrel of the fall. We both looked forward to their return south for winter, when they abounded. Driving through the rural, bleak farmland of southern Georgia, we'd make a game of counting them. Sometimes there'd be a dozen sitting on power lines between Osierfield, where Milton lived, and Baxley, my hometown an hour away.

I sat down in the grass to watch these Montana kestrels, on a mountain flank strewn with boulders made of thick, gray, petrified filo dough. The rocks were mottled with at least four different colors of lichens: sea-green, mustard, chestnut brown, and the green of old dollar bills. Crumbly mosses growing there reminded me of kitchen herbs, but tasted like old shoes.

The two kestrels converged on a forty-foot pine snag. As they hunted, diving for what appeared to be grasshoppers, I scribbled field notes. Every two or three minutes one of them swooped for an insect. I watched closely. I saw one touch the ground, pause there, then lift and bank wildly in a yard of space the same distance above the ground. When she flew back to the tree, she landed on a different perch and ate, bobbing her head, picking at the food in her talon in a sedate and elegant way. A third bird joined them.

The kestrels fed further and further up the mountain. I had pulled off my boots at the first rock, to pick cheatgrass burrs out of my socks, and now I followed the kestrels barefoot, creeping below the ridge, thinking to get above them before I crawled across. But I rose too close. One bird broke from the pine and flew out over the shady canyon. The other disappeared. I walked back toward my boots. It was 7 P.M. now and I was hungry. A band-winged grasshopper sputtered away from me, its red wings leaving an audible trail.

The mountain felt soft and warm to my tired feet, and I thought about how you get to know a place. It is a reciprocal process of incorporation, of adding one life to another: an exchange.

First, you bathe there—my son and I, arriving cross-country to Missoula, had stopped east of town to swim in the cold Clark Fork River. This morning I'd done the same, plunging into the glacial lake when we'd first arrived. I didn't even think about it; I just went in.

Then you go barefoot, or naked if you can.

Then you eat and drink from a place. Then you sleep with it. Then you stay.

A sharp stone punctured the sole of my foot and I grimaced. Two kestrels lifted from a grassy meadow below, a tiny bowl divided down the middle by an ungulate trail, like the line pregnant women get on their bellies, and floated to pines rooted in the drainage. When they flew they went *killy, killy, killy,* then kept silent. For the first time I was higher than kestrels.

The sun set. Where it struck Flathead, a gaseous ball of white-hot fire seemed to boil the water. The mountain ridge on the mainland, worn and blue, made a fence around the sun. As I walked, mule deer warily lifted their heads from late grazing, and ten honking Canada geese, winging home, sealed shut the day.

The viewing of the body took place the day after Grandmama died. All afternoon I sat within a fluctuating circle of people under the oak in Grandmama's swept yard and listened to stories. Folks came and went, bringing food: chicken and dumplings, a pan of rolls, pound cake. No one cried. We sat in the presence of death and did not mention it.

About 5 P.M. I ironed a nice blouse, used a little of Grandma's makeup, and rode to the funeral home with my first cousin Jimmy. Grandma's casket had been wheeled to the front of the chapel. It was shining silver and gold, surrounded by flowers and huge pots of white lilies. The casket was open, and just the top of Grandmama's head, lying against pink satin, was visible. It looked as if any moment she would raise herself and ask what on earth she was doing in such a ridiculous box. "Help me out of here," she'd say, and I would. Her eyeglasses rested on her lifeless face. What need did a body have of glasses?

There were only a few people in the chapel, all immediate family. They sat contemplatively on the benches. I went and stood beside Grandma, looking in, and Aunt Coot joined me. We had often stood together beside Grandma's bed. My aunt reached down and touched her mother, smoothed her hair, fingered her elfin ears. The undertaker had fixed Grandma's hair special, and she would've liked it. I touched it too. It felt the same, rough and wiry. Her ear was cold, frozen in place. Her hands were cold. A few days before, I'd removed fingernail polish that one of the nurses had painted on, and was glad I had.

We sat and sat. People started to come — people from Spring Branch community who'd known Grandma all their lives. Her neighbors. Nieces and nephews. Distant kin. I tried to meet them all, following genealogical lines until I was exhausted, fitting people into a framework of history and place that included me. "You have to be Lee Ada's daughter," someone said to me. "You look just like her."

During the funeral the next day I sat beside Uncle Percy, the son who'd never left the home-place. Most of the time he twiddled his thumbs round and round, motion without purpose, but once I looked over to see a tiny spring flowing from his eye. On the other side, Aunt Fonida's body rocked and shook with her silent tears. Uncle James, the Baptist minister, recited Grandmama's favorite Bible verse — Chapter 1, Verse 16 of the Book of Ruth: "And Ruth said, Entreat me not to leave thee, or to return from following after thee: for whither thou goest, I will go, and where thou lodgest, I will lodge: thy people shall be my people, and thy God my God."

I rode with Aunt Fonida in the slow burial procession, following the glossy, black hearse from Spring Branch Church along a clay road that turned toward Carter Cemetery. Behind us a long line of cars crept past the houses of Grandma's neighbors, farms she'd passed all her life, places she'd stopped to visit. It was her last journey of this world, back to a clayhill where she'd chosen to be buried, beside Granddaddy, among all the dead of that country.

That evening in Hank's cabin on Wild Horse Island, when I dragged my sleeping gear out into the dark field, the sky was a hand-painted bowl, silver on black, and I circled the edge of Hank's property like an animal, sniffing out a good place to bed down. The grass was dry and stringy.

To the east a strange, amorphous glow crowned the tallest mountain. Could the Pleiades look that huge? I found the Dippers. The Milky Way was a sash tied across the revolving sky. It was so thick with stars it looked like cottage cheese. As I stared up, a raptor's dark shadow winged noiselessly past. An owl. Not long after I went to sleep the hooves of a galloping wild horse, thudding against the ground, woke me, but I returned immediately to sleep.

At dawn I headed toward the canyon where I'd last seen the kestrels, passing through the orchard I'd stumbled upon the evening before. There were no more than fifteen trees in the orchard, mostly apple, some pear, and all thick with fruit. The wild apples were no bigger than a child's fist and reminded me of apricots. Just as I had entered the grove, a fruit hit the ground. It seemed both a gift and an invitation, sour and delicious. I had shaken the tree and gathered a handful, gnawing at them as I traced the pretty trees.

Now a coyote bounded from the orchard, toward the drainage, and I smiled at the rugs of beaten-down grass beneath the trees. On the ground not an apple could be found. I shook loose a few and came out onto the prairie. Five mule deer watched from a wale of land, attracted by the thudding of the fruit. Their antlers were silhouetted against a pink promise of sun.

Meadowlarks, birds truly gifted with voice, sang all about. Then, in the middle of that, a coyote howled. I instantly crouched in the grasses that were fat and silent with dew. Just below, in the drainage, a coyote barked a reply, followed by another 150 feet northeast of me. A yelping commenced, punctuated by long, mournful howls that came from a coyote that I could see through the trees, poised on the next hill. On hands and knees I inched closer, staying behind small pines that invaded the prairie in absence of fire. It would not take long to learn the voices.

I knew that my presence—early out, the sun no more than thin streaks painted above dim, dark-green mountains, signified something to them. I knew that the coyote conversation told of my presence as much as it told their own, just as a hollerer in the great Okefenokee Swamp back home sings not only to locate himself to his neighbors, but them to him. I was connected to the coyote through lengths of song-rope, and to hear myself in animal song humbled me. I knew then, much as I resisted the island, that in one brief visit I had become part of its legacy: in vanishing grass lines my feet laid against the earth and in the unrecorded songs of coyotes. And having heard the songs and been met with trails, neither could I go free of it.

Not long afterward a kestrel landed at eye level on a flank ahead. It simply sat, waiting for the dew to evaporate and the sun to warm grasshoppers into motion. No breakfast, yet, for them either. I headed toward a rocky cliff, above the waiting kestrel, and while I was yet three hundred feet away I saw it was a good place. I was on the western side of the canyon where I had observed the birds the evening before, and already I saw two kestrels there. They perched in a snag intertwined with a shorter, live pine, which cradled the dead tree in its arms like an elder. The trees were rooted below where the talus slope leveled into a run of rocks, so that the tree's upper branches brushed the craggy cliff.

When the sun topped the mountain I had to shift positions, crawling up the slope so as not to be blinded. Four or five bighorn ewes, bedded down fifty feet above, watched without panic. From the canyon bottom I heard a clatter and looked down to see the mantle of rock fragments struck by the hooves of a hugely antlered mule deer. Though hundreds of feet below, it broke into a run when it spotted me. Another, following a few minutes behind, did the same. Two kestrels flew out from the rocks below and performed an aerial stunt, flying in unison, making a twirling W, then separating. Watching through binoculars brought the open space into my throat and I felt sick. The glasses had the effect of suspending me in the abyss, and I tightened my feet against the overhanging rock.

All morning I watched kestrels, among the most striking birds on the continent, flashing their copper tails, arrested in flight, the sun washing their slate-gray backs to midnight blue. At one point I counted seven different kestrels around me. The fresh sunlight laid yellow-green ribbons down the backs of the ridges and dusted the meadows gold.

After Grandmama's funeral, after everyone had eaten the last helpings of chicken-and-rice and pineapple cake back at the house, and had fled to their new cars and left all that history that was no longer relevant to their lives, only Mama, Daddy, Uncle Percy and I remained.

I watched until the kestrels had spread across the morning. When I stood to go, tying my sweater around my waist, I saw that the ewes had vanished. A kestrel landed and clung to a mullein stem. The dried stalks stuck up like birthday candles, and here and there a new rosette of hairy leaves grew. I knew that frost would soon kill these, and it would not be long before most of the kestrels would be gone.

I would not be leaving.

In that moment I would have become a kestrel. I stumbled, then folded into a niche of boulder that overlooked the magnificent chartreuse relief of Wild Horse Island. I thought to pray, but instead faces would appear: my grandmother, who

had known the kestrels and would not be there when they returned, and Milton, and my parents. So I cried.

Even as I grieved for my own land and its people, I knew
something else was happening.

The morning had been a movement of such beauty that at
times I had gasped aloud. I had come from wild sleep, sat in
meditation with bighorn sheep stretched behind my shoulders
and rock wrens at my feet, watching a suite of falcons in pano-
ply, their secrets unguarded.

In healing the wounds of my departure from the South, this
place—these Rockies, with their strange bighorn and ravens,
with their chill days steeped in the amber vestiges of summer—sidled its way into my heart. I knew that I thawed to it:
the tears showed me that.

Thus I made my way to the cabin, red-eyed, rent by the creatures of unfolding mountains. That is the way love grows, I
knew. To deny it would be an unnatural act. That's when I knew
I would take the West as a lover, and that I would be devoted
to it, and faithful for a time.

But I wouldn't stay.

Mary Q. Steele

The Living Year

(TENNESSEE)

March: I went up to the wildfowl reserve at Hiwassee Island to say good-by to the geese. But I was too late. Only a handful still floated on the water of the inlets, those who were ill or injured or for abstruse reasons of their own had decided not to make the long trip to Manitoba. Some mallards, tidily paired, a few black ducks, a coot or two, and three blue-winged teal—these were all that were left of the great flocks and rafts of wintering birds.

The gulls were still there, and the crows. Eight great blue herons stood about, knee-deep in water along the edge of the island. Something, perhaps a muskrat, went zigzagging among them, some creature perfectly aware that any one of them might stab it with a vast bill and swallow it whole, and each heron in turn bent its head with great dignity, with forbearance, to watch this foolish and frantic progress, as old men watch the antics of children. The twigs of the trees were spatulate with spring.

The geese were gone but I was not sorry to have come. White-crowned and white-throated sparrows whistled in the brush piles and a pheasant cackled from the hedge-rows. The day was grey and gradually the clouds lowered and thickened.

When the rain began it did not come in drops, the air simply grew damper and damper and condensed on the lenses of binoculars and telescope until at last it was obvious that it was useless to stay any longer.

All that qualifies me as a just person is lack of an umbrella. In truth I rather like being rained on, the less than subtle reminder that in the scheme of things I am no more privileged than a frog. Next to life itself, water is the most astonishing phenomenon the universe has to offer and rain is its loveliest manifestation.

There may come a day when rain will fall upon the earth only where technology decides it is needed, and only when it will provide least inconvenience. Scientists will order it as they will order the genes of unborn babies, and men will have become, I think, something rather more, and something a good deal less, than men.

I am almost sure I will be dead before it happens. I am glad to have come up to say good-by to the geese on a day when the wind still blew where it listed, from the four quarters of God's will.

April: This is the twelfth of April, the miracle of miracles. Had I been granted the power to work wonders, this is the wonder I would choose to work. How foolish and tawdry and banal other miracles would seem, water into wine, weeping statues, even waking some poor soul from his long sleep. For the world that has grown old and wrinkled and feeble is suddenly made young and vibrant and beautiful enough to break the heart.

What gives these hours their faërie quality, makes their beauty transcend any other, is the poignant knowledge that in addition to being supernatural, they are so brief-lived, are going to be gone long before I can really comprehend they are here.

It is the trees. For a few hours, over the hills they are defined in a kind of embroidery, a kind of pointillism, gold, amber, rose, topaz, emerald, rust, crimson, dusty green, honey, scarlet. It will not last a week.

If I lived in a treeless land, no doubt I would make do with something less cosmic, would be content to turn water into wine.

May: Along the banks of the river and of ponds and creeks, turtles cluster like scales on a fish, close and over-lapping, to enjoy the sun. Piled one on top of another, big ones on little ones and little ones on big, they bask and sleep in the warmth.

But it is not too deep a sleep. Let me shut a car door or appear on the river's edge, or let the sun flash off my binoculars, and they are gone in a series of quiet splashes. "Sliders" we call them locally from this habit, the sleek way they leave the bank and enter the water.

I walked as quietly as I was able to the river, along an abandoned ferry slip, but it was not quietly enough, and they went, one after another, from the place where they had been napping on the roof of a half-drowned chicken shed wedged against the bank.

I was disappointed. Not that I couldn't see them as well as I might wish with binoculars or telescope, but simply that it seems foolish not to be able to sneak up on creatures so deeply asleep, so oblivious to anything except the heat of the sun and the sound of the water.

I stood for a while enjoying those things myself, and a small wind, and the new leaves of willows, the squeaks and rasps of grackles and redwings. It was marvelously peaceful.

But something was not right. Something was uneasy-making. Something was there I had not counted on.

At the edge of the weathered wood of the shed a middle-sized turtle still sat, still warmed, watching me out of an enigmatic yellow eye. The thoughts of a turtle, said Emerson, are turtle. And I was disconcerted to find that I had been these last few minutes turtle. He stared beadily on, and after a bit I turned and walked self-consciously away.

June: In the long twilight of the longest day I spent a while grubbing weeds out of the border in front of the hydrangea bushes, a task which has for so long included only the interesting middle section that the dull ends have both disappeared under a flood of ground ivy. Once again I worked at the middle portion, which has as one advantage that there is much less to do there. And it had as another on this particular evening one of those chance meetings I will remember with pleasure all my life.

For I lifted my head and there in the quince tree not two feet away sat a young thrush. The bird was suspicious and alert but not truly afraid. Its plumage was still indefinite, its tail still something under adult length. It had legs like a night nurse, straight, thin and covered in white stockings. It watched me out of a liquid black eye and tilted its head slowly. And I moved slowly closer. I could see the white skin around its eye, the small bristly pin feathers about its mouth, the flicker of breath in its throat.

The parent bird spied us, cried out a marvelous note of warning and the young one went, in an awkward flurry of panic, bumbling among the branches and diving into the hydrangeas.

I was not unhappy to see it leave. Who would want a longer or closer inspection than I had had of it? What is wildness for if not to make some difference and erect some barriers between us?

And I remembered another such June evening, years before, when I had wandered outside and been attracted to a bush which rattled and shook with birds. When I got within a couple of yards of it, the bush exploded, a vast number of fledgling wrens zoomed out into the air, and in confusion seized the nearest substantiality they could find. They clung to my hair, my sweater, the bagging knees of my jeans. For a haunted moment in the twilight they embraced that which they had been trying to escape. Stricken, neither of us knew what to do. And then something happened; though I was still frozen, something released them and triggered them into helter-skelter flight.

July: I have come across a new flower—new to me, I mean, it has been here all along but in the way of humans, who always suppose they are seeing more than they are, I had overlooked it. And now I have gone scurrying through my books to put a name to my new discovery.

It is *Amianthium muscaetoxicum,* a tall white spire of flowers arising from a cluster of long slender leaves. A native American plant, called fly poison in the forthright native American way. ". . . a pretty species of Asphodelus," William Bartram spoke of it gently, as he spoke of most things, most of which he saw, since he lacked all arrogance.

Now that I have seen it and named it I find it everywhere, *Amianthium muscaetoxicum*, fly poison, crow poison, bunchflower. I look at it with special pleasure. I know its name.

I wonder about this urge to ticket and categorize everything I meet. Once I was a bit ashamed of it. If it delights my eye and gladdens my spirit to see the roadsides lit with these creamy clusters of flowers, what difference does it make that the thing has a name and place in a botanical key? Suffice to enjoy it.

One of the reasons I am so compelled is communication, of course. If I tell you of the lovely pink flowers growing by the wayside, you and I are less than equally charmed by them. But if you and I both think of marsh pinks growing by the wayside, then we have truly shared something beautiful, something unique. (Latin names are supposed to take us a bit further, but they don't always. Nomenclaturists vacillate like the rest of us.)

There is another reason, a deeper and more diffuse and less easily articulated reason. Perhaps there is something after all in the old dark ancient notions of the names of power, that some essence resides in a name. Now that I have named this plant it is in some peculiar fashion, from then on, mine. I have possessed it somehow by labeling it: *Amianthium muscaetoxicum*, fly poison, a pretty species of asphodel, in my power.

August: Someone has run over a possum on the road, and crows have gathered to scavenge. One of them is a partial albino; its wings are white, and I smile to see it, for I recognize it. It has been around the neighborhood for several years. On the ground with other crows, sitting in the top of a pine tree, flying along the mountain's edge, it is marked, distinctive.

I hear about albinism a good deal, but for myself I seldom encounter its victims. One winter, an evening grosbeak came to the feeder, a male bird with his black plumage bleached to platinum and the mustard-yellow to cream, an amazing and beautiful sight.

He died in the ice storm that year, and so did the one-eyed field sparrow and the chickadee with the twisted foot and the thrasher who dragged a useless leg. It horrifies me sometimes that these creatures which give me so much pleasure are made individual to me only by being marred or maimed.

September: When I visit the seashore, one of the books I always take with me is a fat, green, boxed volume called *South Carolina Birdlife*. It is the queen of bird books, handsomely illustrated with paintings and photographs so evocative of the Low Country that I can hardly bear to shut the pages; crotchety and full of a kind of fierce, lovely jingoism: few birds have been able to resist the urge to visit South Carolina.

But the feature that attracts me most I have never encountered in another state bird guide: a purely gratuitous rendering of the Latin names of the avifauna into English.

Thus the common starling is listed as *Sturnus vulgaris*, which the authors dutifully translate as common starling, without comment. Nor have they anything to say about the Florida grackle, "*Quisculus quiscula quiscula* (a quail a quail a quail)" though an error twice-compounded deserves some notice, I would think.

Once in a while they provide a helpful addition. The lapwing, for instance, is denoted *Vanellus vanellus* and the reader is informed that *vanellus* means a little fan, in reference to the winnowing noise of its wings. The subspecific name of the belted piping plover is *circumcinctus* which is translated as "surrounded, *i.e.*, belted." And they are moved to remark the endearing appropriateness of *Clangula hyemalis*, a little winter noise, for the old squaw.

But they maintain a stiffish silence about such flights of fancy as "*Capella gallinago delicata* (a star in the constellation Auriga, a hen, delicate)" for Wilson's snipe. Or for the gull-billed tern, *Gelochelidon nilotica aranea*, "a laughing swallow of the river Nile pertaining to a spider."

I am myself charmed and delighted by some of the names;

by *Chordailes minor,* "a smaller evening musical instrument," for the night hawk; by *Bombycilla cedrorum,* "the silky-tailed inhabitant of the cedars," for cedar wax-wing.

I am more than charmed, I am in fact reassured. I am distrustful of scientists, not altogether certain I want to go where they seem to be taking us. It is encouraging then to come upon this streak of poetry and imagination in the cold of the laboratory. There must be some redeeming qualities in the cast of mind that devised the name *Calidris canulus rufus,* for the American knot, the reddish sandpiper, up to its knees in the waves, vainly commanding the tide to halt. I like the humility that so often often comes up with names translating simply "some bird" or "unknown bird." And oh, the dreaming magic of *Dendroica petechia aestiva,* the tree-dwelling, island-loving Eastern yellow warbler, pertaining to summer.

October: October for the most part is a limp and lackluster month here. The oaks still keep their green, but the leaves are dull and dry; no amount of rain will make them lively, will wash away the dust.

Bloom is sparse and hesitant, woodpeckers cry out, the pears thud to the ground and their bruises ferment. The wasps and yellow jackets carouse on the juice and then lie about on their backs giggling and kicking feebly. The days are mild, hazy, and shadowless; the nights are tame.

But evenings are another matter. Then the air is clear and yellow, tinged with bronze. Among the oaks the outlines of more precipitate trees take on a new grace and a new emphasis. Reflected from their fallen leaves, the light, strong, sad, uncompromising, comes strangely up from the ground.

November: I went to the wildfowl refuge on Hiwassee Island to see the geese. I don't often go during the season, not wishing to run the risk of being shot. Not wishing, either, to see the geese shot. Besides, the gates of the refuge are closed and locked; so I must climb the high bluffs and look down on the river and the island. It was a grey day with a cold wind, and the geese would not move, would not get up and fly, would only squat on the sand bars looking off toward the mountains or, in the water, tip up, showing their white petticoats and revolving slowly head down. They would not even speak, only here and there a single bird honking, not the lovely, wild, bugling chorus of a moving flock, the deep, sweet, spine-tingling music. One of the reasons I don't go up on the cliffs very often is that once or twice I have been so caught up in that rush of wings and voices above my head that I have nearly gone over the edge—a clumsy and rejected Leda, come near to putting off anybody's knowledge or power.

Below the cliff a great blue heron swept by, croaking to itself in its toad voice. I squatted by my telescope. Across the river a man in a small boat tended a trotline, moving from one floating plastic bleach jug to the next one, hauling up the empty hooks. When he leaned over, his jacket slid up his back revealing several inches of bare flesh. In the trees winter birds moved about: myrtle warblers, purple finches, a winter wren, a fox sparrow. In a bush by my side a small brown spider tidied her web, tightening a guy wire here, a stray cable there, dropping some tiny carcass wrapped in silk. Mid-November is late for spiders to be about—by my reckoning, not hers. While I watched her some ducks flew by, talking among themselves in little purring crooning notes. I never knew what ducks they were, but I have never forgotten that soft murmur; if I ever hear it again I shall recognize it.

Close to this place is a dead tree. In the years I have been coming here it has lost every branch and now stands a stark pole, ready to break to pieces in the next storm. Woodpeckers often hitch up and down it while I sit here waiting for the geese, but on this day a big red-tailed hawk perched on its top, looking down at the river with the gaze of terrible anguish that hawks can wear. I sat watching him, and after a moment he turned his head and watched me. When he left, the dead tree swayed back and forth for a full thirty seconds in reaction to the thrust of his feet.

Coming down off the hill carrying my telescope, it occurred to me, as it had a hundred times before, that I am one of the lucky ones. This is all I have so far in my life wanted or needed.

But I cannot help wondering what will become of people like me when the world is cemented over.

December: Down in the hollows, in what we call the "coves" of the mountains, it is always spring. Water runs everywhere, even in the drought of August, even under the freezing moon of January, and there is a hopeful freshness and wetness to the air that speaks of spring. One day before Christmas I go down into one of these drains to get some hemlock cones for a wreath for my door. Almost everything in sight is evergreen— hemlocks and pines and hollies, laurel and rhododendron, arbutus and wild ginger and partridge berry, Christmas fern and ground pine and wintergreen, mosses and lichens.

The witch hazel is bare, but it is blooming, covered with fringy yellow blossoms and surrounded by their strange nonscent, as though every smell but that of cleanliness had been washed away.

The big-leaved magnolia has dropped its foliage too, and the woods are strewn with two-foot-long leaves of a curious newspaper-grey. The upper side is a warm golden brown, but something in the leaf's boat shape causes it to land nine times out of ten with its underside uppermost. Until the leaves blend in with the rest of the compost, the woods have a littered and garbagy look.

Now on this chilly drizzling day I have come slipping and sliding down the steep rocky path, out of the winter woods, spare and bony and dry, into this semitropical garden along the creeks. It is the birds which most clearly indicate the season— kinglets and white-throated sparrows and purple finches. But even the birds sense that April promise, and suddenly the kinglets flash their ruby crowns; above the gurgle of water they burst suddenly into that astonishing song, too big by far to issue from this tiny creature and flowering sweetly on this spring-time air.

January: We made a rough trellis for the clematis to climb on—a pole with one crosspiece. The carpenter bees found it right away and used the crosspiece for a nest. All summer long when I worked in the yard I could hear those infinitesimal jaws gnawing away. As far away as twenty feet I could hear it.

The other day in a moment of whimsy I took down the crosspiece and sawed it open. I don't know what I expected to find in those silk-smooth chambers. Eggs? Larvae? Nothing at all? What I found were five fat queens, five gold-and-black sleeping beauties, waiting for the kiss of no particular prince, for they were already fertilized, waiting only for warm weather.

I was horrified and bound the whole business up with bicycle tape and left it on the window sill in the garage. In the spring four of them emerged. The fifth never woke, but I don't believe I was the cause of her death.

The carpenter bees mumble around the house all summer looking for nesting sites. I don't know what the requirements are or why the clematis trellis proved better than something else. They spent a long time inspecting the lintel and jambs of the back door but rejected that location. Anyway, the lintel was already occupied by carpenter ants, and has been as far back as we've lived here. Sometimes they swarm, a flock of huge winged ants, inside and outside the house. Once I called the exterminators, but the sight of all that long dying repelled me, and I have not done it since. After the exterminators had done their work, I thought the ants must all be gone, but six months later there was a little pile of sawdust under the lintel. I watched and by and by an ant came out of a crack, walked to the edge of the lintel, leaned over, and dropped a wood chip that antipodean distance to the floor. They are still busy there, but we live in tolerance. The swarms have never returned to anything like their size before the exterminators; nowadays I prop the doors open and let them fly.

February: Sometimes I see a bald eagle at the wildfowl reserve. Sometimes it is soaring over the pines, an imperial bird, crowned, lordly, stern ruler of some cloud-kingdom. And sometimes it is standing on a sand bar eating a dead fish, diminished to a rival carrion-eater by the crows who stand around it making raucous remarks. Nevertheless, they themselves are dwindled to grackle size by the eagle's hugeness, and they keep a respectful distance.

But once, and once only, I saw there a golden eagle, a vast dark bird shawled in brass. It too sat on a sand bar and ate dead fish, for it too scavenges. Yet it is also a fierce predator, can strike and carry away young and grown birds of every variety, even raccoons and foxes.

The whole place knew it. When the eagle rose and flew over a grove of cedars, suddenly the world erupted with crows, herons, jays—screaming, wheeling, circling, crying with fear. I have never, before or since, seen such a terrible sky, so filled with anger and dread.

March: Any warmish day in December or January the chorus frogs may call. Birds sing for a number of reasons—to attract a mate; to establish a territory and warn away other birds; to communicate; or simply for singing's sake. But frogs sing for one reason only, and what they are saying over and over is "Sex! Sex! Sex!" At least according to Archie Carr, a writer who should know.

It makes a lovely song, a sweet, slow-rising trill, a charming small hymn to procreation. On one of these days I can stand on the edge of the mountain and hear it floating up from every pond and puddle. By the end of March the ponds and puddles are full of eggs, teeming with tadpoles, who have a good chance of avoiding death by freezing, if not by any other means available.

I can waste a good deal of time poking about in the edges of shallow ponds, catching cold and water beetles, hoping to stir up a salamander or a small Loch Ness monster, falling in, creating havoc in the mud. I can never resist; something mysterious is hidden under the layers of dead leaves and silt. When the eggs are laid and the tadpoles begin to grow, I am more drawn than ever and hunker down to watch it happen. And one morning in the middle of March there are the leopard frogs fringing the edge of the water, slender males each clutching his fat female in pop-eyed single-mindedness. Sometimes his embrace is so passionate and long that the lady drowns; he has even been known to drown himself. There is a moral lesson to be learned here, but whether about sex or single-mindedness I have not yet determined.

March: I went up to the wildfowl reserve, to say good-by to the geese. We chose the right day, blue and bright, and the geese were there by the hundred. They were restless and active, flying up and landing, walking about with that proud long-legged walk, calling and calling. The geese make three sounds, their beautiful wild voices, the booming roar of their wings in flight, and the silken hiss when their bodies slide into the water. And on this day of farewell, I heard all three.

There is a field where the marsh hawks quarter and today the geese are feeding there, with the sun on their bronze backs, and one pintail in the midst of them. Among the birds on the water there were three blue geese and one snow, as there often are. Their white heads and necks make a startling contrast with the black ones of the Canadas. They are handsome creatures but they do not have the appeal for me that the Canadas have; there is something placid and domestic about them, those pink bills and feet; their voices are not so deeply fierce and beautiful.

Kildees and one snipe pattered around on the sand bars, the trees crackled and sparkled with redwings, frogs, called from the hollows, and the plowed fields were starred and spangled with chickweed and dandelions and ranunculus. We ate our lunch away from the water, out of the cold wind, and a woodchuck watched us from behind a kind of rampart it had erected in front of the entrance of its burrow. A number of young bulls grazing in the field next to us, rushed down to the fence with brave looks and lowered heads, but when I went up to them and offered the core of my apple and the crust of a sandwich, they retreated in disorder. At the far end of their pasture a deer leaped over the fence, scampered across the corner of the meadow, leaped out again, and disappeared into the pines. If they envied him they did not show it, following his progress with the same earnest thoughtfulness which they had devoted to my consumption of a hard-boiled egg.

There was no sound but the wind and the geese and a far-away barking dog.

It has been a good day. Time and chance happeneth to us all. All sorts of imponderables lie between here and October, between here and Canada. But whatever happens, I have had this good day in which to say good-by to the geese.

Afterword: Among my earliest recollections is of myself standing transfixed by the song of a Bewick's wren. What it was, I did not at age four know or care. I recognized it simply as the essence of an April morning.

From the wren I went on to more momentous occasions. I marked my days by Events, by the sight of wild turkeys rising above a little dark copse of pines; by the seldom-heard calls of chuck-will's-widows; by my first clear close look at ibises; by the spine-chilling sensation of a snake moving unexpectedly under my unwary hand.

As I grow older I find myself returning to the less sophisticated attitudes of four years old. More and homelier things, the stems of grasses and the songs of crickets, seem to me miraculous.

Life, in order to continue, must be at least endurable to its participants. But that it is possible, in spite of implicit horrors, to find it beautiful fills me with astonishment, with gratitude. What I have hoped to convey in these pages is my own sense of how valuable and how fragile it is, this tiny spark in an eternity of darkness, and how greatly to be treasured in whatever manifestation.

Christopher Camuto

Old Growth

(NORTH CAROLINA)

> To preserve wild animals implies generally the
> creation of a forest for them to dwell in or resort
> to. So it is with man. . . .The civilized nations—
> Greece, Rome, England—have been sustained
> by the primitive forests which anciently rotted
> where they stand. They survive as long as the
> soil is not exhausted.
>
> HENRY THOREAU, "Walking"

When a Cherokee dreamed of snakes, he was
treated for snakebite upon awakening. In these
forested mountains, mind and body were as intimate as night and day, and a decoction of heart-
leaf and snake tongue—hepatica and walking
fern—might protect the dreamer from the mis-
steps of his waking life. This dreaming was not
symbolic but an unadorned intrusion of the real.
The rattlesnake in the mind was the rattlesnake
beside the path, a being with a spirit indepen-
dent of human confusion. Such was indigenous
respect for the thing itself, a habit of mind that
leaned toward observation of the other rather
than projection of the self.

This is old growth in early May, a few odd days
in woods that never felt an ax, the rarest kind of
place in North America, a fragment of true for-

est. Such sacred groves would be in these mountains, which fended off history as long as they could, hid red wolves and red men as well as ancient trees and soils with their attendant life, intact places where creation progressed as it was inclined to before the great disturbance.

The Cherokee, like all native easterners, were first and foremost forest people, and their thoughts were forest thoughts. The green thought in a green shade was not a literary invention. The forest was the source of their deepest beliefs and best medicine. But the power of native medicines did not come solely from the chemical properties of plants. Cure came, in part, from the places where plants grew. The business of roots and herbs was a philosophic enterprise, part of a way of life in situ. There once was a topography to the way people thought and behaved. The possibility of a cure for something that had gone wrong—for being lost in mind or body—was a gift of place.

The place that mattered most, that was the most powerful, the wildest place, was the deep forest interior, where nothing had been changed by man.

In the southern Appalachians, the way into old growth is always the same: an interstate, to a state highway, to a two-lane blacktop that leads past smaller and smaller towns; then a dirt road to a trailhead at an old logging road—overgrown, you hope—off which a faint path leads you toward the stream you've been listening to since you hit the logging road and from which you can take your bearings, using that stream as a wandering baseline. A half mile up this watercourse you strike the trace of an old trail used by hunters and the few people who know what's hidden on the slopes ahead.

A trail descended from a logging road makes for suspiciously easy walking. Even after such a road has become overgrown and offers only an inviting footpath, you can tell its origins from the odd consistency in its grade and the way it glides along an unnatural contour. That's how the machine got in the garden and the logs got out. But the fragment of trail I'm on now jags through the woods as if it had a more intimate relationship with the terrain, unwinding footfall by footfall along a narrow bevel of least resistance through the tangled vegetation and around sudden brows of rock without altering anything in its path. Unless you adjust your pace to match the jagged surface of real ground, this path will turn your ankle or run the toe of your boot into the constant variation underfoot. A trace of ancient trial and error, a true trail makes choices that are sometimes hard to fathom, thoughtfully looping downslope to avoid a windthrow that disappeared a century ago but jamming you against the tree that fell last winter. It's the narrow, winding path of predator and prey, the way of hunters and warriors, lovers and medicine men. A rare thing now, a true trail, a trail that leads somewhere.

If you set out in the dark, daylight arrives twice at your feet, suffusing at first, unaccountably, from the woods around you, often in a gray mist of ground fog, breath of that nearby stream exhaled into the woods, and then, hours later, falling from overhead, brightly as light through the apex of a cathedral window. This time of day between the first and second light is, like the hours of dusk when night is visibly in the air, a time to observe your misperceptions, glints in the middle distance of that old doubleness of things, subjects and objects as elusive as drumming grouse moving about the morning woods like the Wild Boys, leading you on.

From a rise in the trail I see smoke simmer from a small clearing given over to wildflowers and Christmas fern and bordered by spicebush and serviceberry. But the smoke is strange, rising and then falling again, as if I were watching a short loop of film. Half awake, I lean on my walking stick and watch the smoking old field as I listen to the thoughtful song of a yellow-throated vireo high overhead and wonder about what I am seeing.

So that first kind of morning light hovers in spiderwebs strung between the taller ferns, a thousand smoky auras trapped in globes of dew beaded on silken threads, each array pulsing in a slight breeze I hadn't noticed and reifying, as a forest often does, a fragile interface of fact and impression.

Old growth, of course, is rare, but some survives even on national forest land, hidden both from the appetite of lumber companies and the prurience of hiking guides. The best places are always uphill, toward the great spine of mountains, but the ascent is easy, a stiff walk only if you are in a hurry, effortless if you are not. Off-trail, your pace is dictated by terrain and vegetation and by the way the mood of forest features directs your mind along. I'm drawn to the rock outcrops strewn through every watershed like wreckage from a crash, jagged chest-high shelves of wet stone sheathed in cushion moss that sprout forests of tiny hemlock nurslings that shade the moss that make soil for their roots, a minor symbiosis, another dancing loop. In the woods, life thrives on coexistence.

As I get deeper into the trackless woods, I keep a bold creek on my left and pick my way through ranks of second growth—or third or fourth or fifth, for all I know—impressive if you've never seen the old places or don't spend much time in any woods. But even after fifty years, a reforested clear-cut is still more clear-cut than forest. Managed forests are woodlots.

The root of *forest*—from the Latin *foris*, for "out of doors" and associated with *silvam*, "the outside wood"—takes us back toward Western notions of wildness and wilderness. But in English the word was severed from its roots in the Middle Ages as the original forests of the British Isles were cut down for the pastures and deer parks that profited and amused the nobility. Once that dark, tangled place beyond the pale, forests became merely an extension of culture, still out of doors but no longer an outside wood in the primitive sense that was either threatening or inviting, depending on your cast of mind.

The word devolved back toward its original meaning with the European settlement of North America, where neither Puritan nor Cavalier found the king's tidy woods, cleared for hunting on horseback, but rather the impenetrable forest of the Iroquois and Cherokee, the old wild place of European nightmares, a tangle full of wolves that might devour one's livestock and heathens who might not worship one's god. Here was a continent half covered with a forest as hard to interpret as exploit, the dark outside wood again. So the word *forest* glowed red from the settlers' writings until that forest, too, was cut down and the natural life within it, as well as the cultures that lived astride it, were destroyed. And then the word was tame again.

The older sense of the word is perhaps a trace of a fundamental distinction between what is inside culture and outside of it—that frame of untamed nature that has disappeared, except when, at night, we look into the starlit blackness overhead. Tangled in the etymology of the word *forest* is the trace of a fundamental continuum that degenerated into an apparent antithesis once the Industrial Revolution reduced nature to raw material and then consumer culture turned it into a toy. Lurking beyond the unmarked word *outside* is the keener word *other*, which suggests that a true forest is strange and dangerous, something to be feared and destroyed, not just for profit but also for ideological reasons, for the narrow peace of mind that thrives on monoculture—the consciousness that hated those old tangled woods, and all those tangled languages, and those fabulous people who were different, a consciousness still very much with us.

Needless to say, most of the forest that originally covered the southern Appalachians was destroyed, along with the rest of the eastern forests. The fragments left standing survived by accident or isolated acts of prudence. The paucity of such places is a measure of something lacking in man. The rarity of old growth is unnatural.

The tack I'm on takes me through a tract of fifty-year-old pole timber that contrasts sharply with what's up ahead. I come this way deliberately. If I were blindfolded, I could feel the edge I'm looking for and tell you exactly where the old woods start. There is a threshold beyond which the synesthesia unique to intact forests takes hold. There is nothing like it in the world.

Even blindfolded, I would feel light become an object tangible as the bulky trees that draw the darkness of the forest floor upward, as if compensating for the intruding rays from overhead. I would hear the woody, mellow silence that supports the reciprocal sounds of wind and birdsong between the gusts and notes of which I would hear the shape of randomly well-used space. I would smell time in last century's peaty rot and in this year's first new leaves. Walking across the soft, uneven ground, I would feel even older time roll underfoot as deeply furrowed waves of never-disturbed soil crested in foot-thick mats of sphagnum moss and broke over the faded forms of pre-Columbian hemlocks and tulip poplars ghosting underneath. Standing in the deep pit at the base of a tree recently crashed out of the canopy, I might, still blindfolded, find an arrowhead just by digging with my fingers in the cache of dirt and stone unearthed from the centuries by its upturned roots, testing with my fingertips for the unmistakable scallop of a worked edge.

In old growth, I'd be overwhelmed before I'd taken the blindfold off.

Entering a true forest from second growth is as dramatic an experience as walking into a cathedral from a city street and having one kind of space immediately replace another. The faint trail winds and rises through an old clear-cut, the floor of which is dry and brown and empty in those places where it isn't a monoculture of mountain laurel. But the edge is abrupt, inspiring or heartbreaking, depending on which way you are going. Once you've brought the nave into view, you see how the most refined aesthetics of high culture came from the woods. Shafts of light drop from a height into the unsettling darkness around you as if through high-arching stained glass. You expect music, and once you are another hundred steps farther on that music—variations on the theme of natural silence—rises from all quarters as ground never torn to hell by a skidder operation rolls and buckles into a forested watershed that towers and leans over itself, a place large and intimate as a church.

The depth of field alone will stop you in your tracks, from fields of tiny orange spores periscoped out of the mossy banks aside the trail to the open crowns of 200-foot poplars that check the sky. You start walking like a deer, holding your breath and hanging your steps, turning your head from side to side to find a focal point in this rare glimpse of a complete world, hoping something flushes out of the busy stillness.

The trail, deeply grooved but not eroded, brings you nearly eye level with the thick roots of the big trees that are the most obvious sign of time here. They emerge from mounds of soil tapered up to their flared bases—poplar and hemlock the size of small redwoods, finely chiseled mountain silverbell the size of hemlock and poplar; outsize red maples and sugar maples; yellow birch and buckeye, their tightly wound wood concealing their years; enormous papaw and basswood; smooth-bark magnolia and elegantly prop-rooted beech. All arranged according to some calculus of soil and aspect and centuries of weather. Biomass, in the jargon of ecologists. More life than thought can handle.

More death, too, arrayed in rotting trees strewn about the slopes like seeds and occupying as much space as the standing wood. But it is not the fallen giants, so rare to see, that really draw the eye. It's the faint impression of a log beached in the mossy earth and about to disappear forever that tells you time moves slowly here, but moves, that the woods are made of wood and that this century's saplings are rooted in last autumn's fertile detritus and the faint, fading life of the last millennium.

The phrase *old growth* is recent. An ecological term with some poetry in it, it is nearly an oxymoron in a consumer culture that thrives on waste, except in nature, where it won't do to let trees fall and rot in this way, no more than oil can be left under Arctic tundra or coal in mountains, no more than marshes or beaches can be let alone for the life and pleasures they encourage. The earth must be *used*, we are told, in order to be valuable. No matter that this idea is demented and that the wasteful practices it encourages doom us to progressive impoverishment. The idea goes back to the Puritan Cotton Mather, one of those pious Europeans unhinged by the original American forest. "What is not useful is vicious," the bright-eyed believer declared. Is this true?

Old growth is life and death come round. Not in some textbook cycle, but joined at the hip, dancer and the dance. This is not the swift, unforgiving relation of predator and prey laid out around me. This is older—some strange, formal enfolding of senescence and conception, a beautiful loop worked out a long time ago, ancient as tides, inscrutable as smoke rising and falling in place from an old field.

Contributors

John Lane is a widely published essayist and poet and an expert kayaker. His book of natural history essays, *Weed Time: Essays from the Edge of a Country Yard*, was published in 1992. "Natural Edges," a creative nonfiction piece about his experiences living on Cumberland Island National Seashore in the early 1980s, appeared in W. W. Norton's anthology *In Short: Brief Creative Nonfiction* (1996).

Gerald Thurmond is a sociologist who has written on time perception, aging, and religious movements as well as on the environment. He is an avid birder and teaches a nature appreciation class entitled "Creepy Crawlers" in the Wofford College summer camp for academically gifted children.

Rick Bass has lived in Texas, Mississippi, Vermont, Utah, and Arkansas but has settled on a remote ranch in the Yaak Valley of northern Montana. He is the author of numerous books of short stories; his nonfiction books include his second essay collection, *Wild to the Heart* (1987), from which "Good Day at Black Creek" was taken. *Fiber* was published by the University of Georgia Press in 1998.

Jan DeBlieu lives on the North Carolina outer

banks. Her book *Hatteras Journal* (1987), from which "Hurricane" was taken, has been called "required reading for all coastal conservationists." In 1991 she published *Meant to Be Wild*, which *Library Journal* cited as one of the three best natural history books of 1991. Her latest book is *Wind*.

Wendell Berry, farmer, poet, novelist, voice for all things traditional and wild, lives and writes in Port Royal, Kentucky, where he works his farm. "The Making of a Marginal Farm" is taken from *Recollected Essays* (1980).

Eddy L. Harris is the author of *Mississippi Solo*, an account of his experiences while paddling a canoe the length of the Mississippi. "Vicksburg" is a chapter from that book. He has also written about traveling by motorcycle through the old Confederacy, and his experiences in Harlem. He lives in Missouri and is at work on a book about Paris.

James Kilgo is the author of two books of natural history essays—*Deep Enough for Ivorybills* and *Inheritance of Horses*—and a novel, *Daughter of My People*. He is also an avid hunter, naturalist and long-time professor at the University of Georgia. "Actual Field Conditions" is taken from *Deep Enough for Ivorybills* (1988).

Janet Lembke lives part of the year on the Neuse River in North Carolina. She has chronicled her life there in many books, all published by Lyons & Burford, Publishers, New York. "River Time" is from a collection by the same title that was published in 1989. Her most recent book is *Shake Them 'Simmons Down*.

Archie Carr, the late famed Florida naturalist and herpetologist, was most noted for his work with sea turtles, but also won an O. Henry Award for a short story. "Living with an Alligator" is from his collected essays, *A Naturalist in Florida* (1994).

Harry Middleton, who died in the summer of 1993, was the author of two highly acclaimed nonfiction books—*The Earth is Enough* and *On the Spine of Time*. "Bagpipes on Hazel Creek" appeared in *On the Spine of Time* (1991).

Franklin Burroughs grew up in South Carolina and now lives in Maine, where he teaches at Bowdoin College. He is the author of two acclaimed nonfiction books, *Billy Watson's Croaker Sack* and *The River Home*. "Lake Waccamaw to Freelands" is the second chapter of *The River Home*. Both of his collections have been recently reissued by the University of Georgia Press.

Susan Cerulean is a naturalist and writer living in Gainesville, Florida. She is finishing work on a book about swallowtail kites, from which "Searching for Swallow-Tails" is taken.

E. O. Wilson is Pellegrino University Professor and curator in entomology at the Museum of Comparative Zoology, Harvard University. Among his numerous books are *On Human Nature*, *The Diversity of Life*, and *Biophilia*. "Paradise Beach" is the first chapter of his autobiography *Naturalist*.

Marylou Awiakta is a Cherokee/Appalachian writer and storyteller. Her family has lived in the southern Appalachian mountains for more than seven generations. She is the author of *Abiding Appalachia: Where Mountains and Atoms Meet* and *Rising Fawn and the Fire Mystery*, as well as *Selu*. She lives in Memphis with her family.

Bland Simpson, a member of the acclaimed string band the Red Clay Ramblers, teaches writing at the University of North Carolina at Chapel Hill. "The Great Dismal" is the final chapter in his book by the same name, published in 1990.

Stephen Harrigan is a Texas novelist and journalist and the author of many nonfiction collections. He lives in Austin, is working on a novel about the Alamo, and recently published a collection of essays, *Comanche Midnight*, in which "The Soul of Treaty Oak" appears.

Barry Lopez is the author of many books of fiction and nonfiction, including *Arctic Dreams*, for which he won the National Book Award, *Lessons from the Wolverine* (Georgia), and *Apologia* (Georgia). He lives in Oregon. "Theft: A Memoir" is from his latest volume of essays, *About This Life* (1998).

Janisse Ray, poet and essayist, recently finished an MFA at the University of Montana, where "Whither Thou Goest" was written. Ray has now returned to her grandmother's house in south Georgia.

Mary Q. Steele wrote children's books as well as natural history. She lived in the Tennessee river valley. "The Living Year" is a selection of entries from her book by the same title published in 1982.

Christopher Camuto is the author of *A Fly Fisherman's Blue Ridge* and the forthcoming *Hunting from Home*. He has taught at the University of Virginia and at Washington and Lee University and is book review columnist for *Gray's Sporting Journal*. "Old Growth" is a chapter from *Another Country: Journeying Toward the Cherokee Mountains* (1997).